Uprising at Bowling Green

Uprising at Bowling Green

How the Quiet Fifties Became the Political Sixties

Norbert Wiley
Joseph B. Perry Jr.
Arthur G. Neal

Paradigm Publishers
Boulder • London

Copyright © 2012 by Paradigm Publishers

Published in the United States by Paradigm Publishers, 5589 Arapahoe Avenue, Boulder, CO 80303 USA.

Paradigm Publishers is the trade name of Birkenkamp & Company, LLC,
Dean Birkenkamp, President and Publisher.

Library of Congress Cataloging-in-Publication Data

Wiley, Norbert.
  Uprising at Bowling Green : how the quiet fifties became the political sixties / by Norbert Wiley, Joseph B. Perry, Jr., Arthur G. Neal ; foreword by Randall Collins.
    p. cm.
  Includes bibliographical references and index.
  ISBN 978-1-59451-934-5 (hardcover : alk. paper)
  1. Bowling Green State University—History. 2. College students—Political activity—Ohio—Bowling Green—History. 3. Student movements—Ohio—Bowling Green—History.
I. Perry, Joseph B. II. Neal, Arthur G. III. Title.
  LD4191.O62W55 2012
  378.1'9810977116—dc23

                                                              2011048830

Printed and bound in the United States of America on acid-free paper that meets the standards of the American National Standard for Permanence of Paper for Printed Library Materials.

Designed and Typeset by Straight Creek Bookmakers.

16 15 14 13 12   1 2 3 4 5

Contents

Foreword

Imagine a university campus where there are wide green lawns but students are prohibited from walking across and have to stay on the paved walkways around them. Where students can't kiss goodnight outside the dorms and are expelled for drinking alcohol anywhere, even off campus, except in their parents' homes. Where female students aren't allowed to hold hands with their boyfriends and are locked in their dorms in the evening. Where the president checks to see that the faculty are in their offices by 8:00 a.m., and his wife peers in their windows and relays complaints to department heads if their offices are messy. Where attending faculty meetings is compulsory but only the president has the right to speak. This was Bowling Green University as of 1961.

This was the place where the first student protest of the 1960s happened. It was also the most successful of all student protests: The president was forced to resign, the rules were changed, and an authoritarian, traditional institution was transformed into a contemporary one.

Paradoxically, it might seem, this came about as the result of a rather short and mild phase of collective behavior—a couple of excited crowd confrontations, a few hours of mildly chaotic excitement without violence or property destruction, some speechmaking, a one-day boycott of classes. It began with a playful fraternity water fight, as students gathered outside on the first mild spring day. The authorities became alarmed because a crowd had gathered to watch, but they refused to disperse, and the dean who personally tried to force the students back to their rooms by wading into the crowd and pushing them had little success. On the microlevel of direct confrontation, he was not being obeyed. Emboldened by the disparity in numbers, the crowd backed up before the dean's physical aggression but closed in behind him as a wall of students. As we know from microsociological study of violence, a single antagonist against a group of more than three or four persons is likely to be taken as a weak victim and to be repeatedly and unmercifully attacked, and in this case the disparity was close to one hundred to one.

This was one of the turning points that escalated the conflict. In each case the pattern was the same: The authoritarian officials of Bowling Green, used to overawing everyone else by unrelenting performance of total dominance, could not back down, and continued escalating even in situations where a temporary withdrawal would have defused the situation. At the end of the water fight, one of the young fraternity pledges, full of excitement, came up behind the dean and doused him with a water balloon. In effect it was bringing the dean into the fun of the water fight, but he undoubtedly did not see it that way; it would have been a victory for the students' definition of the situation and a loss of his dignified and authoritative status. With this denouement, the confrontation with the dean ended, and the students rushed away. They were charged up with the energy of a little symbolic victory, and they had a goal: Running across the grass—in defiance of another annoying, trivial rule—they headed for the girls' dorms, where they tried to rescue them from being locked in. Failing at this, they tried a local riot script, to block the highway near the campus, which had been done four years before in a fraternity protest against the drinking rules.

After a few hours of excitement, the crowd action petered out. It could have ended like this, a little upsurge of collective effervescence in the mode of campus ruckuses against authority. These have existed in strict colleges all the way back to the town-and-gown riots of the medieval universities and brawls between drunken students and proctors at Oxford catching them sneaking into college after closing hours at night. The American version was the spring vacation riot, usually at a popular gathering place such as the beach town Fort Lauderdale, Florida, where in the 1950s (and later) thousands of students would gather for revelry during spring break, typically getting into a good-natured riot when police tried to disperse an especially noisy crowd. (In my younger days, the tradition was the annual Labor Day riot, typically end-of-summer partying at Lake George in upstate New York, where local police would try to break up a crowd of noisy students and a few hours' rampage would result.)

But at Bowling Green in spring 1961, another step occurred that transformed the carousing-versus-authorities riot into something more principled and of wider-reaching consequence. The day after the water-balloon incident, a crowd of students gathered outside the main campus building and were addressed by adults—including some sympathetic ones, a campus minister and a philosophy professor, who framed their issue as one of free speech and human dignity. They discussed further courses of action and decided upon a one-day boycott of classes. This was done the following day. The action culminated that evening when a crowd became angry that the student council had vacillated on supporting them; the president tried to disperse the crowd, but he was jeered, and later, as the students milled around and lit bonfires, the president was burned in effigy. But the spring break began the next day and students went home. Things quieted down and a number of students were expelled for their actions. This should have posed an insurmountable obstacle to keeping the protest going, since the emotional power of a mass movement depends on being able to assemble excited crowds and keep up the sense of crisis. Lack of continuity over time is what dooms momentary crowd outbursts to ineffectiveness, which is why student riots had happened from time to time since at least the year 1200 without being more than a colorful tradition.

But two more things happened that kept the Bowling Green movement going and channeled it into serious consequences. One is that the students, dispersing for their break, expanded the network of supporters and activists by proselytizing their parents. Instead of being merely a water fight broken up by a dean, the disturbance was explained as a movement for free speech and freedom from the petty despotism of old-fashioned, authoritarian rules. Parents sympathized; so did alumni, who had experienced it themselves. Influential alumni were recruited, including wealthy industrialists and members of the board of trustees, who again confirmed the annoyances of the Bowling Green regime. Here we see the secret of political success: an expanding network of supporters, reaching those with high social resources and influence. A delegation of students went to the state legislature, complaining to the committees on education (since this was a state university). Since the trustees of Bowling Green State University were in the habit of rubber-stamping the demands of its authoritarian president, the plan was agreed upon in the legislature to expand the board of trustees to include some new, independent-minded members.

At this point, a prudent political operator would have cooled down the situation and offered a compromise. But the Bowling Green president stood his ground and opposed all compromise. The appointment of new trustees became a key battleground. Both sides escalated their efforts. The president had become anathema to the legislature; when they approved the trustee plan almost unanimously, he lost the battle and had to resign.

Why was the president so intransigent? We can see this better in the light of the series of confrontations that made up the escalation points in the conflict. It began with the dean, who, operating in a style similar to that of the president, tried to impose his personal authority on students refusing to disperse from a youthful game. That incident ended with an insult to his dignity, and an emboldening of the students. The third incident, just described, was the president's taking the expansion of the trustees as a personal challenge. In between was a faculty meeting called by the president the day after the mini-uprising adjourned for vacation. The president made an address, monopolizing the floor, describing the students as misbehaving children whom he had spanked and sent to bed. But the same philosophy professor defied custom and demanded the right to speak, going on to attack the entire style of university control. As in his public speech to the students two days before, he framed the issue as one of free speech and human dignity. The petty incidents, and the ostensibly childish behavior of the students, were abstracted into the realm of general principles that everyone ought to be concerned with. The president was furious at having his authority challenged, but although many of the faculty were frightened and cowed by the president, a substantial proportion were energized to organize themselves for further action.

The dramatic confrontation at the faculty meeting led to another escalation, when the president fired the offending professor at the end of the term. Since this was done on Graduation Day, when students and their parents were still on campus, it provided one more emotional shock and one more issue to carry into the larger community. The president's actions gave credence to the interpretation that the underlying problem was one of free speech. Six days later the trustee issue culminated in the state legislature and the president was forced to resign.

In social-movement theory, this interpretative argument is a process of framing specific incidents in terms of a larger interpretation. This might be thought of as an appeal to culture and tradition, but we should notice the connection between cultural framing and expanding networks of alliance. When the emerging leaders (both the adults—the campus minister and philosophy professor—and the students who organized the delegation to the state legislature) framed the issue, it was in the lofty and dignified terms of freedom of speech and rights of human dignity. In part, this was a way of linking themselves to the civil rights movement, a movement that was in the headlines in 1961 as the Freedom Rides were being carried out by students at all-black colleges, despite arrests by police and denunciations by segregationist Southern politicians. The rhetoric of the Bowling Green spokespersons thus framed themselves in the sympathetic position of oppressed African Americans, and framed the university administrators as the counterparts of Southern racists.

More importantly for the local movement, this metaphorical connection acquired additional grounding as a network that allied the grievances of the Bowling Green faculty—being spied on and controlled in petty ways by the president, given no voice in university matters—with the students' grievances against equally petty and omnipresent controls. As the authors, Wiley, Perry, and Neal, point out, the Bowling Green student movement was one of the few 1960s campus uprisings in which there was a strong alliance between faculty and students, and this was a key to its success. Revolt from the bottom is seldom successful, as we see in comparing state revolutions, unless it coincides with and fuses networks with revolt from near the top.

The work of making the link between disparate struggles is done by the use of general and abstract concepts. The ideas of free speech and human dignity were communications across the lines of disparate groups with their own problems, casting them as shared problems. Networks ordinarily are represented as geometric figures linking individuals into larger webs of connections; but this is only a metaphor, and in the flow of everyday life networks are made by the process of repeated communications. Networks with a high degree of consciousness of themselves as a community engaged in collective action are held together because they circulate a shared discourse. The very existence of the self-conscious network which makes up a social movement is constituted by its reverberation of repeated expressions. The rhetoric of free speech and human dignity that circulated at Bowling Green and then through wider networks in Ohio in spring 1961 was a currency of inspiration and energizing confidence.

We might be inclined to think the very terms themselves—free speech! human dignity!—were what carried the inspiration, but it is more sociological to see that the two sides are reciprocal. The words and concepts are regarded with high respect and uplift at that ritual moment because they are circulating rapidly in an expanding, excited network of people in action; and the emotional energy embodied in the words makes them inspiring. The words themselves become Durkheimian symbols, sacred objects that allow a group to focus upon itself and keep itself going in action. Symbols, which are mere words in a book, carry little inspiration if they are read in social isolation, in a mood of flat, detached cognition. It is when they are part of an active process of social circulation that they acquire a halo of emotional strength and commitment. And that is what a successful social movement is for.

Randall Collins

Preface

The Bowling Green State University student uprising of 1961, little noticed as it has been, is quite helpful for understanding the protest sixties. It was the first large student demonstration of the sixties—in fact, the first major student demonstration since the 1930s. It also shows how, at one midwestern university, the fifties transitioned into the sixties. This point will unfold as the book proceeds, but it will be treated most extensively in Chapter 8. The Bowling Green case started as a fifties-style student protest against excessively strict rules. But as the three-day action developed, and especially as the students later argued their case before the press and the Ohio state legislature, the issues changed from lifestyle restrictions to civil rights and civil liberties, especially freedom of speech. The BG case preceded the University of California, Berkeley, Free Speech Movement by more than three years. It was the first protest to argue that students had freedom of speech just as all other Americans. And if there was any issue that overarched the entire sixties student movement it was freedom of speech.

The Bowling Green case was also the most successful student protest of the sixties, for the students forced the rather paternalistic president, Ralph McDonald, into resigning from office. When the students brought their grievances to the Ohio Senate Committee on Education they influenced the committee chair, Ross Pepple, into introducing a bill that was initially meant as a mild rebuke to President McDonald. The bill expanded the BGSU board of trustees from five to seven. McDonald then wrote an outraged letter to the rules committee of the legislature, more or less ordering the legislators to vote against this bill. Here he showed the same authoritarian style he used to run the campus. In other words, instead of just rolling with the punch McDonald used all his prestige to fight the bill, thereby escalating it into a vote of confidence. The legislature responded with a knockout blow, perhaps the most severe that any state legislature has ever given to any college president. The Senate voted 31 to 1 for the bill and the House voted 112 to nothing. This resounding response to McDonalds's letter made it clear that he had to resign. The resignation quickly turned this campus from a behind-the-times, paternalistic one into a moderately liberal, decidedly democratic one. This transition also initiated student freedom of speech into the American university system, although it would take a while for it to spread to other campuses.

About the same time as the Bowling Green events, in spring of 1961, there was student dissent at the University of Michigan over the in loco parentis system. This focused on the dean of women's surveillance and disapproval of interracial dating. A group of students, led by the *Michigan Daily* editor Tom Hayden, lodged a formal complaint with the university administration, including statements from alumni. A university committee, headed by the law professor John Reed, investigated the issue for several months and recommended that the in loco parentis system be abolished. The administration concurred with this recommendation and the offending system was removed, constituting what seems to have been a first in the American university system. The dean of women, Deborah Bacon, was also relieved of her position and sent back to the English department. This was happening at the same time the Bowling Green students were protesting related issues on their campus, although neither group of students knew about the other.

At the time of the Bowling Green uprising, all three of the authors were in the sociology department at the university. We shared an interest in collective behavior, social movements, and the sociology of conflict—all highly relevant to the student rebellion. But we were engaged in other projects, and it took a long time to decide on the present collaboration. Still, our experience with the student uprising was so intense and dramatic it became permanently implanted in our memories.

In writing this book, we therefore drew on our direct experience. We also consulted newspapers and published materials. In addition, we conducted more than a hundred interviews with former students and faculty members who were at Bowling Green at the time of the uprising. The book is based on a wide range of sources, as we sought to construct an overall portrait of the demonstrations, their antecedents, and their aftermath.

Collective memories in the modern world are frequently short lived. There are presently no students, faculty, or administrators at Bowling Green State University who were there during the uprising of spring 1961. Very few on campus today have even a vague awareness of the dramatic impact of this event on the development of the university. Yet the organizational culture on campus at the present time was much influenced by the removal of a president who was widely regarded as authoritarian and micromanaging. The freedoms of students today, the influence of the faculty, and the strong academic programs are all outgrowths of the rebellion and its consequences.

Unfortunately, there are no research reports on these demonstrations, except for an excellent chapter in David Maloney's master's thesis (Maloney 1981, 1–36). This lack is the main reason why we wrote the book. All the participants who might have executed the research were too emotionally involved to do the job at the time. And a large, midwestern student revolt such as our case was so new and inexplicable that it got little national notice. At the same time as these demonstrations there were beer riots on the beaches of Florida, and these did get the national attention. Spring-break high jinks were understandable. But a student demonstration for civil liberties this early in the sixties made no sense to the press at the time, and it went pretty much unnoticed.[1] In addition, scholarly attention gradually shifted to the national wave of demonstrations with a focus on the civil rights movement and the Vietnam War.

The Bowling Green demonstrations began spontaneously without any clear rationale or meaning, but they did last for three days. The three months afterward witnessed a fight between students and administrators over the meaning or interpretation of the demonstrations. The students won this battle overwhelmingly, as parents, the news media, and people in positions of power came to recognize the legitimacy of the students' claims. In the social-movements literature the fight over meaning is called the framing process, and we will interpret the student victory as largely one of skilled framing, particularly with the press and the legislature.

Although there are no scholarly accounts of the demonstrations, other than the brief one in Maloney's master's thesis, there are two histories of Bowling Green State University that treat the demonstrations and provide useful information. These are James Robert Overman's (1967) *The History of Bowling Green State University* and Stuart R. Givens's (1986) *The Falcon Soars*. Overman's book covers the period from the founding of the college until 1963, but includes only brief references to the 1961 demonstrations. Givens's book extends from 1963 to 1985, and while it describes the sixties-seventies civil rights and anti-war protests, it touches the earlier years only in the historical prologue.

There was also an extremely useful graduate student paper, by James R. Gordon, which compiled and commented on the newspaper accounts of these events. This paper was the only convenient source for getting a detailed account of the demonstrations, and we will draw on it extensively. It is entitled "The One-Hundred Days of Bowling Green: March 26–June 26, 1961," and is dated May 1965. Unfortunately, the BGSU archives have few materials from the McDonald years, only four small boxes. Evidently President McDonald took most of his papers with him.

Finally, a centenary history of the university, entitled *Bowling Green State University: 1910–2010* and written by Gary R. Hess, appeared in 2010. Hess has a fourteen-page chapter on the McDonald years and the student demonstration that agrees substantially with our report.

For valuable comments and suggestions on many aspects of this research, special thanks are due to Gilbert Abcarian, Linda Zoe Barat, Paul Bluemle, Ann Bowers, Julianne Burton, Christine Chambers, Randall Collins, William Day, Norman Denzin, Robert Dunn, James Gordon, H. Theodore Groat, Barbara Guyse, Tom Hayden, Kenneth Heineman, Samuel Kaplan, Charles Kurfess, Donald Longworth, Martin M. McLaughlin, Richard Miller, Sue Rautine, Robert Ross, J. A. Skipton, Nicholas Sofias, Winton Solberg, Sherman Stanage, Nella Van Dyke, David Westby, Helen Youngelson-Neal, Paul Wiley, and Monica Wiley.

NOTES

1. Another forgotten campus explosion occurred in the late 1940s at Olivet College, a small school in Michigan affiliated with the Church of Christ. The college had become quite liberal in the 1940s, with some prominent socialists on the faculty, but in 1948 a new president decided to purge the most liberal faculty and bring the school back to "law and order" (*Time*, 1949; *Harvard Crimson*, 1949). There was substantial student protest and an attempt by the liberal faculty to split the college and start a new college in upper New York State. But the attempt was unsuccessful for lack of sufficient funds. When the students went on strike, the president said, "Ninety percent of the student picket line were of a certain race and from a certain section of the country" (*Harvard Crimson*, 1949, p. 3 of Internet version). The "race" was Jewish and the section of the country was New York City. When one of us e-mailed the present librarian at Olivet, in fall 2009, inquiring about documents concerning the controversy, she said there were no such documents to her knowledge and that she had never heard about the school's disturbance. Olivet College has successfully kept any reference to the campus eruption out of its active memory, although there are stories about the incident in the student paper of the time, the *Echo*. Bowling Green did not go this far, but the absence of any research reports has had some of the same effect. The importance of the Olivet incident was that it was the first sign of the McCarthyism and campus loyalty oaths that were soon to come to the American university system (Blauner 2009).

Chapter 1

Background and History

Most of the literature on student uprisings during the 1960s concentrates on only a few prestigious universities. This may be because it is much more shocking when any kind of disturbance occurs at the nation's leading institutions of higher learning. But the Bowling Green case is a part of a larger matrix of student discontent. This uprising occurred prior to those of Berkeley, Wisconsin, Michigan, and Columbia. This priority was perhaps because the social control of students and the crisis of authority were much more intense at Bowling Green than elsewhere.

In fact the Bowling Green demonstration was so unexpected in when and where it happened that it might be good to examine it as a deviant case before going into the story itself. Florian Znaniecki says, "The exception is thus an essential instrument of scientific progress" (Znaniecki 1968/1934, 233), and this case is a glaring exception to what normally happened in conservative colleges in the Midwest in the early sixties. By all the rules of plausibility, the Bowling Green demonstration should never have happened. When circumstances that normally disallow an event lead to its actually happening, it is because there is some cause that has not previously been noticed. When Seymour Martin Lipset and his associates (1956) studied the International Typographers Union as a deviant case, it was a rare instance of a union that had a two-party system and a strong democratic tradition. He was looking for the unexpected cause. And he found it in the fact that this union made it easy to have a free press within the union community itself. The nature of the typographer's job made printing presses easily available, and this availability made it easy to have multiple, uncontrolled newspapers. These newspapers, in turn, facilitated a two-party system and a tradition of free elections.

The Bowling Green demonstrations also would never have been predicted, given the circumstances. Let us list the conditions that made this demonstration unlikely, and see if they lead to an unnoticed, unexpected cause.

1

(1) *There was little protest in the fifties and early sixties.* Studies of student protest in the fifties show that protest was uncommon (Keniston 1960; Van Dyke 2003). McCarthyism seems to have paralyzed politics on campuses as well as in more public venues (Stouffer 1955). Also, the United States was in a cold war against the Soviet Union, and attention was generally focused on external threats rather than on campus issues. The patriotic stance was to criticize the Soviet Union and refrain from criticizing the United States, including its universities. The Bowling Green demonstration did occur in 1961, when the fifties were over, and in some ways the civil rights movement, led by Martin Luther King Jr., started the protest process in the mid-fifties. Still, student protest itself did not seriously begin until near the middle of the sixties. The Bowling Green demonstration was the largest demonstration of the sixteen years after World War II. Given the campus tranquility of the early sixties, this demonstration seems to have come out of nowhere.

(2) *Protest occurred on the coasts, not in the hinterland.* Harvard University was the major college for protest, little that there was, in the fifties (Van Dyke 2003, 235). The University of Chicago also had sporadic protest. Toward the end of the decade the University of California at Berkeley was becoming a protest center. Other coastal universities also had some protest in the fifties. But the hinterland, particularly the Midwest, had little student protest. The radical political parties, both Socialist and Communist, were concentrated in coastal cities, and the universities in these cities may have been influenced by the proximity of these political forces. The children of liberal and radical parents were also more likely to be found in the large, coastal universities. Jewish Americans in particular were overrepresented in the radical political parties, and their children were overrepresented among the leaders of the sixties protest movement (Rudd 2005). Bowling Green had few Jewish students, and the leaders of the demonstrations, to the modest extent that there were leaders at all, appear to have included no Jews, except for one woman in the group that presented grievances to the legislature.

(3) *Bowling Green was an unusually strict, repressive campus.* Bowling Green was a state-funded university but it was located in one of the more politically conservative and traditionally religious sections of Ohio. The governors appointed the trustees, but they tried to choose people who would represent the local culture of northwest Ohio. At Bowling Green that meant trustees who were sympathetic to conservatism and conventional morality. It also meant that Bowling Green State University had strict rules concerning alcohol and relations between the sexes. In loco parentis rules took an extreme form at Bowling Green.

The students knew the rules, both from official documents of the university and from public knowledge, although there was no way of knowing ahead of time how aggressively these rules were enforced. No doubt many of the students felt reasonably comfortable with the rules, although many others did not. Still, campuses of this conservative nature do not have demonstrations, let alone large ones. Liberal campuses, which give a lot of freedom to the students, do have demonstrations. But highly regulated campuses, although they might have some grumbling, remain pretty quiet. In other words, a major demonstration in 1961 might have occurred at some large, coastal university or even at the midwestern University of Chicago. But a conservative institution such as Bowling Green was an extremely unlikely place.

(4) *No protest infrastructure.* A protest infrastructure is a set of student groupings that might lead to or be useful for staging a protest. Examples are student organizations that are oriented toward changing society or altering the status quo, such as groups for pacifism, racial justice, civil liberties, or women's rights. These groups raise political consciousness on a campus, and they also provide a steady supply of leaders. Behind such an infrastructure, in the families of students or in neighboring communities, there are often liberal religions, publications, trade unions, or egalitarian wings of the Democratic Party. Liberal, especially coastal, universities had the right kind of demography for a protest infrastructure. A relatively rural, traditionally Protestant, midwestern campus such as Bowling Green had no such infrastructure. It had duly elected student leaders, usually in allegiance with if not informally selected by the administration. These student leaders did not lead protests. If anything they attempted to deflect whatever dissatisfaction there might be. Even the well-organized Catholic students at Bowling Green were conservative, largely because their chaplain, Father John Ollivier, was extremely opposed to protest.

The fraternities at BGSU were the closest thing the school had to a protest infrastructure. These groups organized and led the torchlight parade against the drinking rules that became the 1957 traffic-blocking demonstration—to be discussed in more detail later in this chapter. But this was not a political, sixties-style demonstration, as we will explain more fully in Chapter 8. This was a protest against the strict lifestyle rules, and it had all the earmarks of a fifties demonstration. If anything, the fraternities, given their goal of shepherding students through school with as much fun as possible, and then into conformist jobs in the power structure, would serve as an obstacle to the more populist sixties demonstrations.

So, lacking a protest infrastructure, Bowling Green again seems an unlikely place for a large demonstration. The fact that it did have such a demonstration evokes difficult questions. We will return to these questions in Chapter 7, Explanations of the Crisis. But for now, let us suggest that the extreme unlikelihood of a Bowling Green demonstration, the overdetermined quality of this school's passivity, turned out to be the very source of the demonstration. The administration tried so hard to prevent student dissent, and constructed such an authoritarian apparatus for doing this, that they became their own gravediggers. The pent-up student dissatisfaction needed just the right mixture of conditions, what is called the "perfect storm," to explode with civil disobedience. And the similarly dissatisfied BG alumni, working in such institutions as state government and the press, were also available to support such a demonstration. We will refer to this perfect storm as the combination of intense student solidarity and the skilled framing of public communication. This will be our theoretical explanation. But we must first go through the rather complex narrative, before presenting the explanation itself.

The demonstrations of 1961 were unscheduled events that emerged on what was perceived by administrators as an orderly campus. The uprisings lasted for three days and were the most successful of the student protests of the 1960s. The coalition that students formed with the faculty eventually succeeded in forcing a controversial president out of office. About one-third of the faculty, including several departmental chairs, sided with the students. The only other campus with this strong a student-faculty coalition was the University of California at Berkeley (Blauner 2009, 233–242) in the mid-sixties, but in Bowling Green's case it was more out in the open.

After the demonstrations in late March, there were three months of maneuvering in which the students took their case to the press and to the Ohio state legislature. The university administrators also attempted to influence the press and the legislature, but they were much less effective. Finally, the president lost a showdown vote in the legislature, as mentioned earlier, and had to resign.

Perhaps the best causal explanation for the uprising was that the university's lifestyle rules were excessively strict for a state university, funded with public money, and that consequently the administration was ripe to lose a publicity battle. As Overman says in his history of the university,

> By 1949, and to a greater extent by 1957 and 1961, [parental standards] had changed. The student body was now more cosmopolitan, and a fairly large percentage came from larger cities and from higher-income families. Standards had also changed. Family discipline was, in general, less strict, and the children were given much greater liberty. In many families social drinking was a matter of course. When the children from these homes entered college, neither the parents nor the children could see any reason why they should not continue to have the same liberty to which they were accustomed. (Overman 1967, 185)

The demonstrations opened a window so that the press and the public could see what was happening at the university. Once the press revealed the discontent of students and faculty with the administration, and the out-of-date rules, the public and the state legislature soon lost confidence. The university's president also made several serious mistakes during the three months of jousting, which hastened his departure.

The student uprising at Bowling Green State University was not an isolated event. It was part of a national development. But it followed a pattern that was unique to Bowling Green. The uprising was an outgrowth of a crisis of authority that evolved within the university, but it also built upon the conflicts and contradictions that were deeply embedded in American society. While the immediate disturbance lasted only three days, its ripple effects extended beyond a decade into the future of the university.

A NOTE ON BOWLING GREEN
STATE UNIVERSITY'S HISTORY

BGSU's history, we will show, led right into a series of student demonstrations, beginning after World War II. In retrospect these demonstrations look like practice for the big, game-changing demonstration of spring 1961. At the time, the earlier dissent looked like more or less normal student dissatisfaction with a strict school. An additional factor was faculty stress, caused by the transition from being a teachers college to becoming a full-scale university. This created rising expectations for the faculty as they chafed for more academic freedom and scholarly voice. In other words the students and much of the faculty were both feeling oppressed, and it should be no surprise that they shared an interest in liberalizing the university.

In response to the need for teachers in northwest Ohio, Bowling Green State University was founded in 1910, and classes began in the fall of 1914. It was initially a normal school, offering only two years of college and specializing in teacher training. One argument for founding this school in Bowling Green was that the town was dry (that is, it forbade the sale of alcoholic beverages): this was deemed appropriate for a predominantly girls' school. Then in 1921 the school became a college, with four years of schooling and a bachelor's degree. From its beginnings until 1935 the school specialized in producing teachers, with the result that most students were women and the curriculum consisted primarily of education courses. In 1935 the college became a state university, with an expansion of the liberal arts and the addition of a business college and some master's degrees. These changes attracted more male students, and in 1938, for the first time, the number of males equaled the number of females.

When the state revenues declined in 1933 as a result of the Great Depression, the legislature gave serious consideration to closing Bowling Green and turning it into a mental hospital. In response, the university enlisted the support of elites in the neighboring towns of northwest Ohio. Leaders in these communities lobbied for the preservation of the college, and in 1934 the legislature decided to keep the school as it was. The importance of this threat is that it made the college more closely allied with the neighboring communities, which also supplied most of its students. These communities were small, highly religious, and culturally conservative.

In the years following World War II, colleges and universities grew significantly. The educational grants provided to returning veterans had dramatic effects on higher education. Millions of men and women who served in the armed forces during the war were rewarded with generous educational benefits. At the same time, the economic prosperity following the war permitted an increased proportion of men and women from working-class backgrounds to obtain a college education.

The rapid growth spurt of BGSU as a result of World War II seems to have been greater than in other American colleges of the time. Enrollment in 1944 was 1,349, but it jumped to 4,472 by 1947, a larger increase than in comparable institutions. Along with this came similar growth in faculty and buildings. Frank Prout was the school president from 1939 to 1951. It was during the second half of his administration that the university saw the beginning of about fifteen years of student unrest, including a series of student demonstrations.

As Overman says,

> In October of 1949 the first of a series of student strikes and demonstrations occurred. These were to recur at intervals for a number of years. Several reasons were given for these disturbances. Among them was too much faculty domination of the Student Senate, lack of freedom of expression in the *B-G News,* and restrictions on the social use of cars. Although most students denied, in public, that the rules concerning the use of alcoholic beverages were a factor, many admitted in private that they were a major cause. At least these rules received the most publicity in the newspapers.
>
> The fundamental, basic cause underlying all others was the growing feeling on the part of the students that they should have more liberty and less stringent controls. They felt they were capable of regulating their own conduct. They believed they should have a stronger voice in determining University policies and greater freedom to criticize. This attitude was particularly strong among the veterans. (Overman 1967, 147)

Overman mentions a "series of strikes and demonstrations" beginning in 1949, but his only concrete reference is to the one in 1957. Evidently, between 1949 and 1957 there were some kind of modest student eruptions that did not have much impact on the press. These may have been led by the fraternities, since fraternities led the 1957 demonstration. Given that McDonald cleaned out the archives for the fifties, it is a lot harder to check on Overman's comment. Overman was a math teacher and an administrator for this entire time, and it is unlikely that his comment could be in error. Short of combing through the school paper for the entire period, all we can do is accept Overman's comment as an accurate account of a relatively low-level series of protests—what he called demonstrations and strikes. The one in 1957, though, was widely reported in the press, including the *New York Times.* And by the spring of 1961 the students believe there was a long "riot" tradition, even though some of the details are, at this point, obscure.

It should be added that Overman wrote his history, useful as it is, without any scholarly footnotes or documentary references. He had been at the university continuously from its founding, most of his years as the liberal arts dean, and it appears he wrote his history from memory. He was not an historian, so it can be overlooked that he did not have an historian's skills. Still, to not have any archival material from the fifties and to make no mention of this, that is, to refrain from warning future researchers, does seem like a scholarly lapse. Givens (1986), who was an historian, also worked without '50s archives, though he too makes no mention of that fact.

Concerning the 1949 demonstration, a participant, William Day, who later wrote for the *Toledo Blade,* said in a letter to one of the authors,

> The student problems at BG actually started in the fall of 1949 when then President, Frank Prout, with the approval of the BG Board, approved new car rules. These said that coeds were not permitted to ride in cars on the BG campus at any time, unless accompanied by a parent, legal guardian or with special permission of the University President. This rule came about, according to Prout, because of complaints he had received from parents of coeds. The parents said that coeds were put at risk by riding in cars driven by male students, many of whom were WW II veterans and were older than the normal male students. The car rules lead to an aborted student strike that fall, and was page 1 news in the *Toledo Blade* and *Cleveland Plain Dealer,* among other newspapers.
>
> The student strike ended quickly when female student were warned not to participate, and some male students were unaware of the effort. The strike against the car rules was the result of the expulsion of two prominent students caught riding in a car. Instead of the strike being billed because of the car rules, it was decided that the strike would be billed as Freedom of the Press (censorship of the student newspaper of which I was the editor at that time) and freedom of the student senate of which James Galloway was the president. This effort by students ended with a relaxation of administrative supervision of the *BG*

News and the student senate, but no change in the car rules, which were later on modified. (Day 2001)

Notice how the students shifted the emphasis from car rules to freedom of the press and the student senate. This definition of the demonstration seems to have been a case of ordinary putting your best foot forward. In 1961 the grievances were again continually reformulated, although this time it was because American society at large, after the civil disobedience of the early civil-rights protestors, had redefined issues in the direction of civil rights and civil liberties.

In another place, Overman comments on the 1957 demonstration:

The first student riot occurred in 1949, during President Prout's administration. A similar disturbance took place early in the morning of Friday, May 24, 1957. The chief cause of the earlier (1949) riot was the resentment of the students against the strict regulations concerning the use of automobiles and alcoholic beverages. By 1957 the automobile restrictions were much more lenient, but those on the use of alcoholic beverages had become even more stringent.

Early in May of 1957, two fraternities were disciplined for serving alcoholic beverages at off-campus social events. This action was supported by the Inter-fraternity Council and by an editorial in the *B-G News*. No disturbances occurred at that time. However, at one o'clock in the morning of Friday, May 24, a torchlight demonstration started on campus protesting the action taken against these fraternities. About 300 students participated and, after touring the campus, congregated on East Wooster Street in front of the President's home. Since this street was also U.S. Highway 6, the crowd caused a traffic jam which soon extended for over half a mile. University police and city police, city firemen, sheriff's deputies, and state highway patrolmen were soon on the scene, and a series of fights started in which several received minor injuries. Finally, the traffic jam was broken by driving several large trucks through the crowd. By 3 a.m., the crowd dispersed and order was restored. (Overman 1967, 183–184)

A student remembers the 1957 demonstration as follows:

The 1957 riots were organized by fraternities. The demonstration was a minor one until the Bowling Green City Fire Department showed up. Before that it was just a bunch of disgruntled students and fraternity members. The addition of the Fire Department kicked things up a notch. Things really escalated when Don McFadden, a member of Pi Kappa Alpha (Pike) and others took a fire hose from the Fire Department. Don also took the Fire Chief's hat, put it on, and turned the fire hose, which was being used for crowd dispersal, back on the members of the Fire Department! Needless to say, this action electrified the crowd and kept the riot going for at least another two hours. A while later both city and campus police were able to drive the crowd away and regain control of the situation. (Glynn 2006)

The riot tradition, as it was called, was etched in the memories of students in 1961, although the memory was neither detailed nor crisp.

The main memory was of the 1957 demonstration with its dramatic torchlight parade and its turning of the tables on the fire department. Still, the 1957 action, after two hours, had been talked down by Dean Elden Smith, and the university knew it could again bring out trucks to stop the students from blocking traffic if necessary.

When Prout left office in 1951 there was a careful search for his replacement. The choice went to Ralph McDonald, a PhD in education whose experience was largely in educational administration. McDonald continued to expand the student body, reaching an enrollment of 6,229 by 1960–1961. McDonald was especially known for raising salaries and increasing the proportion of faculty having a PhD. This made him highly popular with some, but it led to faculty division, as the largest salaries went to those who had completed their PhD. Also there was heavy pressure placed on faculty to finish their PhDs if they had not already done so. Increasing academic qualifications, however, made for a faculty that was perhaps too cosmopolitan for this institution. In other words, the institution held to somewhat archaically conservative rules, even though both the student body and the faculty were changing in a demographic direction that chafed against these rules. Another problem was that by the late 1950s and early 1960s the faculty consisted largely of newcomers.

The demonstrations continued and deepened during the McDonald years. One might expect a new president to gradually liberalize the rules and thereby settle down the students. Instead, McDonald, by and large, made the rules even stricter. This behavior suggests trouble ahead. Throughout the ten unstable years of his administration, the student complaints centered primarily on rules concerning the use of automobiles, alcohol, and the expression of affection (hand-holding and kissing) on campus. Of similar importance were the questions of freedom in student government and in the campus newspaper.

McDonald did liberalize the rules concerning automobiles. In 1951, at the end of Prout's presidency, not only was the use of cars on campus quite limited, but women students were also forbidden to be in automobiles at any time. The latter rule was largely to prevent boys and girls from expressing affection in cars. As Overman says, "This prohibition was partly the result of lack of sufficient parking space on (or near) the campus, but this was not the principal reason. For some time, the citizens of Bowling Green and surrounding communities had complained about petters parking in cars, both on city streets and country lanes" (1967, 145). While McDonald did soften the car rules, as late as 1960–1961 couples were still forbidden to engage in holding hands on campus or in kissing in front of the girls' dormitories after their dates. In addition McDonald made the rules concerning alcohol even stricter. In earlier times the university simply had rules about excessive drinking. Then in 1953 all alcohol was forbidden, both on campus and at off-campus student events. And in 1959 all students, regardless of age, were forbidden to drink alcohol at any time, except when at home with parents' permission. The punishment for getting caught was expulsion.

There was also an unwritten rule in 1960–1961 forbidding professors from drinking in public, that is, in such places as bars and restaurants. For example, the liberal arts dean Emerson Shuck told new professors that "your home is your castle," meaning it is all right for you to drink in your own residences. Newly hired professors were told that being caught drinking in downtown Bowling Green was grounds for non-renewal of contract and dismissal. Faculty members who did have parties in their homes felt uncomfortable about putting their whiskey bottles out on the curb as trash. Some would drive out of town, to a nearby state park, and put the bottles in those trash containers.

During the McDonald years, in summary, the students were becoming more worldly, urban, and unhappy about the strict rules. McDonald responded primarily by making the rules stricter. In addition, he succeeded in improving the quality of the faculty, but he did not permit an increased degree of control by the faculty in the affairs of the university. Dramatic changes were occurring in both the students and the faculty at the same time that the administration was holding on tightly to notions about conventional authority and morality.

The focus of Chapter 2 will be the three days of demonstrations themselves, originating in a fraternity water fight that escalated into a major uprising. Administrative attempts to use repressive measures were unsuccessful, and this series of events, set in motion by responses and counter-responses, culminated in the eventual resignation of a university president. Before the episode ended, all constituencies of the university became involved.

These included the faculty, all of the administration, the news media, the university's board of trustees, and the Ohio state legislature. What started out as an unfocused demonstration led to the development of a specific list of student grievances. The president of the university called a faculty meeting to elicit faculty support for suppressing the students. A confrontation at this meeting between the president and a faculty member resulted in the subsequent firing of the faculty member. The events set in motion had enduring effects on the growth and development of the university.

The need for remedial action may sometimes persist for very long periods of time before anything is done. The students did not have it within their power alone to change the repressive measures that had been instituted by the administration. But when they obtained the support and involvement of the faculty, major changes were brought about within a relatively short period of time.

In Chapter 3 we pause to look at the larger context, the sixties protest decade. This will allow us to continue the narrative with a firmer footing in historical reality. In this chapter we fit Bowling Green into the stream of events that constituted the sixties. After doing this we take on the causal question of what brought about the sixties. The cause of the Bowling Green demonstrations is fairly clear, but the cause of the national turn to student protest and counterculture is less clear. We use the key social theorists, Emile Durkheim, Karl Marx, and Max Weber, as well as a look at post–World War II American history, to tackle this question.

In Chapter 4 we examine the values, orientations, and basic life commitment of the constituencies engaged in the conflict. This will involve foremost a focus on the personalities of President Ralph McDonald and his adversary, Sherman M. Stanage, an assistant professor in the philosophy department. In addition, we will review some of the major ways in which the composition of the student body and the faculty had changed by the early 1960s.

In Chapter 5 we will consider the communication resources or "voices" of the major players—the students, administration, and faculty—in this drama. These voices, both in form and content, changed enormously after the three days of demonstration. The students, after decades of being kept silent, became loud, public, and articulate. The administration continued with its tried and true methods, but its voice became repetitive and ineffective. And the faculty gradually found a new voice and newly opened channels for expressing this voice.

Some of the ripple effects of the student upheaval and the removal of an authoritarian president will be examined in Chapter 6. Foremost among the immediate changes was the way in which the faculty seized the opportunity provided by a power vacuum and took control of the university. After an interval of a two-year search, William T. Jerome was selected as the new president. His administrative style may be summarized around the notion of the president serving as a catalyst to maximize the use of talent at all levels of organization and to promote the development of an innovative and creative university.

The ripple effects also included a continuation of the student tradition of protests. As was the case at major colleges and universities across the country, the students at Bowling Green addressed unnecessary social control measures, and the exclusion of students from consequential decision-making within the university. Before the decade was over, the students had won the right to be represented on all major committees and councils within the university. The student protest and demonstrations during the 1960s were less about the internal structures of the university than about the events that were occurring in the larger society.

In Chapter 7 the major explanations of the student upheaval at Bowling Green will be reviewed. Special emphasis will be given to the combination of solidarity and framing, two forces that draw deeply on sociological theory. The unusual combination of these two forces explains BG's status as a deviant case.

Chapter 8 will consider explaining the transition from the fifties to the sixties as it occurred at Bowling Green. Nationally this was a complex transition, but at Bowling Green you could actually see it happening. The Bowling Green demonstrations were transitional in two senses. Temporally they occurred just as the fifties were passing into the sixties. But they also showed how the nature of the issues and the strategic moves of the students were changing. We are not saying that the Bowling Green case caused the sixties, though it undoubtedly had some influence. Rather this case shows how the sixties differed from the fifties at BG. The difference came about by shifting in midair so to speak, as issues, tactics, and leadership changed from a fifties to a sixties style.

Chapter 9 is also on how the fifties became the sixties but now we are looking at the larger culture in the United States. The sixties might seem like a sharp change from the fifties, but there are a lot of continuities. This chapter shows how minor social contradictions grew in the fifties and became the highly conflictual issues of the sixties.

The conclusion argues that the McDonald administration was destroyed by several powerful waves of opposition, an overdetermined conclusion to its reign. The major force, though, seems to have been an early surge of what became the sixties wave of feminist liberation.

Finally, there are three appendices. One is a statement framed in the existential language of Sherman Stanage's classes. The student author composed a list of issues as they would have been formed by Stanage. This statement is in a distinctly post-fifties consciousness. On the other hand, despite the existential phrasing, the key message seems to be "Give us our American rights, our privacy, and let us alone." Second, we reprint Ralph McDonald's speech to the faculty. This statement was one of the major moves on the part of the administration. It is formed in the old voice that was, at that very time, becoming ineffective and obsolete. It explains why the protest happened in terms that make the administration completely blameless. It is nevertheless well constructed and is vintage Ralph McDonald. He had the spellbinding style of an experienced preacher.

The third appendix is a report of a recent interview with Robert Brinza, who was one of the nine students who went to the statehouse to air grievances to the legislature. The interview was conducted in March of 2008, but, despite the lengthy time interval, it gives a gripping description of how the students walked into the legislature and captured the legislators' attention. Brinza plays the role of the classic anthropological informant for us. He tells us that the students were met with mixed responses at the time, but that their main impact was in bringing about the trustee-expansion bill. The near unanimous passage of this bill, three months after the student visit, brought about the deposing of the McDonald administration.

Chapter 2

The BGSU Student Uprising

There were recurrent complaints about President McDonald among both students and faculty in the 1960–1961 school year. For students, the complaints centered on the rules and regulations, while for faculty, the concerns were with their lack of influence in the governance of the university. An example of these complaints was the belief that McDonald set the prices at the candy counter of the student union. He probably did not, but there was a widespread perception that he kept his hands on all decisions and would not delegate authority to anyone. Both the faculty and the students were griping, and sometimes they were griping to each other. There were also frequent references among students to the 1957 demonstrations, when traffic was blocked on U.S. Route 6, which bordered the campus. The demonstration precedents were somewhat mythologized but had a basis in fact, and they were a constant reference point for the restive students.[1]

In November 1960, John F. Kennedy gave a cocky speech in nearby Toledo, just a few days before he was elected president. The Kennedy style was informal and culturally liberal, and this had an effect on student attitudes. The passing of the Eisenhower years and the shift to the Democratic Party made it seem as though there were new possibilities, both in the nation as a whole and on the Bowling Green campus. The New Left had not yet quite appeared, but the fifties Beatnik movement, with its preoccupations with authenticity and existentialism, was still in evidence. The city of Toledo, which was only twenty miles north of Bowling Green, had coffeehouses in which one could hear long-haired beatniks recite their poetry.

In addition, the civil rights movement, including the Montgomery, Alabama, bus boycott and the more recent student sit-ins, had been going on for several years. Kennedy had reached out to Martin Luther King when King was in jail, and this gesture made civil disobedience seem less like breaking a law and more like stating a moral truth. Just the previous spring there had been a small civil rights demonstration in front of the downtown Woolworth, attended by Bowling Green students and the Toledo NAACP.

By late winter of 1961, there were frequent student rumors about a spring demonstration. There was even a projected date, Sunday, April 9, which would appear in whispers and graffiti on campus. And there was a plan. It was known that as soon as a demonstration began, the administration would lock the women into their dormitories, preventing them from joining the group that had begun the demonstration. No one asked if this lock-up might be illegal. The women, perhaps even more than the men, were getting increasingly unhappy on this campus and ready to protest. Organized feminism would not appear until later in the sixties, but the underlying demographics of increased divorce rates, premarital sex, female employment, later marriage, and fewer children were already creating cognitive dissonance for women.

The four women's dormitories were together in what was called the Founders Quadrangle. The plan was to go to Founders first, liberate the women, and then block traffic on U.S. Route 6, a major link between Cleveland and Chicago. The traffic blocking was as far as the plan went, but it was somehow expected that the stalled traffic would break the administration's back. The plan and the date were actually in the realm of mythology. There was no one appointed to start the demonstration and no political organization to get things rolling. Of course, everyone, including the administration, knew of the plan and the date.

In fact the planning and the incantation of dates had been around at least since the 1957 demonstrations, appearing every spring and then disappearing when nothing happened. There was no good reason to believe this spring would be any different. The demonstration talk was a ritual that did little more than blow off steam. But this time an unexpected convergence of events actually created the conditions for the demonstration. And it did so, as it turned out, two weeks early.

THREE DAYS OF DEMONSTRATIONS

Sunday, March 26, was an unseasonably warm day in what had been a chilly month. It was sunny, and the temperature hit 72 by early afternoon. The cabin fever of a tough winter lifted immediately. It was a time to be out and celebrating. Townspeople were taking walks and Sunday drives. Students were strolling around and shouting at each other. Wraps were left at home and a summery show of bodies was in evidence. It was as though spring had been skipped and we'd gone right into summer. There was the sound of loud radios, both in dorms and in automobiles. Cars full of students were circling campus and driving slowly along Wooster Street, the heralded route of the demonstration plan. Students were calling from cars, and some were leaning out the windows or even sitting on car roofs. The weather was making people high spirited and a bit rowdy. It was clearly a day of spring fever, and perhaps part of the exuberance was in the anticipation of the predicted demonstrations, fourteen days hence.

The First Day. One of the attractions on this afternoon was a water fight between the pledges and members of Sigma Chi fraternity. The pledging had just been completed and the water fight was meant to be a male-bonding ritual. The frat houses were at the periphery of the campus on fraternity row, adjacent to a playing field the frats often used. Though on the edge, they were still physically part of the campus. The water fight had ten to twenty men on each side, rushing each other with buckets and sometimes balloons full of water. It was good, clean fun, so colorful and exciting that it began to attract a crowd of onlookers.

At Bowling Green the fraternities and sororities were composed of the student elite, both in socioeconomic status and in the eyes of the administration. These young men and women were campus leaders, and, in later life, they frequently became economically successful, loyal alumni and alumnae. The frats were capable of high jinks, however, and there was constant friction over the clandestine use of alcohol at their parties.

Water fights on fraternity row were a tradition at Bowling Green, and this one was going according to expectations. One difference, however, was the size of the crowd. The good weather and the tingly atmosphere conspired to make the water fight an intense attraction. The two frat groups, pledges and regulars, hammed it up for the crowd, ambushing each other and dancing around like circus clowns. The fight had gone on for a couple hours and the weather was getting a little cooler, but the crowd if anything had gotten bigger, and the fight showed no signs of stopping. Word went out that fraternity row was the place to be.[2]

By late afternoon the crowd of several hundred, almost all of whom were students, did not seem to want to disperse, even though the afternoon was approaching the dinner hour. At this point several campus police appeared and announced that the water fight was over and the crowd should go home. Most of the fraternity boys did not leave, however, and some continued to throw water, even in the presence of the police. Nor, with all this excitement, did the crowd start breaking up.

There was a standoff between students and police for some time, with the police obviously not wanting to escalate things. Then the dean of men, Wallace Taylor, came from home and appeared on the scene to take charge of the situation. His long leather coat made it clear he was boss. Taylor repeated what the police had said, that it was time to leave, but he said it with long-practiced authority. Still the crowd did not budge, nor did the water fighters go back to their house.

Taylor was unaccustomed to this kind of disobedience, and he proceeded to push back the crowd of perhaps five hundred single-handedly in the attempt to clear the field. As he walked toward the onlookers in one segment of the circle, they would recede a bit, but the other segments moved forward and got closer in. Then the dean would move to another segment, again physically pushing the onlookers back, but the rest of the circle would move forward. The dean, who was obviously unskilled at crowd control, was inadvertently tightening the circle around himself. It was unclear where all this was going. But the tension suggested that something might happen.

Then, to everyone's surprise, one of the pledges snuck up behind the dean and hit him on the head with a balloon full of water. This was so unexpected and shocking that no one did anything for a moment. It had to sink in. Then the balloon-thrower began to run, the dean and the police started running after him, and the crowd followed the police. When the crowd started running it seemed to crystallize into a unified body. Almost instantly people started shouting, "Founders, Founders," as in the plan. Some of the crowd continued to follow the police, but most of it ran toward Founders to get the coeds. The unlikely and largely imaginary demonstration had actually begun, and it was ignited not by student rowdies but by a dean who had overplayed his hand.

The group that went to Founders, just a couple of minutes away, got there too late. The doors were already locked, preventing the women from joining the demonstration. Still, there were enough demonstrators to block traffic on Route 6 for a while, until the crowd started walking through the campus. The central event of the one-night 1957 demonstration had been the blocking of traffic after a torchlight parade, from about two to three in the morning, at which time the half-mile traffic jam was broken by driving several large trucks through the crowd (Overman 1967, 184). The plan this time was to again make traffic-blocking the central tactic, but this demonstration turned out to be much more reflexive and "talky" than the previous one, centering more on the discussion and articulation of grievances than on marches or traffic-blocking.

A crowd of about five hundred to one thousand went to the student union, which was a natural rallying point. President McDonald and his wife had just eaten dinner in the elegant Carnation Room of the union, and he went out to meet the crowd. He "spoke to the group about the pops concert, the firing of the Alpha Tau Omega head resident, the drinking regulations and various other grievances" (*BG News,* March 28, 1961). McDonald later reported in his March 29, 1961, speech to the faculty that "It was a good natured group."

Some of the group went to downtown Bowling Green, about a half mile from the campus and another traditional rallying point for demonstrations. But most of it circulated around the campus in a seemingly random pattern. First, they went to the library, then back to the union, subsequently to the commons, where, coincidentally, there was a fire in a boiler room, and finally back to Founders. Most of the girls had to be in their dorms by 10:00 p.m., so this was a natural time and place to conclude a demonstration. The crowd broke up by ten fifteen.

But before moving to the second day, we should comment on how Dean Taylor inadvertently started the uprising. This will be a theoretical parenthesis but it is necessary to capture how the dean changed the political dynamics. A crowd had assembled to watch the water fight. On a repressive campus a crowd is always a danger to the administration. Crowds seem to intensify group consciousness. In addition, while students might be afraid of reprisals if they disobey the rules alone and as individuals, a crowd is harder to police. If a crowd breaks the rules, it is more likely to get away with it. This emboldens people in crowds. For this reason a crowd is precisely what the students needed to actually begin the much-anticipated "riot."

From the administration's point of view, crowd control meant, first, not allowing any crowd, or at least any uncontrolled crowd, to form at all. In this case the warm weather was unpredictable, so it functioned as an "act of god" to create a crowd. This was the first condition for starting a demonstration. Still, the crowd had acted in a normal way throughout the two or three hours of the water fight. In other words, it was an ordinary audience rather than a volatile crowd. If the administration had allowed the afternoon to move along, the weather to cool off, and the water fight to end, the crowd would have dispersed naturally.

What formed the audience into a self-aware crowd was the arrival of the campus police. The police addressed and confronted the now alert crowd. Also, the original relationship had been between the crowd and the water fighters. This was an ordinary binary relationship, formed for entertainment, much like that between the audience and performers at an athletic contest or a concert. What the police did was reconstruct the psychology of the situation. What had been a peaceful relationship between the audience and the performers now became a tense and repressive relationship between the police and the crowd of students. The purpose of the police's arrival was to prevent a riot, but it started moving things in that direction, that is, toward a riot.

The dean arrived because the crowd had been refusing to disperse. It was defying the police. His arrival, as we have pointed out, poured oil on the fire. Dean Taylor further unified and angered the crowd by his physically pushing people around. He would place his hands on their shoulders and give them a shove. This slowly made the crowd into a noose around his neck and prepared the way for the spark that started the uprising.

In terms of classic social theory the police and then the dean transformed the crowd into a self-conscious, personalized assembly of people, and an emboldened one at that. In formal terms, the dean changed a "crowd in itself" into a "crowd for itself." Initially the crowd was an audience of individuals. The psychological connection was between the audience members, taken as individuals, and the water fighters. There was no connection among the audience members, except for the superficial one of being together at a performance. They were like an audience in a movie theater, that is, together physically but not psychologically or socially. To change them into a self-conscious assembly or crowd for itself, they had to be treated as a crowd for itself. The dean treated them as an organized group, a corporate entity, and in doing so he made them into an organized group.

The crowd was now consciously conspiring to undermine the dean by taking one step backward and five steps forward. They knew they were defying not only the police but also the overconfident dean. But they could do this risk-free because of the confusion of the situation and the anonymity of the crowd. When the dean treated them as a unified entity and they thus began to act as a unified entity, they underwent an important transformation. They became a kind of organization with a division of labor and a shared consciousness, that is, a crowd for itself. The division of labor had to do with the way the segments of the circle took turns going backward and forward. The shared consciousness had to do with a growing "Let's get the dean" mood. This kind of crowd, as we will explain later, is the sort of thing the great theorist Emile Durkheim had in mind when he discussed how ritual can construct (and reconstruct) reality. A crowd for itself is a ritual crowd. It can act jointly. It can change "reality" by symbolizing and acting in novel ways.

The behavior of the now demonstrating students subsequent to the duel with the dean bespoke a new confidence and a new "voice." We will continue to discuss the sequence of the demonstration, from day to day, but the crucial transformation occurred over the water fight. From this point on, until President McDonald resigned in June, the students stayed, psychologically, in the same assembled state the dean had put them in. They now had a new self-awareness, a more vivid consciousness, a bolder voice, and an almost magical power to reconstruct the reality, that is, the meaning of the reality, of the university. We will discuss this process in more detail in the theory section of Chapter 7.

The Second Day. On Monday, the second day of the demonstrations, students attended class as usual. They had planned to resume the demonstration in the dining halls at 5:00 p.m., but because of the presence of police they gathered outside the union instead. Some went downtown and "ran wild," according to one newspaper report, but the majority gathered around a public speaking system in front of the union. At this point the demonstration turned from action to talk.

An early speaker was Rev. James Trautwein, vicar of St. John's Episcopal Church, which served the campus. Trautwein said, "I am speaking to you as a mediator, not as a representative of the university faculty nor as a representative of the student body." He suggested three possible courses of action for the next day, Tuesday: that the students stay in their rooms and refuse to attend classes; that they attend but refuse to answer when spoken to; or that they go home. Trautwein's talk elevated the moral tone of the demonstration. He was a local clergyman and therefore an authority figure. He spoke of "mediating," which implied justice on both sides of the dispute, and he recommended following paths of civil disobedience. The civil rights movement had been going on for several years; Trautwein's language suggested that this demonstration too pertained to civil rights.

Another speaker, who was the head of the philosophy department, was Sherman Stanage. He would gradually become the central person in the faculty wing of the demonstrations. He told the students that he was proud of their behavior that evening in front of the union. He noted that they had been orderly and had listened quietly to numerous speakers. Stanage also observed that many were in accord with what the students were doing, as long as they remained peaceful. Stanage further noted, "Bowling Green can grow up in this moment if you will let it" (Gordon 1965, 4). Other speakers urging peaceful activity that evening were Wallace W. Taylor, dean of men; Bernie Casey, senior and star football player; Clark Tibbits, student body president-elect; and Murray Ferderber, student newspaper columnist.

This evening of talking resulted in the decision to boycott classes the next day, Tuesday. But more importantly it initiated the central quest of the demonstration—to search for the purpose and meaning of the actions. The speeches by two preachers, Rev. Trautwein and Dr. Stanage, who was a Methodist minister as well as a philosophy professor, framed the demonstration in moral, if not religious, terms. This began a move away from the traditional grievances, which had centered on automobiles, alcohol, and women's hours and only secondarily on newspaper censorship, student government, and other civil liberties issues. The administration wanted to label this a beer riot, motivated by spring fever and fueled by outside agitators, but the participants in the demonstration were defining it in increasingly elevated terms.

The Third Day. On Tuesday there was a class boycott, which seemed moderately successful, though there are no statistics on how it went. About three hundred students sat on blankets on the lawn in front of the union, listening to portable radios, playing cards, limbo dancing, and enjoying the picnic-like atmosphere. The administration made no attempt to break up the boycott, although the usual treatment of unexcused absences would prevail, namely, that only one absence per course per semester would be allowed. The usual number of allowed absences in American universities at that time was "twice the number of semester hours, minus one," so Bowling Green's absence rule was one of its extreme control measures. Not all the boycotting students were out on the lawn. Some were in their dorms or out and about, and others even went home for the spring vacation a day early.

The Gordon (1965) report observed that while the students maintained their classroom sit-out, fraternity, sorority, and dormitory representatives in an extraordinary session drew up a list of ten of the most serious grievances for presentation to the student council that afternoon. Recommendations of the council were to be presented to the student body at 4:30 p.m. and to President McDonald in the evening (6). As Gordon said,

> Student Council action Tuesday afternoon apparently failed to satisfy Bowling Green students. The 10 most serious grievances were not determined and council merely promised to consider grievances at a special meeting more than two weeks hence. A crowd awaited Student Body President Keith Trowbridge outside the Union about 5:30 p.m., and he made an unsuccessful attempt to gain the crowd's acceptance of the postponement.

A few minutes later President McDonald appeared and ordered the students to disperse within ten minutes. In response, he was jeered and booed. Police moved in to break up the crowd, which then re-formed on another part of the campus. As the size of the group grew, so did its activity. The president was burned in effigy, and students chanted, sang songs, heard speeches, and lit a bonfire. Eight students were dismissed for Tuesday night's activity (five of whom were later cleared), and thirty others were questioned after vacation. One of the dismissed said "his only mistake was in not staying in the dorm" (Gordon, 12). At about eight thirty President McDonald again ordered the crowd to disperse, the police moved in, and the campus quieted for the evening.

On this third day of the demonstration, the one before spring vacation, there was clearly a breakdown in communication. The student council, which had a reputation for being friendly to the administration, could not agree on its list of grievances. This meant the demonstrators could not communicate with McDonald, and Rev. Trautwein's mediating process could not be carried out. As a result, the proceedings became aimless on Tuesday night. At about nine McDonald took the extremely serious step of reading the riot act to the students, which was the equivalent of declaring martial law on campus. So ended the third day.

IMMEDIATE AFTERMATH

The students left campus for their homes the next day, Wednesday, and the administration heaved a sigh of relief. Vacations usually dissipate student unrest, and there was no reason to think this vacation would be any different. Students normally lose their momentum during these intervals, and administrators regroup. The return of the students after several days at home is typically a return to business as usual on campus.

But this vacation was different. Already on Tuesday, the day of the class boycott, some students had returned to their hometowns early and were talking to newspaper reporters. The Bowling Green demonstrations were big news in Ohio, and everyone wanted to know the what and, more particularly, the why of events on campus. The one thing most students had decided during the three days was that their protest was not about beer and sex. They were calling for reform, academic freedom, civil liberties, and an atmosphere of fairness on campus. In addition, the word *crusade* was used with increasing frequency.

Nor was it a secret in Ohio that Bowling Green State University was a strict, conservative campus, more like a private, Bible Belt college than one supported by public funds. In particular many liberal Protestants and Jews and probably some Catholics as well were wondering whether the Bowling Green administration might be somewhat out of date, if not of dubious legality. The expression of this concern was soon located on the editorial pages of the *Toledo Blade,* possibly the most powerful newspaper in the state and certainly the most important one in Bowling Green's northeast Ohio.

During the vacation week, then, the demonstration continued in another form. Students talked to their parents and to people in their communities. There was continued talk to reporters and letters continued to be written to editors. And, most portentously, some began to talk to state legislators, to make plans for sending delegations to the capitol and to see the governor. Far from acting guilty, the students sensed a moral advantage, and they made full use of it. They returned to campus not with less but with more momentum.

Back on campus, another important event occurred the very afternoon the students were leaving. President McDonald addressed the faculty concerning his interpretation of the demonstrations. McDonald spoke to the faculty at what was called at Bowling Green a faculty meeting. These meetings were not in any sense controlled by the faculty. There actually was a faculty senate on this campus, but it met only when called by the administration, and it had not met for a long time. Faculty meetings themselves were called by the president and were forums at which McDonald would address the faculty about some issue he felt was pressing. The faculty itself, like the moribund faculty senate, did not call the meetings, control their procedures, or even speak at them. The meetings were more like high school assemblies at which the principal would address the students. In addition, attendance was compulsory.

On this occasion, Wednesday afternoon the week of the demonstrations, the issue was the demonstrations themselves and why they had occurred. By now it should be obvious that the main question concerning these demonstrations was not what had happened during the events of the three days, but why it had happened or what caused it. The students themselves had gone through several waves of explanation during the three days in question. These began with the disputed lifestyle rules concerning drinking and boy-girl relations. They evolved into issues of autonomy, freedom, and civil liberties. And by the third day of the demonstration they were approaching philosophical and moral ideals that evoked the tones of Christian existentialism. On Tuesday, Sherman Stanage's students distributed a manifesto entitled "We Want to Be!" (see Appendix A). The thirteen demands on this list included such items as "creative expression," "high academic standards," "individuality," "not being machines," "dialogue," "communication," and "evaluated rules." In other words, the students kept purifying and systematizing the goals of the demonstration. They were also anticipating the anti-machine theme that would pervade Mario Savio's famous "Put your bodies upon the gears" speech at Berkeley in December 1964.

When McDonald addressed the faculty he explained the demonstrations as a combination of spring fever and relatively childish complaints about sound rules. He also blamed student outsiders, suggesting there was an organized plan to recruit them from other campuses. In addition he blamed the press for inflating the story with exaggerated and inaccurate details. He blamed, without actually naming them, Trautwein and Stanage for addressing the students the second night, bringing up the idea of grievances, and dignifying the protest. Finally, he blamed the state legislature for underfunding the school, creating campus crowdedness and making the students uncomfortable with the inadequate facilities. He made no concessions and advanced no suggestions about reform or liberalization. After speaking for about forty-five minutes, he concluded by asking the faculty to exert an orderly influence on the students when they returned to campus (see Appendix B for McDonald's speech). McDonald had started out a bit tentatively, but he gradually became quite relaxed and fluent. His talk may have been too unyielding and spread the blame around too much, but it was McDonald at his best, and, at the conclusion, he had every reason to believe he had checkmated the students with his oratory.

At one point early in his speech he glared at a young woman, an instructor in the physical education department, who was sitting in one of the front rows of the hall, taking notes. He asked her who she was and what she was doing there. McDonald normally met with all the new faculty as they were hired, and he had probably met this young woman the previous spring, but he had evidently forgotten what she looked like. He confronted her with the obvious implication that she was not supposed to be at the meeting, that she was either a newspaper reporter or some other person of untoward purposes. The young instructor explained her status in an embarrassed and flustered manner and McDonald accepted her explanation.[3] But the flow of his remarks had now been broken and an element of suspiciousness had been revealed.

When he had concluded his talk there was no question period or opportunity for faculty members to speak. Instead, he was preparing to dismiss the assembly, as was his usual practice at these meetings. But on this occasion one of the faculty members, Sherman Stanage, of the Monday night address to the student demonstrators, began to speak. McDonald tried to silence Stanage, and they went back and forth, negotiating Stanage's right to speak. Once Stanage managed to get the floor, he disagreed with the president and took the side of the students. There is no record of exactly what he said, but in a letter to the authors (October 1, 1998), who were all three in attendance at the meeting, he gave the following recollection:

> I remember very distinctly what I said immediately after Mac's speech. I stood up as he finished and said, "President McDonald, I rise to speak in behalf of a vanishing ideal of Bowling Green State University—the ideal of free speech." He demanded several times that I sit down, but I refused to do so (even though Brian Sutton-Smith, who was seated next to me, kept tugging at my pants leg and imploring me to sit down). Finally McDonald changed his mind and said (dismissively), "those who wish to stay and listen to Mr. Stanage can do so, but the rest may leave." There was a commotion caused by a few persons. I remember especially John Coash, Chair of Geology, and Donald Kleckner, Chair of Speech—persons trying to rush out as quickly as possible. The reason for the commotion was that persons around them were keeping their legs in place and were not allowing these persons to leave very easily. Some persons almost fell as a result of their rush and the condition of no easy exiting. I remember reading from the copy of the student leaflet which I had. In fact this leaflet was a genuinely existentialist document written by a student in my existentialism seminar that semester. The leaflet was entitled "WE WANT TO BE!" I said, "The students have asked us for bread and we have given them stones.... All they want us to do is listen to them and to their concerns...."

After Stanage's speech the faculty meeting ended, and the emotions of the audience were quite tangled. McDonald had given the expected address, in which he had rejected the concerns of the students, explained these concerns in an unflattering manner, and ordered the faculty to maintain an orderly campus when the students returned. Stanage, in contrast, had taken the side of the students and expressed their concerns in a highly idealistic fashion. In addition, by breaking the faculty meeting rule and insisting on speaking, he had argued for free speech by seizing it. In other words, the faculty heard both extremes, the president's unyielding argument against the demonstrations and Stanage's rather principled argument for them. There was a thicket of emotions in the audience, but perhaps the most immediate feeling was for Stanage himself. He had demonstrated an extraordinary degree of courage in defying President McDonald and speaking for the students, but his action was also quite risky, if not foolhardy.

A noteworthy feature of this McDonald-Stanage struggle was that Stanage introduced the ideal of free speech as the main issue of the demonstration. Not only did this dignify the protest, but it also introduced what would become the major issue of the student sixties—of the Free Speech Movement at Berkeley, for instance. This incident also began the change in the structure of "voice" on this campus, which we discuss at some length in Chapter 5.

Bowling Green State University was not a bastion of democracy. It was a highly paternalistic if not an authoritarian institution, and this power structure had not changed a great deal since the old normal-school days. President McDonald's nickname was Black Mac, because he always wore black suits and had had the dining room in the president's residence painted all black. Black Mac was not known for either sharing authority or tolerating dissent. On the contrary, he and his loyal administration did not hesitate to punish disobedience or deviance. Stanage had engaged in the most disobedient and deviant behavior ever heard of on this campus. And even though he had gotten away with it for the moment, there was an unspoken question of what would happen to his career as the spring progressed. For the time being, though, he was the hero of the liberal faculty, for he had galvanized faculty dissent and support for the student ideals.

TWO MONTHS OF MANEUVERING

The students returned to campus on Wednesday, April 5, one week after they had departed. They had used that week to fight the battle for public opinion, for a favorable press, and for a sympathetic ear in the state legislature. To show how this politicking proceeded, it will be necessary to quote extensively from Ohio newspapers (as reported in Gordon's research). Initially most Ohio newspapers accepted the administration's side of the story and spoke against the students. In a March 29 interview with Harvey Ford, the *Toledo Blade*'s education editor, McDonald gave the following interpretation of the demonstration:

> President McDonald explained the student outbreak by saying it began as a simple expression of student high spirits in spring weather on Sunday night. Sensational and inflammatory radio reports of this encouraged the students to turn a spring prank into a major crisis, he said. And in order to justify their conduct students were now digging up all sorts of grievances which had been far from their minds when the troubles began. (Gordon 1965, 9)

During the same week as the Bowling Green demonstrations there had been actual student beer riots at Fort Lauderdale, Florida, during spring break. These were clearly hedonistic, irresponsible, and not principled in any way. They were quite sensational and had captured the attention of the national press. When the Bowling Green story hit the papers on Monday the 27th, it was inevitably seen as related to the Florida riots, particularly since the Bowling Green administration was suggesting this interpretation.

Among the headlines were the following: Police Fear New Riot at Bowling Green U: 7 Arrested As 2,000 Stage BGU Protest; Police Quell Bowling Green Student Antics; Bowling Green Riot Blamed on Spring Fever; Student Rioters Defy Prexy; Students Go On Rampage (Gordon 1965, 3).

But the students expected this and they just kept telling their version of the story. The students were gradually successful, and by Wednesday the 29th the press began to show a slight shift toward the position of the students. The *Lima News,* in a bylined story, said,

> Several professors, who asked that they remain anonymous because of reprisals, indicated they supported the students in their peaceful actions to gain recognition. Reports indicated that between one-half and two thirds of the faculty favored the student activities and complaints. The students, many who said they were afraid to openly participate because of various pressures, charged that the professors did not have freedom of speech. (Gordon 1965, 9)

More significantly, as Gordon points out, "Only *The Toledo Blade* hinted that there might be more to the trouble at Bowling Green than was readily apparent. The editorial was called 'Cold War at BGSU.'"

> These college or university students, after all, are on the threshold of adulthood and they should begin holding better rein on their exuberance. But universities should keep the same thing in mind in shaping the restraints placed on student activities. If universities are inclined to ride herd with an iron-fisted approach, or if they make it impossible for one student body to enjoy the same freedoms and pleasures that another is permitted—as many BGSU students and alumni say is the case—then the schools are encouraging a sort of campus cold war that helps no one.
>
> It is notable that BGSU is the only one of Ohio's six state-supported institutions where boisterous demonstrating has occurred in the past few days. If it is merely a case of an over-abundance of school spirit, then it probably should be tolerated as long as it is vented in moderation. But if what has taken place at BGSU is a reflection of an underlying resentment by the student body over what it may regard as abnormally strict irritants placed by the administration in

the path of normal campus life, then the matter should be looked into before it sparks more serious uprisings that could detract from the main purpose of the University. (Gordon 1965, 10–11)

Interestingly, the daily paper in the town of Bowling Green itself, the *Sentinel-Tribune,* was not as anti-student as one might expect. The town was very fearful of downtown riots, but there had not been many of them in this round of demonstrations, and the paper was attempting to be evenhanded. On Thursday, the day after the *Toledo Blade's* "Cold War" editorial, the *Sentinel* reprinted that editorial with this explanatory note: "It is being reprinted because many *Sentinel-Tribune* readers otherwise would miss it. In Bowling Green and main routes the *Sentinel-Tribune* has 80 percent more circulation than *The Blade*" (Gordon 1965, 13). Also on Wednesday, March 29, the first letter to the editor appeared, from a Bowling Green senior to the *Wooster Daily Record*:

> The physical aspects … have been described quite accurately in the papers I have read. The deeper motives behind this demonstration, excluding spring fever, have been touched on vaguely.…
>
> Eventually the dissatisfaction (newspaper censorship, inflexible rules, lack of student authority) of the student body had to be released, and unfortunately the only channel open to them was through a non-destructive demonstration. This channel … was effectively closed.
>
> We followed the advice of some of our more realistic professors and kept destruction out of the demonstration. In response we were treated like delinquents and locked in our respective dorms. (Gordon 1965, 14)

That same day the *Greenville Daily Advocate* interviewed two students and reported, "It was learned that the students are presently asking their parents to write state representatives and senators to intercede on the part of the students." And on March 31, in a page 1, byline story, *The Akron Beacon-Journal* described Bowling Green's problems as "long brewing" and said that "Akron area students interviewed maintained that they are conducting a real fight for principles. Grievances are many and varied, but they all boil down to one thing: The students feel that, given a little more latitude in conducting their own affairs, they can show the administration they are responsible young people."

The *Akron Beacon-Journal* supported its feature story with an editorial: "Has the rein been held too closely on young adults? Have communications … broken down? Is there a real basis for what some students describe as grievances? The key to the trouble may be not so much that the rules are enforced but the MANNER in which it is done" (Gordon 1965, 14).

On Monday, April 3, the students made their first representations to the state legislature.

> The setting moved to Columbus as a dozen BGSU students appeared before the House Education Committee in an informal hearing to ask for a legislative investigation of their grievances. The students also meet with Senator Ross Pepple, R.-Lima, Chairman of the Senate Education Committee. Senator Pepple suggested to Miss Ericksen, who was expelled for her part in the demonstrations, that she write to House Speaker Roger Cloud, requesting an investigation.
>
> Dr. McDonald, meanwhile, sent word to the students that he would meet with them to discuss grievances, if they would return to the campus. (Gordon 1965, 17)

And the next day, Tuesday, April 4, newspapers across the state reported that President McDonald had told legislators he would be "happy to meet with the students," realizing the problems were "not of the Ft. Lauderdale type and worthy of discussion" (Gordon 1965, 18).

The students, then, spent the vacation working the press, their parents, and the state legislature. By the end of the vacation many newspapers were still siding with the administration, but the students had encountered striking success in the battle of words. Important papers were cautiously siding with them, legislators were carefully listening, and President McDonald was reversing his original position and admitting that some grievances were legitimate.

On Thursday, April 6, the second day after the vacation, the press carried a significant story about Senator Pepple. "'United Press International in its dispatches reported that [Sen. Ross] Pepple said he thought increasing the number of members of Bowling Green's board of trustees might prevent any future demonstrations.' He added, 'This was the second disturbance at Bowling Green. One of the newspapers yesterday said that 90 percent of the present professors were behind the students. So I thought it might be good to increase the board. This could give University President Ralph W. McDonald more help and better advice'" (Gordon 1965, 22).

Pepple's comments had two errors. The estimate of 90 percent professorial support for students was high. And Bowling Green had had at least two previous demonstrations (in 1949 and 1957). Still, the point of the story was the trial balloon about increasing the size of the board. And Pepple's comments certainly did not side with McDonald. President McDonald had enjoyed solid support from the board of trustees throughout his ten years in office, despite his relatively authoritarian administrative style. Basically they let him do what he wanted, and they obviously approved of what he did, including the way he did it. Four of the five trustees had been in office since the mid-forties, and the fifth had been appointed in 1956. Pepple's idea about adding two members to the board was clearly a move to cut McDonald's power with the board and to make it more responsive to the students. It would also inevitably be interpreted as a message of disapproval, if not of no confidence, in the existing board.

During the latter two months of the spring semester, the students kept improving their position in the campus cold war. This was due to the well-crafted and self-confident way in which they framed the story with the press and the legislature. McDonald was listening respectfully and also beginning the careful process of softening the rules. For the faculty he reactivated the faculty senate. Public opinion seemed to be swinging predominantly toward the students, and the press gradually took a more sympathetic stance in their direction. The *Toledo Blade* became increasingly pro-student. And there was a new element in the mix when "the *Sentinel-Tribune* scooped the competition with a story that Ohio's Civil Liberties Union has been asked by representatives of the Bowling Green State University faculty to investigate alleged suppression of civil liberties on the campus" (Gordon 1965, 29). These complaints suggest that the administration might have been breaking the law.

One might expect that the parents of the students would generally support the administration, since the latter acts for the parents (in loco parentis). The strict rules were in fact regarded by the administration as what the parents did want. And there undoubtedly had been times (for example, in the mid-thirties, when the imperiled university had appealed to local support) during which the university was in tune with local mores. But over a period of time the student culture, and probably that of the neighboring towns as well, had become more emancipated. Students came from all over, both in and out of state, to take advantage of Bowling Green's low costs and fairly easy entry standards. They came from Toledo, which was a trade-union town and the turf of the liberal Republican *Blade*. In fact, this paper read for the most part like a liberal Democratic newspaper. Many also came from Cleveland and Akron, which were substantial cities. And a significant number came from New York, to take advantage of the moderate out-of-state fees. In other words, many of the Bowling Green parents were Kennedy Democrats themselves, fed up with the stodgy Eisenhower years, doing such new dances as the twist, and enjoying liquor as well.

To get some idea of what the parents thought about the campus war, one of the authors of this book asked his 114 students in early May 1961 about their parents' attitudes. At the beginning of the demonstration the parents were 35 percent pro-McDonald, 11 percent pro-student, and 54 percent neutral. By May they were 24 percent pro-McDonald, 43 percent pro-student, and 33 percent neutral. (The students themselves were, at the time of the questionnaire, 3 percent pro-McDonald, 82 percent pro-student, and 15 percent neutral.) This was obviously not a methodologically perfect questionnaire, since it was given to a captive audience. Nevertheless, its finding of a substantial (32 percent) swing to the students fits the more general finding of a pro-student shift in public opinion.

During the remainder of the spring semester the trends continued as indicated so far: the students became consolidated in their desire for a more liberal atmosphere; the press continued the turn toward the students; the administration started liberalizing the rules and giving more authority to the faculty, the students kept lobbying in the state capital; and the legislature continued to show concern about Bowling Green's outdated controls over the students.

All the indications were that Bowling Green might well modernize its rules and institutions in a way that would make almost everyone happy. The students would breathe easier, the faculty would feel more like university professors, the citizens of Ohio would feel like their colleges were up to date, and the administration would be more in tune with other university administrations across the country. It is true, McDonald had made a strategic error in making the drinking rules stricter for the students, not to mention the recent rule against professors drinking in public. And he had a series of other rules and practices—about class attendance, boy-girl relations, the student newspaper, students' rights to make public statements about the university, among others—that were behind the times. But all these could have been changed.

Perhaps the underlying problem was the poor handling of power—being clumsy with it, wanting too much of it, not delegating it enough, and not sharing it with students and faculty. What McDonald and his administration needed to do was adopt a more democratic and respectful attitude toward power. They could not make any more mistakes, as when the dean of students overplayed his hand at the water fight or when McDonald acted too inflexibly at the beginning of the demonstrations. All they had to do was hang on and they all would get to and through the summer successfully. Then Bowling Green State University could start anew the next fall and McDonald could steer a stronger university for the remainder of his career.

FATEFUL ERROR: FIRING STANAGE

But this was not to be. Instead, McDonald made still another serious mistake just as the semester was ending. It is a maxim in academia that you make your unpopular decisions after the students leave, particularly for the summer. Students might keep their bad mood for the week of spring vacation, but the three months of summer are normally long enough to outlast them on almost anything, particularly with the seniors leaving permanently. But McDonald made his mistake on graduation day itself, when the students (and their parents) were still on campus.

Recall that Sherman Stanage had been the central faculty member during the demonstrations. His students had constructed existentialist goals for the demonstration even before it had begun. He had spoken the second night, congratulating the students and urging them to continue their dissent. He defied President McDonald by speaking at the faculty meeting, saying the students had asked for bread, but "we" (i.e., McDonald) had given them stones. He was a central symbol to the informal organizing process the faculty had engaged in during April and May. Still, Stanage was not well known to the public, for his speech at the faculty meeting had not been leaked to the press. The entire faculty knew about it, and they had talked to many of the students. But the citizens of Ohio and the legislature did not know of Stanage's central role.

Stanage, who was the chair of the two-person philosophy department, was on a year-to-year contract, which meant he could be fired at any time. But his credentials were good and his job evaluations were positive. Being selected as department chair also strengthened his position. The administration could hardly have liked his pro-student behavior during and after the demonstrations. But this could not be used to criticize his professional performance or career. And of course many of the faculty and students were strongly in his corner and regarded him as a hero. It looked to everyone as though Stanage could not be touched by the administration. His job was secure and his position at the university, although perhaps now as something of a gadfly, was solid. No one would have predicted that McDonald would take the risk of firing him.

Nevertheless this is exactly what happened. As Gordon describes the administrative action on June 3, 1961:

> Sherman Miller Stanage, 33, Ph.D., father of four, teacher of philosophy, assistant professor, department chairman, Danforth Scholar, former paratrooper, climbed the stairs from the first floor of the Administration Bldg. and entered the second-story office of Vice-President Kenneth H. McFall.
>
> It was commencement weekend. Seniors and their parents were touring the campus on this Saturday morning. Dedication of the Overman Hall science building, including unveiling of a portrait of J. Robert Overman, one of Bowling Green's original faculty members, would take place within the hour. Dr. Stanage sat opposite the vice-president and was advised that "he would not be asked to continue beyond next year as a member of the faculty ... on the unanimous recommendation of the deans."

Professor Stanage describes his reactions as follows:

When I was called into McFall's office, he handed me a letter of dismissal. I read it and left. I was in his office only about 10 minutes. This is the first time I had talked with Dr. McFall directly about anything concerning my disagreement with the president. Always I had talked with Dr. McDonald before. Beneath the secretary's initials on the letter is written in ink: Approved, Ralph W. McDonald. I had been given no reason to believe I would be dismissed from the University. I have every reason to believe the action was entirely retaliatory and vindictive. (letter to authors, November 1, 1999)

The liberal faculty, already organized into collegial and friendship group-ings, had engaged in informal organizing as soon as the demonstrations began. Throughout this period they were holding confidential meetings with as many as forty faculty members in attendance (*Bowling Green Sentinel-Tribune,* June 5, 1961, p. 1). Howard Brogan, chair of the English department, Richard Carpenter, also of English, and Grover Platt, of history, led them. The dismissal of Stanage boosted their organization, but their goals were much broader than protesting Stanage's firing.

The *Sentinel-Tribune,* under a modest headline, reported, "Faculty Objects to Stanage Dismissal." Headlines over Associated Press and United Press International stories were considerably stronger:

"60 BG Professors Flay McDonald for Stanage's Ouster"—*Freemont News Messenger*
"BG Prof Claims He Was Purged"—*Sandusky Register*
"BG Prexy Assailed by Faculty"—*Alliance Review*

The Associated Press noted, "Bowling Green State University Professor Sherman M. Stanage said today his dismissal from the faculty was a 'retaliatory action' for speaking out for students' rights, following the pre-Easter demonstrations which rocked the campus" (Gordon 1965, 32–33). Stanage had been given an additional year to look for another job. And the administration said the dismissal was due to Stanage's failure to institute a satisfactory program in religious studies, which was part of philosophy at Bowling Green. But hardly anybody believed them.

As one of the preceding headlines says, there was a pro-Stanage petition signed by sixty faculty members, out of a 225-person faculty, the weekend of his dismissal. Among the nineteen signatories who made their names public were the chairs of five departments: English, political science, sociology, psychology, and education.

In addition the faculty members were talking to newspaper editors, to the ACLU, and to the members of the board of trustees. In particular, a group of faculty visited trustee James C. Donnell of Findlay, Ohio, CEO of the Ohio Marathon Oil Corporation. Donnell listened respectfully to the presentation and later began to withdraw support for President McDonald. Subsequent to the meeting with the faculty delegation, Donnell held a meeting with the Bowling Green State University alumni on his staff. When Donnell asked them about conditions on campus they spoke strongly against the university's administration. From then on Donnell began siding with the students and influencing the other trustees.[4]

On the first day after Stanage's dismissal the press generally backed the administration, but once the sixty-person petition came out, the press, led again by the *Toledo Blade,* began questioning the action. A few days later there was a pro-McDonald letter, signed by 115 professors (and twenty-seven administrators), including seventeen chairpersons. But this letter looked like it might have been managed by the McDonald loyalists, and it was rather ignored by the press.

McDONALD'S DOWNFALL

McDonald clearly had overreached himself in firing Stanage, and in the subsequent days the president's ship sprung huge leaks. Already on June 7 one newspaper had abandoned McDonald. The *Napoleon Northwest Signal,* which had editorialized two months earlier that "we're on Dr. McDonald's side as he faces the barricades (against students)," changed its mind on this day and asked, "What does he have that BGSU can't get along without? This is certainly an unhealthy situation ... isn't it about time the state, which owns and operates BGSU, instigated a stiff investigation of the policies of Dr. McDonald? We wonder what mystic power Dr. McDonald holds over the trustees of that venerable institution" (Gordon 1965, 35). The reference to McDonald's "mystic power over the trustees" was quite topical, because two days later, on June 9, the state Senate voted 31 to 1 to enlarge the board of trustees to seven members. Also on that day, Frank Kane, one of the bill's sponsors, revealed Dr. McDonald's correspondence with the Senate Rules Committee concerning the bill. McDonald said the measure would tend to "cause irreparable damage to the university ... and predicted that there will be demonstrations of unruly students on other campuses if the General Assembly doesn't take firm action and defeat the Pepple Bill and thus demonstrate that legislators believe in an orderly campus" (Gordon 1965, 39). With this correspondence, McDonald put all his prestige on the line. By defining the bill as an invitation to further student demonstrations, not only at Bowling Green but at other Ohio universities as well, he virtually ordered the state assembly—which would vote on the bill twelve days hence—to defeat the bill.

In the meantime, the feeling at BGSU was that McDonald, after having fired Stanage, had taken a turn for the worse in the campus cold war. In a bylined column in the *Canton Repository*, the writer said, "There's a camouflaged feeling on the campus of Bowling Green State University that Dr. Ralph McDonald may be living on borrowed time as president of the institution of 6,000 students" (Gordon 1965, 40). During the next week and a half there was continued jockeying over the several issues that were in the air, but with a 31 to 1 vote in the Senate, it was obvious that the House would also back the disputed bill. It came on Wednesday, June 21. "Newspapers today reported the unanimous passage (112–0) by the House of Representatives of the bill to increase the number of University trustees from five to seven."

Reported the Associated Press, "The bill is aimed at making the board more receptive to student opinion." The next day, the *Toledo Blade* editorialized, "The troubled academic atmosphere at Bowling Green has been given further recognition in Columbus. It does offer an all-important opportunity to get at a primary cause of the University's difficulties: a weak board of trustees which permitted an alarming situation to develop by turning over to an arbitrary president virtually all of its policy-making decisions."

The editorial concluded by stating that instead of an investigation, state legislators "wisely chose to strengthen the board. This gives BGSU's trustees a new mandate to re-establish effective control over the University and to resolve a destructive dispute" (Gordon 1965, 45).

On Saturday, June 24, McDonald resigned his presidency. He did this at a meeting of the board that was considering the dismissal of Stanage. Some people were surprised at McDonald's resignation, but it is difficult to see how he could have done otherwise, given his unanimous rebuke by the state assembly. His resignation was the effective end of the lengthy twelve-year student-administration power struggle at Bowling Green.[5]

A more moderate administrator, Ralph G. Harshman, was immediately put in as McDonald's replacement. Stanage was, after a decent interval, reinstated as department chair. Others whom McDonald had demoted were restored to their previous positions. And the students returned to campus much happier and more tractable. Bowling Green went through the rest of the sixties much as other Ohio campuses did: with the normal amount of civil rights and anti-war demonstrations (Maloney 1981) but without the wasteful lifestyle disputes of the McDonald years. And the faculty, although divided by the pro- and anti-McDonald petitions of 1961, conducted themselves like a reasonably self-assured group of university professors.

The conclusion to these events is pretty simple and obvious. McDonald resigned and things were normalized at BGSU. Less obvious is the "why" of all this, for just as the students soul-searched over why they were demonstrating, the researchers must take a close look at the interpretation of these events. In doing so, a closer look will be given to the personalities and constituencies of the conflict and the ripple effects of the events set in motion by the student uprising.

NOTES

1. An earlier version of the material in this chapter was presented as a paper at the annual meeting of the American Sociological Association, San Francisco, 2002.

2. One of the authors, Norbert Wiley, who lived near campus, was taking a walk with one of his children, and he chanced upon the water fight. The description is based on his observations.

3. Her name was Mary Jo Freshley, and, in a letter to the authors dated August 3, 2001, she gave the following recollection: "I believe the reason I was questioned about my attendance at the faculty meeting was because I was taking notes for myself (to see if I could make some sense out of the dialogue later). The press was not welcome at this meeting as I recall so I am sure President McDonald really did feel I was a 'spy' of some sort. Many of my friends afterwards had a great time teasing me about my infiltration of the meeting."

4. James Donnell, who is long deceased, left no records of his attitudes toward President McDonald and the events of spring 1961. But his assistant, John A. Skipton, wrote the following to the authors on September 8, 2001: "My role was solely to inform Mr. Donnell what I was hearing from personal friends, Kenneth Krouse, Bill Day and Harvey Ford of the *Blade*. Being aware of the desire of a faculty group to confer with Mr. Donnell, I urged him to do so. I was not present at the meeting. Shortly after Mr. Donnell's meeting with the group, Mr. Donnell and Mr. Carl Schwyn (another trustee) met to discuss whether any action by the board was necessary. An auto accident prevented my accompanying him. I do not know any specifics of their conversation. My own impression is that Dr. McDonald did not use University assets wisely, whether of money or of personnel. I detected some feeling that some administrator's spending was spending more for aggrandizement than for academic improvements."

5. On the day he resigned, McDonald phoned William Day of the *Toledo Blade,* who was a BGSU alumni. As Day told the authors (letter, July 9, 2001), "I received a phone call at the *Blade* from McDonald in which he said that he held me and the *Blade* personally responsible for his problems at the University and for his decision to resign. I was just able to tell him that I disagreed with his comments before he hung up."

Chapter 3

Overview of the Sixties

Now that we have presented the main events of the Bowling Green uprising, it might be a good time to enlarge the point of view and locate these incidents in the history of the sixties. A social event is defined partly by its context, so this chapter will sketch the context. This digression will allow us to frame the story and look at its reverberations over time. When we return to the main narrative in the next chapter it should have a more historically grounded foundation.

The sixties have been written about many times, but the Bowling Green story, which was the first major protest of the sixties, has never been recorded. Bowling Green's protest got only moderate press notice at the time it occurred, and it may not have had a lot of influence outside of Ohio. On the other hand, the Bowling Green story gives a good picture of how the sixties hit the Midwest, including mid-size, more traditional schools. It shows a highly American protest in the sense of indigenous issues and the American style. This style was neither Old Left nor New Left. In contrast, it was a form of indignation as old as the *Common Sense* of Founding Father Thomas Paine. This style also resembles the simplicity of the 1870s farmer-labor Populist movement. In addition, the BG uprising shows how the fifties became the sixties at Bowling Green, how a demonstration that began with fifties issues, tactics, and style quickly transformed into a sixties model (more in Chapter 8). The first part of this chapter will be a description of the sixties, showing how the BG case fits into the pattern. The second part will be a causal section exploring the question of what caused the sixties.

DESCRIPTION OF THE SIXTIES

Figure 3.1 gives a timeline of the sixties, locating several of the main events and turning points. This is not meant to be a complete picture of the decade. We list just enough points to contextualize the Bowling Green story. We abbreviate names to squeeze all nine entries onto a single line.

Figure 3.1 Timeline of Sixties Protest Movement

Civil Rights	HUAC	BGSU	Port Huron	FSM	HIGH SIXTIES	SDS Splits	Kent State	Econ. Stagflation
1960					1965			1970

For some purposes, the fifties were a long decade and the sixties started "late." But for our purposes in this chapter, the political sixties were a long decade, positioned between two events. The first, which initiated the sixties, was the African American civil rights movement. This began in earnest in December 1955 with the boycott of the segregated Montgomery, Alabama, bus system, a movement led by Martin Luther King Jr. At the other end, the point which concluded the sixties, which were already winding down, was the recession of 1973–1974 and more importantly the "stagflation" which it initiated. This was an unprecedented combination of high unemployment and high inflation, a combination for which the American government had no effective measures.

The American economy had been enjoying the long postwar expansion from the late fifties until 1973. Perhaps one of the reasons the sixties could be a student protest decade was the availability of well-paying jobs and discretionary income. In fact, the prosperity years coincide almost exactly with the enlarged decade of the sixties. Most students did not have to worry much about income during their student years or, as they probably thought, about a job afterward. All that changed with stagflation. We well remember students in the early seventies saying resignedly, "The protests are over; it's time to pay the bills."

The fifties were a politically quiet decade for the most part. Left-of-center political expression was intimidated by anti-Communism and McCarthyism. The hearings of the House Un-American Activities Committee (HUAC) and the aggressiveness of the FBI scared both Communists and ordinary liberals. No doubt the fact that the Russians got the atom bomb in 1949 and the Korean War began in 1950 added to the fear of Communists. The ordinary politics of interest groups, in which the forces of big business and their allies were constantly trying to suppress liberalism, was also central to the apolitical nature of this decade. In fact, ordinary politics was probably a factor in why there was so much anti-Communism, particularly when Communism was so weak in American society. To some extent, anti-Communism was an excuse for the forces of the Right to intimidate the forces of the Left, including ordinary liberalism.

Yet in addition to anti-Communism, World War II created pro-liberal forces in the politics of race. African Americans had fought in a war that was constantly called a war for freedom. For Roosevelt, the war aims, as stated in a 1942 radio address, were for the "rights of men of every creed and every race, wherever they live" (Foner 1998, 223). Blacks, who were still afflicted by Jim Crow laws and customs and were not allowed to vote in the South, wanted to know where their freedom was. So this cause, racial equality, was the one liberal current that grew in the fifties. The 1954 Supreme Court ruling that desegregated schools, *Brown v. Board of Education,* gave official sanction to the African American desire for freedom and equality.

There were small black demonstrations throughout the early fifties. But race did not become a central issue until Martin Luther King Jr. began to lead the Montgomery, Alabama, bus boycott. This was the first strong drive for racial equality, and it got enormous publicity. In a sense this action was saying, "If segregated schools are now illegal, then segregated seats on the bus should also be illegal." The momentum of this boycott increased during the twelve months that it went on, and it concluded with a resounding victory for African Americans. The Supreme Court, in December 1956, ruled that segregated buses were illegal. An additional result of the bus boycott was that Martin Luther King became a great leader. In the remainder of the fifties there were continual demonstrations, but race relations turned largely on court challenges to educational desegregation. Perhaps the main event was when President Eisenhower sent federal troops to Little Rock, Arkansas, to ensure desegregation—and when he said Southern segregation was hurting the American claim of being morally superior to the Communists.

When the lunch-counter sit-ins began in March of 1960, African Americans invented a new tactic. A sit-in was a form of passive aggression or non-violent resistance, suggestive of the auto workers' sit-downs in the 1930s, but applied to a whole new range of targets. The sit-ins bordered on civil disobedience, a tactic that would be widely used in the sixties. The bus boycott was also a new tactic, though blacks would not usually have the numbers to make boycott a successful measure. Sit-ins required only a few determined and courageous individuals.

The next event on the timeline is the anti-HUAC demonstration in San Francisco. This occurred in May of 1960, just weeks after the first lunch-counter sit-in. HUAC had subpoenaed a Berkeley student, Douglas Wachter, who was a member of the Communist Party. Wachter was a political activist and a member of SLATE, a student political party and precursor of the Free Speech Movement. Calling in full-grown adults with regular jobs and lives behind them was one thing, but calling in an eighteen-year-old student was another. SLATE was able to rouse over two hundred students to attend the hearings in the San Francisco city hall. HUAC's first mistake was to go after a student at all. Then, when most of the two hundred protesting students were unable to enter the crowded hearing room, they stood outside in the lobby and sang the Battle Hymn of the Republic. A policeman with a fire hose threatened the students. He was reported to have said, "Do you want some of this?" (Free Speech Movement Archives). The students, using quick political thinking, said yes. Then the police lost their heads and hosed the students down the eighteen stairs, risking the students' limbs and providing graphic publicity for the national press and TV.

The next day, five thousand people, mostly stevedores, marched around city hall to protest the police overreaction (Free Speech Movement Archives). This turnout, along with evidence that the police had acted wrongly, turned the press and public opinion against HUAC. It did not help HUAC when they made an obviously rigged propaganda film that blamed all these activities on a Communist conspiracy. The film, *Operation Abolition,* was shown all over the country, and it seems to have influenced enormous numbers of liberal young people to come to the Bay Area and Berkeley, where the action was.

The controversy over the hearings taught two lessons to political youth. One was that students had the power to demonstrate. They had not done so in any numbers since the 1930s, but once it was obvious they had this power, they continued to demonstrate throughout the sixties. The second lesson was that if you could get the police to overreact, which did not seem very difficult to do, you could win the publicity battle. In addition you would have the new and glaring issue of police misconduct. The hearings also showed how labor (in this case the longshoremen's union) could support the students. This student-labor connection would again appear when the Port Huron Statement was put together at the United Auto Workers retreat facility in 1962 near Port Huron, Michigan. It would also appear in the major anti-war marches in San Francisco, New York, and Washington, D.C.

We are now almost to the point where the Bowling Green demonstration occurred. As we mentioned, the BG students had a simmering demonstration history, so all it would take was the right spark at the right time. In the spring of 1960, as we mentioned, there had been a civil rights sit-in at the downtown Woolworth in Bowling Green. This had been organized by the Toledo NAACP, but it did include BG students. Being on the students' own turf, it gave an example of how to use civil disobedience for a political cause. The BG demonstration tradition did not have up-to-date tactics, but this sit-in introduced a new kind of politics.

The Bowling Green demonstration occurred in March 1961, about a year after the anti-HUAC demonstration and the lunch-counter sit-ins. The BG students were influenced by these occurrences, particularly by the sit-ins, but the demonstration was primarily fueled by the local protest tradition. Since World War II this university had been having trouble softening the old-school-marm, teachers-college rules enough to keep up with the times. It continued to be too strict for the expectations of the students. Their demonstration began as an ordinary spring fever eruption, but it quickly fell into the anti-strictness groove of earlier BG demonstrations. Then, as the three-day demonstration continued and the students tried to formulate their issues, the culture of the sixties descended upon this campus. The students began to define their issues and tactics under this new influence, civil rights and civil disobedience. In fact, the Bowling Green students made their own rural, midwestern contribution to the culture of protest.

The Bowling Green events got a lot of publicity in the state of Ohio, but only a little elsewhere. There were small stories in the *New York Times* and a few other big-city newspapers. But the events were too spread out, from March to June, to constitute an easily packaged story. The biggest feature, that the students ended the fight by forcing the unbending President McDonald to resign, was not given widespread press because it happened three months after the demonstration itself, and the causal relation between the uprising and the resignation was too strung out and indirect to make a crisp narrative.

The next major sixties event was the Port Huron Statement, in which sixty-two students, with the backing of the League for Industrial Democracy, founded Students for a Democratic Society (SDS). This statement was a year or two in the making, but its actual appearance was in June 1962, over a year after the Bowling Green events. There is no visible connection between the Bowling Green uprising and the Port Huron Statement. Nevertheless, the statement had an uncanny resemblance to the populist mind-set of the Bowling Green students.

In the statement itself the main historical reference is to the civil rights movement. The cause of racial justice and the tactic of civil disobedience were major reference points for the SDS founders. Otherwise, the statement reads as though its signers thought they were initiating the sixties, and in a sense they were right. The Bowling Green events may have gotten brief notice in the University of Michigan newspaper, but they would probably not have had much impact on the SDS founders. We recently asked several of the statement's signatories about the BG demonstration, and none of them remembered having heard of it at the time. In other words, although the Bowling Green uprising initiated the stream of sixties demonstrations in a chronological sense, it did not do so in a cause-effect sense. This stream was reinvented in fall 1963 by the Free Speech Movement of UC Berkeley.

The Port Huron Statement is also something of a definition of the New Left. This idea had been around since the late fifties, and C. Wright Mills published an influential "letter" to the New Left in 1960 (Mills 1963, 247–259). In it he said trade unions and the working class were no longer the agents of radical reform, at least in the United States. Instead, he said, the radical agency was now the cultural or intellectual class, especially the students. He also said organized Marxism was no longer viable in the United States. Instead he advocated a simplified and humanistic form of Marxism, which he refers to elsewhere (Mills 1963, 98–101) as plain Marxism. This was a point of view rather than an organization.

This ideology was a lot like Mills's own liberal politics, and also like the American Populist tradition of the late nineteenth century. Populism nowadays has come to mean any ideology that ordinary or average people advocate and that operates in a grassroots rather than a top-down manner. Today this even includes various kinds of right-wing ideology, such as George Wallace's American Independent Party, a segregationist Southern Populism, or Richard Nixon's silent majority. But in the late nineteenth century Populism was a movement centering on the American Midwest, and springing from a farmer-labor coalition.

This was essentially an egalitarian movement that advocated regulations on big business, particularly as this force affected farmers and workers. The Populists wanted more favorable prices, not just for the labor of workers but also for farmers in the commodity (products sold and bought) and credit (interest paid on loans) markets. The Populists also wanted dignity for their members. Among the ways Populism differed from Marxism was by including conflict in the commodity and credit as well as in the labor markets (Wiley 1967). The original Populism then was identified with the lower half of the population, organized in a bottom-up or grassroots fashion and advocating economically egalitarian goals.

The Port Huron Statement had a simple and commonsense quality, resembling such American egalitarian statements as Tom Paine's *Common Sense* and the Populists' platform. As we mentioned, we find the implicit ideology of the Bowling Green students similar to that in the Port Huron Statement. The BG students used generic value words such as *rights* and *liberties,* but there was little political or economic theory behind these ideas. The students wanted equality, privacy, and a minimum of bureaucratic controls or university regulations. They did use incipient sixties ideas such as civil disobedience and student rights, but they used these ideas in a simple and unsophisticated fashion. Later in this chapter we will talk about the larger problem of solidarity or morale in the entire United States, and how the sixties eruptions may have been brought about by a lack of communal values in this country. In this view, industrialization and bureaucratization were chewing up elementary human values, or what Emile Durkheim called solidarity.

The next event on the timeline is the Free Speech Movement (FSM) at the University of California, Berkeley. The Berkeley students had been activated by the 1960 HUAC hearings. SLATE continued to organize liberal and leftist politics on this campus, and its power, initially quite modest, began to grow. The race issue also continued to smolder at Berkeley. In the summer of 1964 there was a voting drive, Freedom Summer, to register black voters in Mississippi. About one thousand volunteers from the North came to Mississippi for this project, many from UC Berkeley. The California university system had a rule against on-campus political activities, including those concerning race issues. This was taking the in loco parentis idea quite a stretch. The no-politics rule was especially galling to those students who had just risked their lives for racial justice in the Mississippi Freedom Summer.

This situation came to a head in September 1964, when campus police arrested students who were distributing political literature from tables at the main entrance to the campus. When the police brought an arrested student into one of their cars, the protesting students surrounded the car and sat down. The police, afraid to just start their cars and run over the sitting students, were trapped on Sproul Plaza—along with the arrested student, Jack Weinberg—for thirty-six hours. Finally the students negotiated a truce with the administration. This surge of protest continued throughout the fall and spring semesters at Berkeley. The main issue was free speech for political purposes. This was the first widely publicized demonstration of the sixties, although it was three and a half years after the Bowling Green demonstration. The tactics were civil disobedience, passive resistance, and the sit-in—all lessons learned from the African American civil rights movement.

To continue the overview of the sixties, the "high sixties" of 1965 to 1968 were characterized by an increasingly popular anti-war movement and the growth of student protest, particularly as organized by SDS. Among the major university protests were those at Wisconsin, Cornell, Michigan, Columbia, Chicago, and Harvard, although there were dozens more on lesser-known campuses. There were also large race and anti-war protests in New York, Washington, D.C., San Francisco, and other major cities. Each of these events was important and complex, but in this overview we cannot give these events the attention they deserve.

The high sixties were a sharp arc, with a narrow rise-and-fall curvature. Student protest became bigger and stronger quite rapidly, but also quickly began to split into ideologically opposed factions. As the New Left increased in size it rapidly became more like the Old Left, that is, divided by warring Marxist positions and wasting its energies on internal struggles.

Perhaps the June 1969 SDS convention, at which the organization split into three parts, marked the end of the classic sixties. The meeting was held in the dingy Chicago Coliseum, just south of the downtown, and it was characterized by disorganization and tension. There were about fifty literature tables ringing the main hall, each representing an "ism" of some kind, and each poised to participate in the takeover of SDS. Anger and hissing prevailed at this meeting. The largest faction was the Progressive Labor Party, a splinter off the Communist Party which was initially Maoist and then Stalinist. PL had the numbers, but they did not control the mike. The people from the national office, led by Bernardine Dohrn and Mark Rudd, had the administrative power, and they more or less controlled this convention.

Progressive Labor did take over SDS after this convention, but SDS itself was pretty much ignored after being taken over by a sect. The two smaller factions were Revolutionary Youth Movement I and Revolutionary Youth Movement II, the former of which would become the Weathermen. After some months many of the Weathermen went underground with the intent of promoting a revolution.

Despite the breakup of SDS, local campus protests continued, as did large anti-war rallies. Still, the hopeful spirit of the student sixties was barely alive. By 1970, despite the dissolution of the national office, the SDS at Kent State University in Ohio was highly organized and also quite militant (Rudd 2009, 210). Kent State was near industrial Akron, a union town. This pushed the Kent State students toward national issues and national power, a condition quite different from that at the more rural Bowling Green State University. The Kent State demonstration, at which the Ohio National Guard fired into a crowd, killing four students and wounding nine others, occurred on May 4, 1970. These killings were a chilling factor, for they marked the escalation of the system for fighting back. The Ohio National Guard seems to have lost its head and this might have been a freak incident, but the significance was not lost on the student population. Then two black students were shot and killed and twelve were injured at Jackson State University just ten days later. These incidents meant the government was capable of going all the way to killing people to stop protest. A precedent had been set. The killings were met initially with massive reactions from the national student population, but they also had a braking effect on further protest.

Between 1971 and the recession of 1973 there was continued anti-war protest, but the end of the sixties was in sight. By the economic stagnation of 1974 the protest movement was pretty well choked off, and when the Vietnam War was concluded with an American defeat in 1974, a major issue of the sixties was resolved.

Throughout the sixties the students kept getting tougher and more inventive, but the forces of law kept going down the same path. The student progression went something like this: peaceful assembly, marches, civil disobedience (e.g., blocking traffic), passive resistance (e.g., lying down), breaking windows, throwing missiles at police, and waging violent revolution (e.g., making bombs). The authorities, with fewer but more hard-edged moves, responded by denying permits for assemblies, making arrests, infiltrating political groups, employing nightsticks, and finally shooting people. In addition, the FBI COINTELPRO unit ignored civil liberties when they infiltrated and attempted to disrupt liberal political groups of all kinds.

When the students decided to turn to violent revolution, as the Weathermen did in 1970, they reached the final move. Not only was this the ultimate tactic, it was also futile with this small a group (under a hundred) and such limited weapons. At this point the authorities had overwhelming power, and the back-and-forth struggle was effectively over. Another way of viewing the sixties, then, is as a set of escalating tactics on the part of both students and authorities. Both sides also gradually broke the rules, more and more as time went on. This all came to a natural end at the same time the sixties were bumping into an economic downturn, perhaps itself strong enough to stop the decade.

We have now concluded a descriptive narrative of the sixties, placing the BG uprising in the initial if not the initiating position. The BG case was the first large student demonstration since the 1930s, and also the only major case between the fifties civil rights movement and the Free Speech Movement of 1964. The BG uprising was also a test case. It showed that student protest was not only a workable idea, but that students had a lot of power. The question then for other American students was how to use this power and for what purposes.

The Bowling Green case also shows how American the sixties were. This period of protest was part of the broader tradition of American reform (Hofstadter 1955; Foner 1998), going back to farmers' tax-related Whiskey Rebellion of the early 1790s. Over time the language of protesting students shifted from the ordinary populism of the Bowling Green demonstrators to the Marxism of the late SDS. But the core issue of justice in American society was there the whole time, pervading the movement from beginning to end. The language was the packaging and this changed, but the issues themselves, of a good and decent society, remained the same.

WHY THE SIXTIES?

We now shift from an overall description of the sixties to an examination of what caused them. In Chapter 8 we will show that the sixties came to Bowling Green in the middle of its demonstration. Not too long after BG, the reformist currents of the sixties also came to many other campuses. We can pretty well explain how and why they came to Bowling Green. But why they came to the rest of the country is another question. No doubt the advent of sixties reform had several causes, but we would like to explore a cause that has not been adequately looked at. The usual list of causes includes: the rise of the race issue; the economic prosperity of the time; the large number of students attending universities; the growth of inquiring, non-vocational majors in the humanities and social sciences; the unpopularity of universities' in loco parentis role; and the decline in anti-Communism after the Senate's censuring of Senator McCarthy.

Part of the momentum of the sixties also came from the early stirrings of the Women's Liberation Movement. Women in the protest movement, particularly those in SDS, complained about not having equal status with the men. But women were still a large and an active part of the student Left. In Chapter 9 we will show the importance and near dominance of women in the Bowling Green demonstrations. The women's movement was largely the result of late-fifties and early-sixties demographic trends, which gradually heightened the political consciousness of women. The demographic infrastructure was well along by the beginning of the sixties, but the consciousness superstructure did not click in much until the mid- or late sixties.

An additional causal factor we would like to examine is a particular imbalance that grew in the United States in the 1940s and 1950s. A certain internal moral insensitivity came about because of the great concern with foreign policy and external danger during those years. The forties were dominated by World War II, and the fifties were dominated by anti-Communism and fear of the Soviet Union. The people of this country believed, rightly or wrongly, that to address these threats they had to close ranks and suspend the process of self-criticism and internal reform. As a result, social problems went unattended and a fear of self-judgment and reform dominated the American conscience.

But by 1960 the Cold War was warming a touch, and the new Democratic president, John F. Kennedy, seemed open to at least a moderate amount of reform. When campaigning for the presidency, Kennedy's mantra was "We've got to get this country moving again." This was, no doubt, a deliberately vague promise, open to several interpretations. But one possible interpretation was social reform itself, in the direction of civil rights and a decent living for everyone. The civil rights movement, spearheaded by blacks in the South, had been going on for several years by the late fifties. The historical moment, then, was one in which reform was overdue.

To understand the reform atmosphere of the 1960s era, it will be helpful to take another look at Durkheim. In particular, his theory of solidarity, which we have already used to explain the dynamics of the Bowing Green demonstration, has implications that can help explain the start of the sixties. To explore this we will have to discuss abstract concepts at some length. After this theoretical interlude we will get back to the sixties and show with better precision how the demonstrations played a useful role both at Bowling Green and in the larger society.

Thus far we have shown how the Bowling Green students found a great deal of cohesion, self-confidence, and consciousness in the protest process. They achieved a solidarity that made them into a tightly knit group with a strong self-definition and visionary ideals. It is obvious how this would feed rebellion. But given that this solidarity spread to more and more campuses as the sixties moved along, the question arises whether this student solidarity may, in some way, have been good for the society as a whole. Did society need this student communalism and its new values? And if so, why did this need appear? Or to put it another way: why the sixties?

We will approach this question by distinguishing two ways in which Durkheim used the concept of solidarity. In his book *The Division of Labor in Society*

(1933/1893), he distinguishes mechanical from organic solidarity. By *mechanical* Durkheim means the cohesion a society gets from shared values and beliefs. His example is the hunting-and-gathering tribes from primitive Australia, which were still present as recently as the late nineteenth century. In these communities, everyone engaged in the same male and female activities, the men hunting and the women preparing food and caring for children. There was little division of labor, other than the one based on gender, but there was a strong and densely packed set of beliefs and religious myths. In the United States the closest thing to this belief system might be isolated small towns in which everyone has similar religious and cultural beliefs.

Durkheim contrasted this solidarity with the kind he called organic. This latter kind was based on the division of labor and the mutual usefulness that this division generates. A large industrial country has a wide variety of industries, as well as institutions such as government, religion, and education. The functions of these entities all fit together, more or less, into a mutually contributing set of roles. They create a solidarity or cohesion based not on cultural attributes or beliefs but on specialization and exchange. Of course, all large societies also have plenty of inequality (often intensely disputed) and social problems. The solidarity of the division of labor, organic solidarity, has some features that work against moral solidarity, even though for the most part the organic is a kind of internal glue or cohesion.

The reason Durkheim distinguished these two kinds of solidarity was his belief that as societies evolved in an industrial direction, mechanical solidarity declined and organic solidarity increased. They had an inverse relationship. This was his idea of social evolution, and he regarded it as the normal tendency of social change. For Durkheim the solidarity of exchange gradually overtook and made unnecessary the solidarity of shared beliefs—mechanical solidarity.

Having made this distinction, it should be noted that the "tone" of the two terms, *mechanical* and *organic,* is somewhat misleading. Most students of Durkheim immediately think he got the terms reversed. For, in the ordinary way we use words, shared beliefs seem "organic" and economic togetherness seems "mechanical." But Durkheim did have a certain logic in his choice of words. A clan, united by shared beliefs, can, if the external food supply runs short, separate into two groups, each of which goes its own way. Each part can survive without the other. This lack of interdependency seemed "mechanical" to Durkheim, and that is why he chose this word. And a larger society with a division of labor has various functions, much as a living organism has different functions. Industrial society resembles an organism in having a variety of "organs," each of which contributes to the survival of the whole. We will continue to use Durkheim's terms as he invented them, but at times we will use what seem to be more comfortable terms: *functional* for organic solidarity and *moral* for mechanical solidarity.

Another problem with Durkheim's theory is that the division of labor, given its usual industries and moral limitations, does not really generate its own solidarity. A large economy is usually cold, impersonal, and ineffective at satisfying the wants and needs of significant segments of a population. People do not identify with a large society merely on the basis of its functions and institutions. It seems as though shared values and beliefs do not really get replaced by the division of labor. Instead, a society with an elaborate division of labor continues to need a shared morality and communal ideals. It seems obvious, for example, that you cannot have a legal system, particularly a system of criminal law, without widespread agreement on the morality underlying this law. But more than this. A society, no matter how industrialized, seems to need some agreement on such basic values as justice, liberty, and freedom. A society also seems to need symbols and rituals for expressing these values, perhaps along the lines of Robert Bellah's "civil religion" (Bellah 1967). The civil religion is a culture, and a culture has to give legitimacy or rightness to a national community. A society exists in its individuals, but it also exists in its own self-image. It has to look right, decent, and OK to itself. Without this self-approval in a culture, by which we mean self-approval from all sectors of a society, including the bottom half, a society is a moral vacuum.

This moral need is especially noticeable in a period of national danger, such as a war, a natural disaster, or a serious economic downturn. In recent years in the United States there have been distinct examples of these dangers. The terrorist attack on the twin towers is an example of a kind of war. Mechanical solidarity—that is, shared patriotism—immediately rose to meet the stress of that disaster. If it had not, the loss would have been much more difficult for the country to sustain and absorb. The Iraq War showed the importance of mechanical solidarity in another way, for the lack of majority support for that war weakened the resources for carrying it through. There was no workable moral consensus for this war, and it was for all practical purposes lost by the United States. And to mention a natural disaster, Hurricane Katrina, which flooded New Orleans, showed how the population had to find a vein of sympathy and altruism to get through that catastrophe. Finally, there is the economic downturn of 2007 and the following years, the biggest downturn since the Great Depression. This reversal needed a restoration of confidence and morale as well as government injections of money to prime the pumps. The lack of mechanical (moral) solidarity was quite noticeable in the way this economic meltdown persisted.

During the 1940s and 1950s, when the Germans, Japanese, and Russians were the enemies, a certain solidarity was generated by disliking these groups. With these external threats, or "out groups," a certain amount of cohesion was developed for the "in group," that is, the United States. Finding an enemy to dislike, and, at times, even scapegoating innocent outsiders, can create a certain amount of moral cohesion for a country, but this kind of cohesion can only work for so long. At some point moral cohesion has to come from within, from a country's own internal processes. The twenty-year period from 1940 to 1960 was too long a time to depend on outside enemies for internal unity. Eventually internal problems would accumulate and moral solidarity would need something more than threats from without.

According to Durkheim, as the division of labor progresses and replaces moral unity, the one remaining moral value in an industrialized society is respect for the person, or what he called the cult of the individual (Durkheim 1964, 407). There may be many mutually conflicting religions, but everyone can agree on the value of the person. The human self—that is, the population of human beings—is a moral center with a fundamental inviolability. It is this respect for the individual which is supposed to underlie criminal law. But respect for the person soon comes into conflict with the way industrial societies treat, or mistreat, many of their individuals and minorities.

The cult of the individual implies a considerable amount of egalitarianism, as well as equality of opportunity (Durkheim 1964, 407). Moral solidarity requires the equality that Thomas Jefferson and Abraham Lincoln called for. If this equality existed, industrial societies could build their moral cohesion on respect for the person. This value could be ritualized in public ceremonies, and it could be the basis for shared morality, dedication, and hopes. But given the widespread injustices of industrial society, the value of the individual cannot easily serve as a moral center and a source of energizing rituals. This door or moral safety valve, which Durkheim attempted to open, is closed by the widespread poverty, homelessness, and misery of many individuals in industrial societies.

We have now got to the point where Durkheim's two solidarities, which he thought of as being in a smooth but inverse relation, look as though they are actually at odds with each other. Organic solidarity tends to diminish mechanical solidarity, but it needs the very force it is replacing. When people attempt to create or revive mechanical solidarity in industrial societies, there is resistance to their efforts. In fact, mechanical and organic solidarity are sometimes in a state of intense conflict. In particular, they were at each other's throats during the protest sixties.

To understand the way the two solidarities are in conflict, it is helpful to introduce a parallel idea from the thought of Max Weber. This has to do with his theory of rationality, in particular the relation between formal and substantive rationality (Weber 1968, 85). For Weber the rationalization of society was the major overall trend of modernization and industrialization. By rationalization he meant about the same as we do by bureaucratization, the rise of large, complex organizations that are organized as efficiently as possible. In these organizations, reason or the cognitive factor is dominant, and such non-cognitive forces as emotion, aesthetics, and morality are placed in the background. Durkheim and Weber are both talking about the industrialization of the world, in their times limited to Europe, the United States, and Japan. What Durkheim referred to as the division of labor, Weber, coming at it from another angle, called rationalization.

Weber introduced a distinction, however, between two forms of rationality, calling them "formal" and "substantive." Substantive rationality directs the industrialization process toward some moral or ideological goal, such as free-market capitalism, socialism, complete equality, or utilitarianism (the greatest good for the greatest number). In contrast, formalization does not have to do with goals at all but only with means. Formal rationality means that the organizational process makes the greatest possible use of two cognitive principles: quantification and regulation. *Quantification* simply means the use of mathematics and numbers, whether the process is producing goods or organizing people. *Regulation* means the most consistent way of using rules, with organizational rules and public law being the major arenas for this rule use. Industries and the bureaucracies by which they are organized do a great deal of quantification to design their fabrication processes, and they also create large bundles of rules to regulate human behavior. Quantification and rules tend to develop together, although they are two distinctly different ways of organizing the world.

Weber thought that the two rationalities, formal and substantive, worked together and were not in conflict. He thought that the goal of industrialization was usually some form of utilitarianism (i.e., satisfying the ordinary needs of a population), and that this goal was attained to a reasonable extent. In other words, he thought capitalism was a good and reasonably just system, just as Durkheim thought that the division of labor was a good and reasonably fair system. Neither envisioned the conflict we are pointing out, which was so dramatized by the sixties.

Just as mechanical and organic solidarity tend to collide at times, formal and substantive rationality also tend to collide. Quantification and regulation are useful for producing abundance, but they say nothing about how to distribute this abundance. The quality of life in industrialized societies can range from that of a complete oligarchy at one extreme, with half-starved slaves doing the work, to complete equality in levels of living at the other. Just as Durkheim's division of labor is the "head" and his mechanical solidarity is the "heart," Weber's formal rationality is the "means" and his substantive rationality the "ends." A system of means can be directed toward a wide variety of ends, from Nazi death camps at one pole to Israeli kibbutzim with their egalitarian living standards at another. Substantive rationality is a different realm entirely from that of formal rationality.

We are saying then that both Durkheim and Weber, two of the giants of sociological theory, described modern societies as functioning rather smoothly. But if you take a close look at their concepts, they show the lines of cleavage in industrial societies. Mechanical solidarity tends to come into conflict with organic solidarity, and substantive rationality (or at least certain forms of it) tends to come into conflict with formal rationality. The concepts of both theorists describe the same internal conflict that makes industrial societies crash at some point. Productivity and justice are two quite distinct principles, and at some point they tend to bang into each other.

There is a third great theorist, Karl Marx, some of whose ideas can help clarify this problem. Marx's writings are complex and there are many ways of interpreting him. We would like to single out the early, humanistic Karl Marx, whose ideas C. Wright Mills called plain Marxism. This was largely a psychological Marx, who thought work should be as fulfilling as possible for the worker. Marx also argued that human labor, time spent at work, created the majority of a product's value. With these premises he argued that the income distribution of a society should be reasonably equal—not flat-out equal but not sharply unequal either.

Marx also called for a kind of psychological democracy, a society in which everyone, regardless of status or job, could feel good about themselves. It seems obvious that ethnic prejudice and other processes that produce minorities would be in conflict with this psychological democracy. The economic Marx, then, who wanted everyone to get a reasonable income, and the anti-alienation Marx, who wanted everyone to enjoy peace of mind, are two sides of the same coin. When Durkheim said that the "sacredness" of the individual was the most available value orientation for an industrial society, he was talking about the same psychological well-being or peace of mind that Marx was talking about.

We are using only one facet of Marxism here, but this is the one we need to make the point. What Durkheim and Weber needed was some idea of a just society. Durkheim did use this idea, but more as an ethereal ideal than as an actual criterion for judging real societies. Marx's just society belongs in Durkheim's mechanical solidarity, his term for a society's value system. It also belongs in Weber's substantive rationality as the moral goal of the rationalization process. This fusion of Marx, Weber, and Durkheim was what Mills was getting at in his criticism of the American power elite, written just before the sixties (Mills 1956). To make our point, then, that the sixties were protesting the lack of a morality or conscience in the United States, we are showing how classical theory helps explain the sixties. To do this we follow Mills in combining Marx, Weber, and Durkheim.

We have now completed the theoretical interlude to give ourselves the concepts to explain the campus battles of the sixties. We will use these concepts to make sense of the sixties puzzle. In Durkheim's terms, the university administrations represented one phase of the industrialization process, and the demonstrating students represented the other. For industrializing countries to continue their mode of production and to command the allegiance of their populations, they have to synthesize their major internal tendencies. The way to do this, as Durkheim argued, is around the sacredness and dignity of the individual. But to consecrate the human person as the core value, the society cannot at the same time neglect and step on individuals. Societies have to work out some form of moral solidarity and, as Marx urged, an acceptable system of distribution. The inequality and the moral vacuum in the United States were major forces behind the student sixties.

In Bowling Green, the student cohesion was an intense state of mechanical solidarity. Even before the demonstrations the students shared the typical beliefs of students in their time and place. But after the demonstrations had raised their consciousness they espoused an idealism and a sense of unity much greater than before. This idealism seemed to be a natural reaction to the over-organized quality of Bowling Green State University. The university had its division of labor, and the students were one strand of that division. The university's idea of how to make the students happy was extracurricular events, particularly sports, and, for the more wealthy and elite students, with the system of fraternities and sororities. These activities were supposed to satisfy the hearts and minds of the students. Of course, the education itself, with its bachelor's degree as a goal, was also supposed to give the student psychological peace. This was all in the nature of the university's organic or functional solidarity, and there was no concern for the moral student in the sense of mechanical solidarity. In McDonald's speech to the faculty, after the first outbreak of the demonstrations, he spoke of the old lady in the shoe spanking the children and putting them to bed (see Appendix B). McDonald may have been trying to inject some humor here, but the choice of words suggests that the administration did in some respects view the students as children.

When students found that assembling and sharing their grievances could give them an intense, almost religious feeling of transcendence, they found what the university had neglected. By assembling and asserting their need for civil liberties, the students gained a sense of shared belief and moral community. This was precisely what the school's division of labor and organization lacked. The official school culture was impersonal, characterized by an almost smug sense of its own rightness and by insensitivity to the problems of its student population. It offered organic solidarity without mechanical or moral solidarity.

It would seem then that Durkheim was over-optimistic, for the division of labor needs moral solidarity to hold it together. If mechanical solidarity gets so low that there is no longer any shared moral consciousness, a vital social resource is missing and many of the society's challenges and problems become unsolvable. This sensitivity first showed up on the American campuses in the 1960s, beginning with the Bowling Green demonstration.

As a point of clarification, we have now used Durkheim's ideas twice, once to agree and once to disagree. His theory of ritual and solidarity as an energizer was useful for explaining how the Bowling Green demonstration got started in the first place, and, once it was started, how it continued to be energized. But Durkheim also had the questionable idea that industrial society, which he called organic solidarity, automatically carried an adequate sense of justice and fair play. Justice for all groups and classes, he claimed, was built into the industrialization process. Durkheim argued on both sides of this question at times, but his main position seems to have been something of a whitewash for industrial morality.

Industrialized societies are quite capable of systematic injustice, and in fact this was the case in the 1960s. Earlier, we used the idea of an economically balanced society, drawing on C. Wright Mills's notion of plain or humanistic Marxism, to correct Durkheim on this issue. We might say we used Durkheim for "supply" but not "demand." "Supply" has to do with the amount or degree of moral sensitivity. The student movement of the sixties generated a large amount of solidarity and moral concern. Durkheim's theory of ritual explains this well. But "demand" has to do with the need of society for moral correction. Durkheim's theory of the sacred self was moderately helpful here, but Marx's approach to egalitarianism was more helpful. Durkheim was somewhat blind to the lapse in equality and justice in industrial society. It is common to pick and choose ideas to explain a problem (in this case, the "Why the sixties?" problem). We picked and chose from the array of theory in the sociological classics of Durkheim, Marx, and Weber.

As we said earlier, we think the reason why there was a need for mechanical solidarity in the sixties, both on the campuses and in the society at large, was that there had been twenty years of scapegoat solidarity in American history. Scapegoat solidarity is cohesion that comes from having (or sometimes only imagining that you have) an outside enemy. It is a form of cohesion that has decided limits, particularly if it is leaned on for a long period of time. The normal way of creating internal solidarity is by sharing general values, and in industrial society the greatest value is the inviolability of the individual. If a society begins to treat its population badly and loses respect for the (i.e., each and every) individual, it runs out of moral gas. It has a head but no heart. And no outside enemy can substitute for the inside sense of fraternity.

The lack of a healthy mix of solidarities on the American campus was even more noticeable at the University of California at Berkeley in the mid-1960s. President Clark Kerr described the university in terms taken from economics. For Kerr the university was an economic engine, destined to carry Western capitalism to new heights. As he put it, the railroads carried American capitalism in the late nineteenth century, the auto industry led American capitalism in the early twentieth century, and the university would be the major economic engine in the late twentieth century. He used an industrial metaphor to describe the university, calling it the knowledge industry, with the students as the resource and also, once educated, as the product or output (Kerr 1963, 88). His language was redolent with division-of-labor imagery. The solidarity was evidently supposed to come entirely from the sheer economic efficiency of the university. Kerr ignored moral solidarity all together.

When the Berkeley students returned from the voting-registration campaign in the South in the fall of 1964, they wanted to continue their moral pursuit on the campus. They wanted the university to be a force for social justice in the United States. They did not want to be merely one strand in a bureaucratic apparatus. They wanted to find a place for their mechanical solidarity, their moral outlook and commitments. They represented mechanical solidarity in conflict with organic solidarity. As Mario Savio put it in a speech outside Sproul Hall on December 2, 1964,

> There's a time when the operation of the machine becomes so odious, makes you so sick at heart, that you can't take part; you can't even passively take part. And you've got to put your bodies upon the gears and upon the wheels, upon the levers, upon all the apparatus, and you've got to make it stop. And you've got to indicate to the people who run it, to the people who own it, that unless you're free, the machine will be prevented from working at all. (Cohen 2009, 327)

Savio's often-quoted lines describe the collision between protest and the university, between the moral and the functional, between mechanical and organic solidarity. By 1964 this dialectic had moved to the point of physical confrontation. But it revealed not just a problem of the 1960s campus: it revealed a cancer within industrialization itself. Modernization and industrialization and bureaucratization have limits. When they collide with core human values they are going too far, and there will be a backlash from the forces of moral solidarity. This struggle, so visible at Berkeley in the fall of 1964, was already visible at Bowling Green in 1961. As we will point out later, you can see the '50s transforming into the '60s at Bowling Green. Underlying this transition was the struggle of moral solidarity against functional solidarity.

CONCLUDING OBSERVATIONS

This discussion of the sixties and the place of the Bowling Green events therein suggests some tentative observations:

1. The inclusion of the BG story fills in and enlarges the story of the sixties. The first major student demonstration on a campus is usually thought to be the UC Berkeley Free Speech Movement of September

1964. But the BG demonstration occurred in March 1961, three and a half years earlier. Themes introduced at BG appeared again, presumably because they were in the air, in the Port Huron Statement, and in Mario Savio's famous anti-machine speech at Berkeley.

2. The BG case shows how American the sixties were. What could be more apple pie than rural Ohio? The sixties began in small-town academia, caused by stresses in what had been teachers colleges. These resembled student restiveness as it stretched back to colonial days.

3. The BG case shows how accurately the Port Huron Statement captured what students were thinking. This statement, although more sophisticated, was quite close to the mentality of the BG rebels. The BG events were at the simplistic end of the sixties. By the end of the decade events had proceeded to the opposite pole, both in tactics and issues.

4. Bowling Green links the fifties to the sixties. There were lots of smallish and often unrecorded student demonstrations in the fifties. These usually had the same local, homemade quality as the Bowling Green events. With Bowling Green in mind, it might make sense to take a closer look at student protest in the fifties (and late forties).

5. The sixties may have been one of the causes of feminism, but feminism was also one of the causes of the sixties. The feminist demographic processes were happening in the late fifties and early sixties, already producing cognitive dissonance (Betty Friedan's "problem that had no name") for women. Feminist consciousness itself did not click in until the mid- to late sixties. But the infrastructure was producing feminist social forces and influencing the sixties before women brought these forces to full awareness, finding the name of the problem and dissolving the cognitive dissonance.

6. We will not draw conclusions from the theoretical discussion in the latter half of this chapter, but one suggestion is that theory often works best when ideas are grabbed and combined, expediently, from whatever sources look good. We did this picking and choosing from the Marx-Weber-Durkheim batch of ideas. Also, concrete, as opposed to abstract questions, such as why the sixties occurred at all, can give a powerful drive to theoretical analysis.

Chapter 4

Personalities and Constituencies in the Conflict

Now that we have a broader picture of the sixties and Bowling Green's place in that larger drama, we can return to the smaller drama in northwest Ohio. All major segments of the university became activated before the upheaval on campus ran its course. The events set in motion had volcanic effects on the subsequent development of the university. Both the university's identity and its internal dynamics were sufficiently changed to allow no way for the university to return to its pre-1960s status. The faculty had achieved a level of power and influence that was atypical of state universities; the students won rights and privileges that changed the tenor of life on campus; the power and authority of the central administration came to be tempered in a variety of ways.

There were four primary constituents in the controversy that erupted in the spring of 1961. The leadership and symbolism of President Ralph W. McDonald and his administration were foremost. McDonald had notable strengths. Perhaps his major achievement was that he enlarged the university significantly, both in buildings and in people: Bowling Green came to dominate both the town and the northwest region of Ohio. On the other hand, McDonald's style of leadership, his attempt to impose his own moral values (not hiring atheists, for example, or forbidding alcohol), and his use of university resources to reinforce his privileged position were causes of student and faculty discontent.

An equally strong and symbolic personality surfaced with Sherman M. Stanage, an assistant professor of philosophy. It is quite rare for a non-tenured assistant professor to become a major figure in a campus power struggle. But Stanage was a charismatic, Socratic figure, and he had an extraordinary impact on students. On most Saturday mornings he could be found drinking coffee in a corner of the university union. He was available for a continuation of class discussions with students on an informal basis. Students were instructed on phenomenology and how to use the philosophical method in examining their personal values and commitments. His existential and phenomenological approach had a galvanizing effect on faculty colleagues as well as on students.

There were no overriding uniformities in the students who came to play a part in the campus politics of Bowling Green in the 1960s. There was no activist type, scholastically or demographically. If anything, the protesters were distinctly average students. In addition, most of the students were simply spectators, if often quite interested spectators, to the events that were transpiring on campus. Only a very few played an active leadership role of any kind. Commenting on the national context of student protest during the 1960s, Kenneth Keniston (1969, 310) states, "Whatever we say about student dissenters is said about a very small minority of the six million college students." This observation applies in some respects to students at BGSU, as well as to students at other colleges and universities. But the students' role as observers did not mean that they were apathetic or indifferent to the issues of concern. On the contrary, those who were playing active leadership roles were articulating the typical sentiments of BGSU students in general.

The students who did play active roles in the uprising, however, gained a valuable set of skills that probably served them well in subsequent career development. Both those who actively supported McDonald and those who did not were refining and elaborating leadership and organizational skills.

During the 1960s, Max Weber's emphasis on value neutrality as an academic ideal fell by the wayside. The authentic pursuit of knowledge does indeed require objectivity, but the problems selected for investigation, the methods employed, and sometimes even the conclusions reached are neither self-evident nor derived from a position of value neutrality. The deep divisions within the faculty during the student uprising grew in part out of differential perceptions of the role of students, the role of the administration, and the role of the faculty in the conduct of university affairs. These perceptual differences disturbed the value neutrality of anyone's views.

The clashing personalities of McDonald and Stanage became both the symbolic and the real focus of the disturbance at BGSU. The dialectic between them was embedded in the social forces that were operating and in the personal biographies of the two men. Their personalities were shaped selectively by their times and social surroundings. Under ordinary circumstances, such contrasting personalities would go their separate ways on a college campus. The bureaucracy would absorb them. But because of the unique conditions of a campus crisis, their worldviews and personalities intersected at the faculty meeting called by President McDonald. The outcome was both dramatic and consequential for the development of the university.

Another personality, somewhat in the background, was the campus Catholic chaplain, Father John Ollivier. Ollivier had a significant amount of influence on President McDonald, and he may have been advising him during the demonstrations and their aftermath. We will include a description of Ollivier's role in campus politics later in this chapter.

RALPH W. McDONALD

From early on, McDonald showed a high degree of intelligence, a capacity for hard work, and a propensity for juggling a number of interests at once. He graduated with highest honors and Phi Beta Kappa from the small, conservative, Methodist-affiliated Hendrix College in Conway, Arkansas. His honors were in English and mathematics, prefiguring his later interest in these fields along with economics. He was not, however, apparently aiming for a scholarly career in any of these disciplines, but leaning toward administration, taking on the principalship of a high school shortly after college.

Following this excursion into secondary education, McDonald quickly found his métier when he went to Duke, earning both a master's and a doctor's degree. These were not in English or mathematics, where he had considerable experience, but in the field of higher education, with an emphasis on administration. He then served as a department head, associate director of the extension division, graduate professor of education, and organizer of graduate activities at the University of North Carolina. Later he took the position of executive secretary of the higher-education division of the NEA, an unusual job for a future university president but one that apparently much impressed the selection committee at Bowling Green. He was an administrator from top to bottom, with only moderate scholarly interest. After his PhD he did not do scholarly research, although he wrote numerous reports and articles on the administration of higher education.

As he advanced in the administrative ranks, McDonald developed a persona that exemplified his central concern with order and decorum. His manner and appearance were somewhat forbidding: black suits, white shirts, dark ties, and polished shoes. He did not drink or swear, and was a devoted churchgoer. In his interactions he focused attention on his dignified and somewhat intimidating manner. It is something of a puzzle, in view of his devotion to Methodism, that he had not directed his career toward an eventual bishopric, at which he would probably have been quite successful. His conservative persona was consistent in all respects. He never raised his voice or showed emotion and was always polite and courteous, the very model of a Southern Christian gentleman. One of the requirements of the selection committee at Bowling Green was that the new president should be a "Christian Gentleman." This phrase has an anti-Semitic ring to it today, but at the time, the early fifties, it probably merely reflected the insularity of this campus.

There were numerous accomplishments under McDonald's presidency at BGSU. Faculty salaries were raised substantially, new curriculum developments were fostered, outstanding faculty were recruited from prestigious schools, and fine new facilities were built. These accomplishments loomed large in the eyes of the board, the parents, and much of the faculty.

The drawbacks of McDonald's administration, however, should also be noted. Probably the most significant was the way in which he exercised his power. It may be that he was a repressed and timid soul who had constructed an armor of aloofness and decorum to protect a vulnerable inner self. Or perhaps he was naturally inclined to a close-up style of administration. At any rate, such habits as prowling the campus at night to make sure that order prevailed, or financially punishing those he thought were in opposition to his policies, are significant to his personality. An instance of the first sort of behavior is the night that Professor Bernard Gundlach was working late, around midnight, in his office, when McDonald used his master key to enter the office. "Why, Professor Gundlach, what are you doing here?" said the president, and Gundlach, a German of high academic standing and a man afraid of nobody, retorted, "Why, President McDonald, what are *you* doing here?" To which McDonald replied that he was just checking to see that the furniture was properly arranged. It is hard to imagine the usual university president doing this sort of thing, and even more difficult to ascertain the reason.

McDonald's micromanagement went as far as assigning faculty office space within departments, appointing or removing departmental chairs, making the final decision on hiring or not hiring new faculty members, and having the final say in faculty promotions and salary. His frequent inspection tours of campus were directed toward making sure the faculty displayed proper decorum in their interaction with students. For example, the chair of the sociology department was instructed to reprimand a new faculty member who was seen by the president with his feet on his desk while talking to a student.

McDonald not only was a micromanager but also showed, at times, a touch of vindictiveness. When Professor Carpenter of the English department opposed an administrative plan to censor the student newspaper, he was scratched from the summer teaching schedule with no reason given. On Carpenter's subsequent meeting with the president, it was obvious that he was being punished for his opposition, although nothing of the sort was ever said. Eventually McDonald realized that the case was bound to become an issue, and he put Carpenter back on the summer schedule. This minor incident illustrates how McDonald worked his control over such matters as salaries, and shows his willingness to take direct issue with those who he thought were against his grand plans for order and decorum.

McDonald made several blunders when the demonstrations kicked off the Bowling Green revolution, and here we shall try to figure out why such an intelligent man turned so clumsy under pressure. One reason for his errors was that he had never encountered such challenges to his position before and so he was not prepared to handle them wisely. He was used to being king of the hill, so to speak; for people to act against his vision of an orderly campus was difficult for him to fathom. Such acts as calling the state highway patrol and declaring a formal state of "emergency" were overreactions to the situation. They turned a molehill into a mountain and, through the rural press, initially made the students appear to be serious rioters and dangerous characters when they were merely disgruntled, and armed with a reasonable set of issues.

When Stanage "stood up in church" and asked that the policies be changed, McDonald's response was to fire the young professor as soon as an excuse could be found. The way this was done, using the grounds that Stanage had not developed a religious emphasis in the philosophy department, did not convince the faculty. But apparently this did not bother McDonald. Amazingly insensitive to the temper of the faculty, he made a ticklish situation into a genuine crisis. Then his fighting against the proposal in the legislature to increase BGSU's board of trustees by two members did not resonate well with the public: Ohioans could see that he felt the present board was not supervising McDonald. One might have expected that the parents of the students would generally support the administration, since the latter acts in loco parentis. The strict rules were in fact regarded by the administration as what the parents did want. And there undoubtedly had been a time, for example in the mid-thirties when the imperiled university had appealed to local support, during which the university was in tune with local mores. But over a period of time the student culture, and probably that of the neighboring towns as well, had become more emancipated. Students came from all over, both in and out of state, to take advantage of Bowling Green's bargain price and accessibility. They came from Toledo, which was a trade union town and the turf of the liberal Republican *Blade*. In fact this paper read, for the most part, like a liberal Democratic newspaper. Many also came from Cleveland and Akron, which were substantial cities. And a significant number came from New York, to take advantage of the moderate out-of-state fees. In other words, many of these parents were Kennedy Democrats themselves, fed up with the stodgy Eisenhower years, doing such new dances as the twist and enjoying liquor as well.

Finally, McDonald's blatant manipulation of salaries did not sit well with either those who received the big increases or those who did not. The president's administrative style had worked reasonably well when everyone was afraid of him, but once the students and Stanage stood up and challenged it, the style's ineffectiveness and inequity became obvious. In other words, McDonald made his style an issue.

Ultimately it seems that McDonald was so smitten by his own success that he could not understand what was happening. He had carefully built an imposing house, but once it was challenged it became a house of cards. He could not discern that his "house" could not be saved from destruction unless he changed his ways. It was never suggested by anyone during the crisis that he resign, only that he give way on certain issues. But giving way was something he could not abide, since he seldom gave in on anything. His eventual resignation, the immediate cause of which was the unsupportive vote from the legislature, was his way of saying that he had been mistreated, misunderstood, and unappreciated, and that he would not stay under those circumstances. But, in his own way, he arranged his departure so that he could return as a member of the faculty, possibly running the show from behind the scenes. Although he took the position that his devotion was to the university, he tried to take good care that his own well-being was protected. Like many heads of institutions, his intelligence was actually limited to planning and procedures, with little awareness of the human factors. And like many otherwise intelligent people, he had significant blind spots, some of which were responsible for his downfall. He could not change his persona, just as he could not change his taste for black suits.

The reasons behind these anomalies of rigid personality, Southern Christian gentlemanliness, and obtuse judgments must remain speculative. We may, however, venture some educated guesses as to how they came about. It seems clear from his career and attitudes that McDonald was a type A personality, a workaholic, totally absorbed in his role. This may have been inherent, simply the kind of person he was, or it may have been a result of his early upbringing and his notion of the kind of person he wanted to be. However, it will be remembered that McDonald was nurtured in a small-town, small-college atmosphere, and that his model for a properly run college undoubtedly stemmed from those early experiences. He apparently envisioned as his ideal a university run by a hardworking, authoritative president, with the order and decorum of a Bible Belt college with the rigorous scholarship and high-level teaching of an institution such as the University of Michigan or the University of Chicago. In addition, there would be as strong a religious component as could be managed in a public university. That all these objectives were incompatible did not seem to enter his mind.

McDonald advanced the above mismatched goals without paying attention to the festering discontent among the students and faculty. When the conflict became manifest, he denied its real nature and, as he put it in his address to the faculty, tried to "spank his children and send them to bed" (see Appendix B). Following his initial misjudgment and denial of there being any substance to what was going on, he continued to make the mistakes that led to his downfall. His eccentric vision for Bowling Green was so dominant that he could not see other ways of proceeding. He lacked the personal flexibility necessary for circumventing the disaster that was in store for him. He was a man of powerful, narrow concepts, who could not handle change, a not unusual personality in people with authoritarian tendencies. He was a victim of his own ideas.

After describing the complexities of McDonald's character, one cannot but mention the touch of tragedy in his story. In analyzing this medium, Aristotle emphasized the presence of a tragic flaw in an otherwise highly gifted personality. For the heroes of Greek tragedy and the later tragic figures of Shakespeare this flaw caused a sharp reversal of fortune in a fundamentally successful life. Tragic heroes are great leaders who have one blind spot, although this flaw has consequences that bring about a failed life. The failure is so great as to be almost incommensurate with the hero's achievements, i.e., almost unjust.

McDonald had elements of Aristotle's tragic hero. He worked hard, was a largely successful leader, and had notable achievements. But his foot was too heavy on the gas and too light on the brakes. He did not know when to soften the power process. Instead, he had a compulsion to keep driving, full speed ahead—for example, in attempting to bully the Ohio state legislature. The ancient Greeks referred to this flaw as hubris, or overwhelming self-confidence; it brought a tragic conclusion to many an otherwise praiseworthy life. At McDonald's most successful moments there was a whiff of Shakespeare's Macbeth, but in the end, at his downfall, there was more of King Lear, prowling into the night, screaming at fate, wondering what had happened.

We must also mention a passing resemblance between McDonald and Clark Kerr, the chancellor of University of California, Berkeley, who would reign over the Free Speech Movement of the Berkeley sixties. While there is almost nothing in common between the two leaders, they were similar in working with a somewhat bloodless "factory" model of a university. They were constructors or builders, who tended to think of the students as materials in their organizational projects. This is a seemingly efficient way to think, but it shows its limits when the students resist the shaping of their spirits.

SHERMAN M. STANAGE

When McDonald was screening the applicants for the new position he had created in the philosophy department, he became quite excited. The application of Sherman M. Stanage seemed to come from the very kind of person McDonald was seeking for the job. Stanage had recently received his PhD in philosophy from the University of Colorado. He had previously been ordained and employed as a Methodist minister. These were impressive credentials in McDonald's view, and Stanage was hired as an assistant professor in a tenure-track position.

McDonald held a firm view that a well-educated person, whether at a state university or elsewhere, should be well trained in the tenets of Christianity. This attitude did not sit very well with Thomas Tuttle, who was the chair of the philosophy department at the time Stanage was hired. Tuttle taught a popular undergraduate course on the philosophy of religion, but the focus was exclusively on his specialty, which was in Asian religions. This was not what McDonald had in mind for religious instruction at his university.

Professor Tuttle had a chip on his shoulder when Stanage arrived on campus. As they got to know each other, however, the two became friends and partners in the academic enterprise. With his deep involvement in existentialism and phenomenology, Stanage had moved far beyond his previous training in theology. While he had little or no interest in developing the kind of religion program McDonald wanted, he did have a dramatic impact on students in his philosophy courses, and he became a valuable colleague to faculty in several departments. Over time, it became apparent that both his personal background and his academic inclinations were at odds with the objectives President McDonald wished to promote.

During his early years, Stanage had lived in Bernardo, New Mexico, which was just a wide place in the road where his father had a grocery and liquor store. The community was entirely Spanish-speaking, so he became bilingual at an early age. When he was seven or eight, his parents let him travel west with strangers. A family had stopped at the store, and had two boys about his age. When they drove back through Bernardo on their way home to Atlanta, they asked if he could go with them to Atlanta for the school year. His parents agreed, and Sherman was required to travel alone by public transportation back to New Mexico after the school year was over.

His father traveled extensively during World War II, and as a result Stanage attended three different high schools: one in Tucson, Arizona, another in Albuquerque, New Mexico, and a third in Northampton, Massachusetts. He was a senior in high school at a very early age, and he subsequently lied about his age in order to enter the army. Because of his proficiency in languages, he was sent to language school to learn Japanese, and then to Hokkaido, Japan, as an interpreter. He served in the 511th Parachute Infantry Regiment, 11th Airborne Division, during the occupation of Japan.

After his military service, Stanage attended the University of New Mexico, where he earned his bachelor's degree with a double major in psychology and philosophy. Two years later he graduated from the Iliff School of Theology with a Master of Theology degree. His teaching career began at Baker University in Kansas. At Baker, he taught both philosophy and religion. After two years, he was asked to leave because of his social activism. He had protested the requirement that every male student at the university enroll in ROTC, and he had taken a group of students to the Lower Rio Grande Valley in support of striking farmworkers.

Stanage had become an advocate for liberal causes and was a strong believer in democratic principles and the quest for social justice. His students thought of him as one of the best professors they had ever had. He was a creative listener, and from his days as a Methodist minister he maintained a pastoral concern for people. He enjoyed exploring ideas with friends and colleagues as well as with students. He was so committed to his ideals and to his professional work that he frequently defaulted on his family responsibilities as a husband and a father of four daughters. Stanage was obviously a most complex human being.

He was greatly influenced by the philosophical writings of Kierkegaard, Wittgenstein, Tillich, Husserl, Schutz, and Collingwood. His approach to students, higher education, and social relationships was shaped by a synthesis of intellectual resources and his personal experiences as director of the Wesley Foundation in Boulder, Colorado, while he was completing his doctorate. He had very little patience with colleagues who only taught courses in the history of philosophy and did not engage students in the doing of philosophy.

His particular approach to students and to life in general was to place emphasis on multiple realities, differential worldviews, and diverse experiences in everyday life. Throughout, there was the assumption that a primary quest of humanity is to find meaning in everyday life. The coherence and meaning of personal lives and the social order are not self-evident, since we do not live in a world with a clearly defined purpose. The basic task of educators is to get students involved in the subject matter, and this requires listening to what students have to say and engaging them in relevant dialogue. It was perhaps his effective implementation of a philosophical approach to teaching that allowed Stanage to touch students deeply and elicit admiration for both his intellect and his personal qualities.

It was when Stanage observed students building bonfires in front of the union and blocking traffic on U.S. Route 6 that he criticized their methods for displaying discontent. Consistent with his approach to teaching, he suggested that if there were grievances, then these needed to be explicitly defined before they could be acted upon. This seemed to be a reasonable, rational way of approaching social conflict, one that Stanage laid out clearly in his subsequent book entitled *Reason and Violence* (1974).

Stanage was as shocked as anyone else when the charges were levied against him and Rev. Trautwein by President McDonald in the faculty meeting. A clash of strong personalities occurred when McDonald refused to engage in a dialogue with Stanage and attempted to adjourn the faculty meeting, and then two months later sent Stanage a letter notifying him of his dismissal. Attendance at faculty meetings called by the president was mandatory, and for those in attendance, the electrifying atmosphere created by the exchange between McDonald and Stanage became permanently engrained in their memories. Stanage's emphasis on dialogue collided with McDonald's emphasis on monologue and obedience to authority. The interplay between McDonald and Stanage galvanized sentiment among the faculty, the board of trustees, and, once it leaked out, the news media.

This was not the usual boring and colorless faculty meeting. A lowly assistant professor was challenging a bigger-than-life authority figure who had godlike bearing and demeanor. In biblical terms, it resembled the youthful David's confronting the giant Goliath. To some of the faculty, Stanage seemed to resemble the historical account of Socrates, who was true to his beliefs, come what may. Stress and discomfort was evident among older faculty members, who had been socialized to accept the primary authority of the McDonald regime. But Stanage later received several phone calls from faculty who congratulated him for his defense of freedom and the right to speak out in an open society.

The large number of new faculty members who had been hired during the previous two years watched in amazement as events unfolded. The meeting was to become one of the more memorable experiences for those who subsequently lived through the events of the 1960s. Neutrality and indifference were not options for the faculty in attendance. All were caught up in the emotional intensity of the moment, and all were required to confront their own values and identities and how they saw themselves relating to the academic enterprise.

STUDENTS

Then as now, most college students were attending school to improve their opportunities in the job market. The basic values being emphasized were, for the most part, materialism and hedonism. The college degree had taken on a magical quality as the key to a good life. The students had taken seriously the Health, Education and Welfare posters prominently displayed on high school bulletin boards showing a connection between level of education and lifetime earnings. But while most students were career oriented, a growing number of them were dedicating their lives to making the world a better place. These were the students who shared the youthful idealism of John F. Kennedy.

The election of Kennedy in 1960 to the presidency of the United States stimulated a great deal of idealism among the youth of the nation. He was only forty-three years old when he was elected, the youngest person ever brought to that office. The aura he gave to the presidency was one of youthfulness, vigor, energy, and idealism. He was the first president born in the twentieth century, and he was regarded as the spokesperson for a new generation (Neal 1998). Becoming involved in political activities had been elevated to a noble enterprise. Kennedy's style was oriented toward enhancing optimism, enthusiasm, and commitment (Rosenblatt 1962). It was easy to identify with Kennedy, and to adopt his values. This curbed many young people's materialistic, hedonistic motivations for going to college.

The student activists at Bowling Green followed this Kennedy pattern in a redefinition of morality. The primary issues of morality were not seen to be matters of personal or sexual decorum. Instead they were identified as those aspects of the social order having deleterious effects on large numbers of people (Lance 1966). Examples included policies promoting the persistence of poverty in the midst of increasing affluence; Jim Crow practices and other racial discrimination in a society proclaiming equality of opportunity; and national resources increasingly allocated for developing new military weapons instead of improving the overall quality of life.

The students of 1960 were a part of the first generation to be socialized by television. The sale of television sets as necessary consumer items escalated after 1950. The content of the programming was highly varied, but only three networks supplied it. Marshall McLuhan (1965) maintained that the social significance of television derived from its creation of "a global village." Almost instantaneous communication from nearly any place in the world became possible. Television entertainment made rapid contributions to enlarging and elaborating pleasure-oriented activities. Both participatory and spectator experiences were greatly extended (Neal 2007). In moving toward more cosmopolitan identities, students were developing an awareness of the world as comprising many cultures; there emerged a greater willingness to question the assumptions of one's own traditions.

The primary reasons for student discontent in 1960 would seem unbelievable to contemporary college students. But then, colleges and universities throughout the United States pursued in loco parentis policies, legally acting in the place of parents. Such policies today are regarded as a violation of such civil liberties as freedom of speech and freedom of movement. In 1960, however, students were not regarded or treated as full-fledged adults. Instead, protective, parental attitudes and policies were followed. And while in loco parentis principles were in operation at most universities, they took an extreme pattern at Bowling Green.

The university took pride in being a residential campus, and this pride took the form of requiring all students to live on campus unless they were commuting and living with their parents. There was zero tolerance of alcoholic beverages, and of coed interactions except under certain approved conditions. Class attendance was compulsory, and all faculty members were required to submit a daily list of the names of all students absent from classes. If absent, a student was required to submit evidence of a legitimate excuse, such as illness certified by a medical doctor or a death within one's immediate family. Not all the faculty felt comfortable with this policy. Some thought it was not their right to control class attendance.

The social control of students by the administration was relatively easy because of the students' atomization. The detachment and discreteness of individual students precluded any form of effective group action. In lacking organization, students were without a framework for concerted action or for registering social protest. Students also lacked a shared consciousness, particularly of what their rights and grievances were. All students come and go as they move through a university's system. Usually the institution is changed very little by them as individuals.

In those rare cases where a coalition is formed between student activists and sympathetic faculty members, however, the grievances become central. And in Bowling Green's case the inflexibility of rules and regulations had become a concern to faculty as well as to students. Further, forces operating in the larger society were in the process of promoting a greater range of personal choices for the individual (Rosenthal 2005). The older forms of traditional morality were being challenged by an increasing concern for social responsibility, freedom of movement, and collective morality.

FACULTY

As a result of the rapid increase in student enrollment at Bowling Green, a large number of new faculty members had been added. It was becoming increasingly difficult for many universities at this time to staff their classes with well-qualified faculty. Successful recruitment at Bowling Green was facilitated by faculty salaries being in the top echelon for state universities in the United States. But McDonald's emphasis upon hiring a well-qualified faculty was incompatible with his micromanagement and authoritarian control of all aspects of campus life. A well-qualified faculty is not necessarily an obedient faculty.

Cynical faculty referred to McDonald's pompous pronouncements as aspirations for creating under his leadership "an Ann Arbor South," or "a Harvard on Poe Ditch." The way in which salaries had been used to elicit compliance was evident in the decisions on salaries for the 1961–1962 academic year. McDonald met with other administrators to place the faculty into three categories: the McDonald supporters, the neutrals, and those who were presumed to have supported Stanage. Since the pro-Stanage petition was under lock and key in a local attorney's office, no one actually knew who had or had not signed the petition, but guesses were made. By allocating nearly all of the funds available for salary increases to those he presumed to be his supporters, McDonald saw to it that some faculty members received as much as a 30 percent salary increase in a single year. Only negligible amounts, or none at all, were given to the dissenters and the neutrals. This departing act on McDonald's part had such disruptive effects that it took the faculty senate and the deans of the colleges several years to smooth out faculty salaries and to make the necessary market adjustments.

The deep divisions within the faculty over the student rebellion and over the McDonald administration persisted as personal hostilities and resentments for many years. The conflict was reflected in interpersonal antagonisms within departments and in campus politics, and occupied a central place in the gossip mill on campus. Informal groups and friendships were often shaped by where individual faculty members stood on the issues of 1961.

A segment of the faculty had seized on student discontent to promote their own quite compatible goals within the university. The more liberal wing of the faculty was disenchanted with the heavy-handed approach of McDonald, but the opportunity provided by the student rebellion permitted them to make their move. A new source of creative and innovative leadership, that of the students themselves, had emerged within the university.

The liberal faculty developed social networks that persisted for several years. Howard Brogan invited a group of liberal faculty members to his home to form a new faculty forum. His idea was to organize a select group that would meet on a monthly basis to read papers and discuss the central topics of their research. At the organizational meeting, Brogan himself presented a paper entitled "The Power of Negative Thinking."

In subsequent meetings, the name of the newly formed organization became Academics Anonymous, in part as a play on the name of another well-known organization and in part to reflect the anonymity of the faculty who signed the petition protesting the firing of Sherman Stanage. Membership in the group was by invitation only and was presumed to include the top intellectuals on campus. The members were primarily from the departments of English, sociology, history, political science, psychology, foreign languages, and economics.

The meetings were collegial and stimulating because of their interdisciplinary focus. Formal papers were read on contemporary research interests as a way of eliciting criticism and feedback, as well as becoming better acquainted with each other. Membership became a source of pride, and a great deal of information was shared about events on campus. There were frequent adjournments to local bars after the formal meetings for a continuation of the discussions. Many of the innovative changes within the university over the next ten years originated from this group's discussions. A large number of subsequent leaders and chairs of the faculty senate also came from the group.

The faculty members hired in the late 1950s and early 1960s were much closer in age to the students than to their older colleagues. Their youthfulness and early career stage permitted them to share a sense of idealism with their students. The older liberal wing of the faculty often served as mentors to the new hires and steered them through the pitfalls of the McDonald administration. The liberal faculty contributed disproportionately to the number of leading academic scholars on campus. They not only interacted with the new hires and invited them to coffee breaks, but they also served as commendable role models.

The experience of two particular historical events had decisive effects on the faculty at BGSU during the early 1960s. One was having served in the military during World War II; the second was having received graduate training during the era in which a fear of Communism was dominant in the United States, when the notion that some Americans had formed an allegiance with the Soviet Union to promote international Communism had developed into mass hysteria.

As members of the armed forces, BGSU faculty members had formerly served in some of the major battles of North Africa, Europe, and Asia. After the war was over, many of them continued to serve as officers in reserve units. All were psychologically affected by their military experiences and had come to believe that life on a college campus was the best that modern society had to offer. The nation had lost its former position of isolation in the world, and international relations had become a major concern. The horizons of the veterans had been broadened by their international travel and by their military service. The result was a much more cosmopolitan worldview than was prevalent on campuses before the war.

The faculty members at BGSU in the early 1960s also had been socialized during the era of McCarthyism on college campuses. Senator Joseph McCarthy and his supporters claimed that an epic struggle was underway for control of the minds and souls of the masses. Public schools and universities were seen as a forum to indoctrinate students with the Communist way of thinking. McCarthy's claims seemed credible enough at the time that professors throughout the country were required to sign a loyalty oath as a condition for employment. FBI agents routinely checked libraries to identify those professors who had checked out books by Karl Marx or other known Communists. Professors who had joined left-wing organizations during their youth or who had had friends who were known Communists were suspected of disloyalty and dismissed from their jobs. Textbooks and library books by American authors, both past and present, were scanned for themes sympathetic to the Communist cause (Neal 1998).

Conformity became the rule of the day both on college campuses and in many other institutional areas (Stouffer 1955). College professors altered their lecture notes to remove any suggestion of subversive ideas. State legislatures enacted laws prohibiting controversial speakers from being allowed on campuses. Banning controversial speakers was based on the view that students were receptive and gullible when exposed to possibly subversive ideas. Only a purification of the system could assure that "American values" would be transmitted and the "American way of life" preserved. The ideals of open inquiry and academic freedom in a democratic society fell by the wayside. The demand for conformity had corrosive effects on the integrity and vitality of the system. Those faculty members who had been deeply affected by the McCarthy-era emphasis on conformity and avoidance of conflict had a great deal of difficulty in dealing with the McDonald-Stanage controversy and the subsequent protests among the students.

We will end this chapter with a brief look at John Ollivier, the charismatic and somewhat mysterious Catholic chaplain. His importance on campus especially during the demonstrations was probably significant, but it is difficult to appraise because he operated with a certain amount of secrecy, particularly in his relationship with President McDonald.

FATHER JOHN OLLIVIER

The pastor of the Catholic group the Newman Club, Father John Ollivier had a close relationship with the university president. He also seemed to be an important person behind the scenes in BGSU politics during the period of the 1961 student demonstrations and their aftermath. In particular he seems to have been talking to President McDonald about some campus issues and acting as a shadowy advisor or "gray eminence." Ollivier kept a low profile with the press, but he was extremely vocal in his Catholic student newsletter, *The Newman Notes*.

In directing his chaplaincy, Ollivier attempted to keep tight control over the Catholic students, although his actual control was probably only over the more committed of them. In the fall of 1960 there was a total enrollment on campus of 6,229. Of these, Father Ollivier said about 1,400 were Catholics (*Newman Notes*, March 16, 1961). No one could have known exactly how many Catholics there were, for there are always people coming and going in large and loosely boundaried religious groups. But still, these figures would make the campus about 20 percent Catholic. This is a lower figure than might have been expected, given that northwest Ohio was at the time about 40 percent Catholic. But Catholics probably did not attend state universities in the same proportions as non-Catholic students did. And some might have decided not to "come out" as Catholics while at Bowling Green. In any case, Ollivier gave all the signs of having considerable power, both over the devoutly Catholic students and as a spokesman for the Catholic Church.

Ollivier resembled President McDonald in his being in the conservative wing in his religious and political views. And both exercised authority in a strict and exacting manner. McDonald was a Methodist version of Ollivier. In addition, Ollivier was opposed to reformist currents in the Church, even though in the early sixties, soon after the BGSU student demonstrations, Pope John XXIII himself called the theologically liberal Second Vatican Council. Ollivier, then, was something of an oddity, even in his own church. But this does not seem to have diminished his authority on the BGSU campus.

Ollivier took the position that "Catholic students are forbidden to study philosophy here at Bowling Green because of the atheistic leanings in that department" (*Newman Notes*, March 16, 1961). When a Catholic philosopher was hired as Stanage's replacement, Father Ollivier wrote, "Dr. Goodwin, presently teaching at DePaul University in Chicago, will be added to the staff of the philosophy department next fall. We strongly urge Catholics to register in the classes he will conduct in the Aristotelian-Thomistic tradition" (*Newman Notes,* May 7, 1961).

The two philosophers that Ollivier said had atheistic leanings were Thomas Tuttle and Sherman Stanage. They were both distinctly liberal, theologically and politically, but neither was an atheist. It is not clear what Ollivier meant by atheistic leanings.

Besides being similar in personalities and beliefs, McDonald and Ollivier seem to have been in some kind of close communication. One sign of this was that Ollivier claimed to have known about McDonald's plans to fire Stanage eight months before Stanage himself was informed of it. As Ollivier put it,

> Dr. McDonald, who hired Mr. Stanage to develop a department of accredited courses in religion, told me last October, several months before the student riot, that Mr. Stanage would not have his contract renewed in June, because he not only failed to establish what he had been hired to establish, but rather proved to be the biggest obstacle to its establishment. (*Newman Notes,* November 12, 1961)

It does not seem possible that Ollivier was prevaricating here, since McDonald could easily have denied the claim. And McDonald's communication to Ollivier was probably not in writing but face to face, most likely in McDonald's office, since the topic was too sensitive for a paper trail. They may have also talked about Stanage's possible replacements. In fact it was a substantial violation of professional ethics for McDonald to have given Ollivier this information before he gave it to Stanage. This incident suggests that the McDonald-Ollivier relationship had a distinctly secretive and high-risk quality to it.

When Ollivier mentioned "accredited courses in religion" in the last quotation, he was probably including the prospect of accredited courses in the Catholic religion, including courses taught by Father Ollivier himself and possibly other local Catholic priests. This was also suggested by another comment he made in his newsletter. This comment is somewhat long, but significant, and it shows Ollivier's belief that Catholics were being mistreated at the university:

> They expressly stated in their complaint to the governor, I had undue influence with the administration. This was ridiculous. But it must be true, they thought, for after all Dr. McDonald had stated that he would never hire an atheist. He had hired a Catholic to teach in the Philosophy Department, (and don't think this didn't start letters flying to various philosophical organizations) and crime of all crimes, Dr. McDonald had committed himself to accredit the Catholic

religion class. These of course are regarded as capital sins in the language of the secularist and the free thinker. And so in their terror of Catholic infiltration, the motto adopted became "Get McDonald at any cost." (*Newman Notes,* November 12, 1961)

If BGSU had ever instituted accredited Catholic religious classes, it would have been a singular success for Father Ollivier. When McDonald resigned, however, this idea was quietly abandoned. But during the period of the demonstrations it was probably very much on Father Ollivier's mind, and the eventual loss must have been severely disappointing.

It should also be noted that Ollivier thought the underlying force behind the student demonstrations and the faculty dissidence was anti-Catholicism. There was widespread concern about Father Ollivier's influence over the philosophy department, but this seems like a rather minor force in the 1961 demonstration and the resignation of McDonald.

Ollivier's role at BGSU, then, was complex. He was quite blunt-spoken and seemingly crystal clear in his views, and he was more than just another college chaplain. McDonald seemed to have great respect for Ollivier, and he wanted to do whatever he could to please him and the Catholic students. The problem was that the school was a public institution supported by tax money. Therefore the line between church and state had to be carefully respected, or the university's policies would be in violation of the Constitution. McDonald does not seem to have been very concerned about this line—or perhaps he drew it differently from others.

Another questionable policy that McDonald tried to follow was to avoid hiring atheists on the faculty. He interviewed all job candidates, and he always asked which church the candidate might be attending. He would ask this in a purely sociable, friendly way. But his purpose was to find out if the job candidate believed in God. The word had long been out that this was part of the job interview, and candidates were advised by friends on the BGSU faculty that they should act religious whether they really were or not. The president's pro-theist policy was illegal, both in the broad sense of mixing church and state and in the more specific sense of violating the State of Ohio's fair-employment law. But it never became an open or publicly disputed issue, instead remaining a game of cat and mouse.

Around this time there was a United Press story that mentioned Father Ollivier:

Five persons formerly associated with the University as students or teachers today sought an interview with Governor Michael V. DiSalle. They brought with them a list of six grievances against the administration of President Ralph

McDonald. Included in the list was the charge that Father John Ollivier, the campus chaplain, exercised undue control over the selection of faculty members through influence on the administration. They said that Father Ollivier, advisor to the Newman Club, a Catholic organization, wrote each Catholic student entering the University a letter saying they should not take philosophy courses. Sources in Bowling Green quoted Father Ollivier as saying a Catholic would be added to the staff of the philosophy department and that this would be accomplished by church officials discussing it with McDonald. (Gordon, 38)

During the demonstrations themselves, as we mentioned earlier, two other religious advisors, Sherman Stanage and James Trautwein, spoke to the students the second day and gave messages that more or less legitimized the demonstrations. Father Ollivier was also invited to speak to the assembled students, but he refused. His position was that the demonstrating students were criminals and should be placed in jail.

Fr. Ollivier's role during the demonstrations and their aftermath, given his closeness to President McDonald, was probably important. But it was largely private: that is, there is no public record of what he may have said or done. Therefore one can only guess how much influence he actually had, and what actions he was taking. He did whatever he could to keep the Catholic students out of the demonstrations, and this meant that he, and those Catholic students who obeyed him, were officially bystanders. But he may have continued unofficially to advise McDonald on the Stanage issue until the end.

If McDonald had not been so decisively delegitimized by the state legislature's votes and more or less forced to resign, Ollivier might have become a political issue in his own right, for he engaged in several questionable activities. But once McDonald resigned it was obvious that Ollivier would quickly lose most of his power with the administration. The new president would treat him as just another chaplain. This meant he was no longer of much interest in the politics of BGSU. He continued to take strong religious positions in his newsletter, but his larger influence disappeared, and he dropped out of sight in campus politics.

Chapter 5

Voices in Contention at BGSU

Another way of viewing the demonstrations and their aftermath is as a set of interacting voices in a dialogue, or at least as a system of communication. In this section we will look back at some things already mentioned, but we will interpret them in a new way. A great theorist of voice and dialogue was the Russian philosopher Mikhail Bakhtin. For Bakhtin, who was writing during the Stalin era in the Soviet Union, dialogue was the most progressive and liberating social process (Bakhtin 1984). It was also totally lacking under Stalin's repressive hand. Bakhtin emphasized the form of dialogue as much as the content. In particular he singled out the qualities of "addressivity" and "responsivity" as influential on the content of dialogue. Addressivity is the way one speaker recognizes or greets the other. In some languages, German and French, for example, a person can be addressed either formally (*Sie* or *vous*) or informally (*du* or *tu*). In others (e.g., in Russian, Spanish, and Continental Portuguese), there are three forms of address, a special one being singled out for extremely close relationships. A close address means a close emotional content.

Bakhtin obviously had the restricted communication of the Soviet Union in mind when he analyzed voice. He was not free to use examples from his own repressive society; to do so would have landed him in jail. So he usually used literary examples, often from Dostoyevsky's novels. This was a politically safe procedure because Dostoyevsky was a conservative and was regarded as acceptable by Stalin's regime. But it is easy enough to use Bakhtin's ideas for an ordinary society: they can apply to the Soviet Union or to the less repressive but still quite imperfect United States. We will draw on Bakhtin's perceptive theory of voice to analyze events at Bowling Green.

There are also sometimes power implications in forms of address. If someone is called "boy" or "missy," he or she is immediately being placed in a subordinate position, and it is understood that he or she will be treated in that manner. People so addressed can fight back in various ways, but if they do not, or do so unsuccessfully, they will remain in the lower position. In the United States Navy, invitations were until 1970 addressed to "officers and their ladies and enlisted men and their wives." In other words, addressive subordination rippled out to families. Addressivity, then, which is based both on customs and on previous communications between the two parties, has a distinct role in regulating what can be said in the communication.

Receptivity is the other person's response to the addressivity. Receptivity is a role, specifically the role of agreeing to a particular set of rules in the communication. Jurgen Habermas is famous for a rather altruistic set of rules he thinks holds when people communicate in a democratic arena (Habermas 1984). The reality seems less altruistic. Receptivity will correspond to the address. If a person has recognized you in a warm, friendly manner, your receptivity will probably be of the same nature. If a person recognizes you as an inferior, you are being implicitly ordered to respond as an inferior. There are sometimes related dialogical forms, such as how far away from each other people stand or how much eye contact they make with each other.

Bakhtin also distinguished a monological from a dialogical form of communication. In a dialogue, each speaker is open to the other's opinions. Assertions are tentative and welcoming of counterresponse. The communicators work together as a team, seeking some kind of shared value. By contrast, a monological style is one in which one person speaks to another as though the other were not there. The speaker makes finished, highly boundaried remarks. No comments, particularly negative ones, are expected. A speech, a sermon, or a scholarly paper is usually quite monological. Addressivity in a monologue is distant, and there are no openings for corrections or other viewpoints.

Bakhtin had the further idea that human beings were themselves dialogues—internal dialogues with one aspect of the self talking to another. This is similar to George Herbert Mead's idea in sociology that the self is the "I" (the present self) talking to the "me" (the past self) (Mead 1964/1913). If your internal conversation is stiff and formal, tending toward the monological, you are not enjoying the full benefits of dialogue. In particular, mental health, as opposed to psychopathology and depression, flourishes when the self can reach uninhibited internal dialogue.

Bakhtin also had the idea that the physical environment—both natural objects, such as hills and lakes, and, more especially, "built" objects, such as buildings, automobiles, and monuments—had voice. These objects have meanings, although the meanings are subject to interpretation. And the meanings can be heard (i.e., decoded) as voice. This is most obvious with negative or power-laden voices, as when segregated facilities told African Americans that they were inferior. The separate swimming pools said, "You are dirty," and the segregated buses said, "You smell bad." The built environment, then, has a lot of social power in its implicit messages to various social groups.

The Bowling Green campus too was full of physical markers that kept the students in their place. One noticeable physical voice was that of the campus lawns. Normally lawns have pathways that facilitate movement from place to place. These include lots of diagonals and cross-paths which allow walkers to get from point to point more efficiently. At Bowling Green, someone had decided not to have many shortcuts through the lawns. Instead, you often had to walk along the perimeter. Walking across the lawns was prohibited. As McDonald's press director, James Gordon, recently recalled, "[McDonald] ordered picket fences for every sidewalk intersection on campus to keep students from cutting through the grass" (*Bowling Green Sentinel-Tribune,* June 24, 2010). When the demonstrations started, one of the first acts of civil disobedience was to create more efficient paths across the lawns. This amounted to "sassing" the lawns and so sassing the administration.

The path-making was also an expression or symbol of student solidarity. When President McDonald resigned and the reformed administration began, one of the first changes was to place shortcuts in the lawns. This was not only a sensible way of handling foot traffic but also a change in the character of the physical voice from repressive to tolerant.

When the campus was in its most student-dominated state, as it was just before the demonstrations, the entire physical environment expressed the power of the administration. There was not just one environmental voice but a whole system of them, and they spoke in harmony. They were a chorus, and they said, "We"—that is, the administration—"are in charge." But when the students began to dispute their subordinate role, the physical voices began to change. There was a clash or disharmony, as some features of the environment still expressed the administration's power but other features began to express the students' dissenting voices. This was a mixed, cacophonous chorus. And after McDonald resigned and the administration turned in a liberal direction, still another campus chorus was heard. It said, "Power is shared on this campus."

One final distinction is the commonsense one between voice as a mode of communication and as the substance or content of communication. A newspaper column or a megaphone or a graffiti site is a mode of communication, and a declaration or disagreement or complaint is the content of communication. This distinction was implicit in the discussion of Bakhtin's concepts.

Keeping these ideas in mind, we will now look at how the communication system at BGSU was completely, if laboriously, transformed during the period of the student uprising. This transformation was permanent—that is, it has continued from spring 1961 to the present time. In addition, it has had an exemplary influence on many other Ohio campuses.

The main actors in this discussion will be the students, the faculty, and the administration. We will not single out leaders or symbolic figures, for we are now talking generically about collectivities and their communications status.

STUDENT VOICE

For many years before the 1961 demonstration the students had little voice in any sense of the word. There were few ways they could express themselves. And in the modes that were open to them, there was little they were allowed to say. In terms of ordinary civil liberties or freedom of speech, they were pretty much forced into silence or into saying things the administration would approve of. The school paper was not free to express critical or unconventional views. And students could not write critical letters to the editor or contribute to negative stories about the university in the various newspapers of Ohio. There were no explicit or formal rules about communication. Instead, there was a blanket rule against improper behavior, and this notion of impropriety was stretched to apply to anything critical of or negative about the university. If the students complained about this rule, they were breaking it. In the Student Handbook (the university's rulebook), in the section called "Conduct of Students," the phrase "high moral and ethical standards" appears three times. This was the major elastic clause the university used, extending it as necessary, as the basis for its various unwritten rules. The punishment for breaking them could be expulsion. The only real voice the students had was civil disobedience, or what was locally referred to as a riot, a word that comes from *roar*.

The riot or roaring tradition was the binary opposite of the tidy communication channels and content that were open to these students. To stay with this analogy, the students had two choices: bleating like lambs or roaring like lions. The options in between, which constituted the range of ordinary or routine communication, were all forbidden. And the binaries fed each other. The periodic "riots" (or rather, the demonstrations, protests, or expressions of civil disobedience) were always curtailed as deviant or criminal acts, and the students were pushed back into the conformist channels. When the return to these channels became too frustrating, the students tried roaring again. No doubt the demonstrations suggested to the administration that only conformist channels were safe. The idea that there should be freedom of speech for students, just as there is for American citizens generally, does not seem to have occurred to the administration.

There is a sense in which all the student demonstrations of the sixties and later were over freedom of speech. Of course, students wanted this freedom to have a particular substantive content (anti-war or civil rights concerns, for example), but at a generic level the fight was over opening the channels of communication and institutionalizing free speech.

At Bowling Green, all this changed the moment the 1961 demonstration began. When the fraternity pledge hit Dean Taylor with a water balloon and then ran to escape the police with everyone following him, the whole voice structure was transformed. The structure itself changed instantly, but the practice had to change little by little via trial and error. It was not very many days, though, before students started saying what they meant and getting away with it.

The obvious analogy was with the way the demonstration at the University of California, Berkeley, began on December 2, 1964. Students were leafleting from tables on Sproul Plaza, near Bancroft Avenue on the south edge of the campus. The tables were positioned to catch the student sidewalk traffic. The university had earlier declared this area no longer legal for student politicking, revoking access to a practice that had long been a student right. When the students refused to comply with police orders to move, a campus police car drove across the sidewalk onto Sproul Plaza to more conveniently arrest the leafleting students. A large crowd of students had gathered around, watching and jeering. When the police car parked, a nameless student yelled, "Sit down." This phrase, which echoed the 1930s sit-down strikes in the auto plants of Michigan, was immediately understood to mean, "Sit down around the police car so it will be trapped. They won't dare drive over our bodies."

The expression "Sit down" was analogous to the watchword "Founders," which created the pathway into the Bowling Green uprising. Once the Berkeley students had sat down, students took off their shoes so as not to damage the police car, climbed onto its roof, and gave short speeches. In both cases, at Bowling Green and then at UC Berkeley, a simple shouted expression was the catalyst for the civil disobedience.

For the Bowling Green students this was a movement back into the riot or roaring mode. The dean had treated the crowd as sheep, but he pushed too hard and turned them into lions. This incident, however, was completely different from its closest BG historical precedent, the 1957 traffic-stopping demonstration. This time, in 1961, Martin Luther King had already inserted civil disobedience into the national dialogue (and legal system), as Reverend Trautwein pointed out the second night of the demonstrations. When Trautwein suggested that the student demonstrations too were a form of civil rights protest, he placed an important "frame" or interpretation on the demonstration. The "riot" had now become civil disobedience. This time the roaring was legal. And the theme of the three days, and the three months of positioning that followed, was the students' finding their voices and exploring their grievances with these new modes of expression. Free speech was explored and tested on the Bowling Green campus months and even years before it was explored at Berkeley, Harvard, Columbia, and all the rest.

It should be remembered that free speech does not always look like free speech. Sometimes it looks like obscenity or anti-patriotism or riot. Obscene words are legal in this country. It is not against the law to communicate through them. It may be shocking or unaesthetic or unpopular, but free speech is regularly tested by pushing it as far as possible, into the zone of rough language, for instance. Flag burning is the same device. People burn flags to deepen the institution of free speech and to make ordinary free speech safer. Not to insult the flag or make fun of patriotism. Civil liberties are tested at the boundaries or extremes, not in the mainstream or at the midpoint. This might seem like a legal technicality, but it is the way rights are given precedent and security in the American legal system.

The forbidding of hand-holding and kisses goodnight after a date was a similar curtailment of free speech at Bowling Green. The kiss is a form of communication or free speech, and its expression has a powerful meaning and function in the lives of young people. The kiss is part of human development in the areas of sex, love, and marriage. People explore their emotions and their commitments with expressions of affection. These kisses have just as much dignity as any other expression of the human spirit.

At Bowling Green as elsewhere, kisses were part of the movement toward adulthood. If students were told they could not kiss at the doors of the women's dorms as a date ended and the couple was parting for the night, they were being deprived of their rights. Certainly a kiss is a message, even if a nonverbal one, and it lies squarely in the area of free speech. In addition, forbidding these signs of affection was an insult to the women, a point we will return to in the conclusion chapter. The "voice" of this rule suggested there was something wrong with women. One reason women were so angry and vocal in the demonstrations and their aftermath was that it was largely a question of their rights.

When a delegation of nine students appeared before the House and Senate committees on education on April 3, 1961, and started the movement toward the board-enlargement bill that would dethrone Ralph McDonald's administration, the group was led in part by two women. There were in addition three other women in the delegation, which made it majority female. These women were quite dedicated to lobbying the legislature, and in retrospect one can see why. They were angry feminists, ten years before feminism became a mainstream issue in the United States. And one might say this early force of feminism was the main factor in establishing free speech at BGSU and putting down the repressive administration. The fact that this university, overnight, stopped being a repressive institution and became a liberal American campus is largely due to the heroic actions of these women and the other student demonstrators.

The administration does not seem to have ever sensed what was happening on this broad political canvas, both in the United States and in Bowling Green. The university was using an out-of-date voice with an out-of-date message. The legal idea of students being protected by school administrations in loco parentis could be given various loadings. At one extreme there could be a minimal amount of protection, restricted to clearly important dangers and risks for the students. At the other extreme there could be a maximal amount of protection, moving the system toward what Erving Goffman called a total institution. Bowling Green had much too much alleged protection for the students. The riot tradition was a constant message from the students to the administration that the alleged protections were actually curtailing their everyday rights.

As many contemporary observers said, and as we observed earlier, Bowling Green was like a denominational college run by some kind of fundamentalist sect. Actually it was run on tax dollars, and the country was at that time asking for more and more freedom and equality in the way in which tax dollars were spent. Right before the BG demonstrations these sentiments were expressed eloquently by the newly elected president, John F. Kennedy, and by the charismatic civil rights leader Martin Luther King. It was these leaders who were changing the country and whom the students were listening to. In a sense, King and Kennedy were the patron saints of the BG demonstrations.

One indication of the administration's misunderstanding of the civil liberties issue was how it responded when several professors complained to the American Civil Liberties Union in April of 1961. The professors were mainly complaining about their own civil liberties, but students' civil liberties were also at issue.

> "Obviously civil liberties are not involved," said Dr. Donnal V. Smith, assistant to the President, concerning the announcement this week that the Ohio Civil Liberties Union would investigate alleged suppressions of civil liberties on this campus....
>
> Dr. Smith pointed out that if we had a regulation that only people of a certain denomination or race could attend the University, we would have a violation. This we do not have, or anything like it. (*Bowling Green Sentinel-Tribune,* April 25, 1961)

Smith, who was presumably speaking for President McDonald, was actually talking about civil rights rather than civil liberties. Civil rights are the rights of special groups such as women, African Americans, or members of minority religious groups. These rights have to do with equality. By contrast, civil liberties come from the Bill of Rights of the federal Constitution: freedom of speech, religion, assembly, and privacy, and so forth. These rights primarily concern freedom rather than equality. If McDonald (and his spokesperson Smith) did not know the difference between civil rights and civil liberties, as appears to have been the case, it is understandable that he would also misunderstand the students' complaints that their civil liberties were being violated.

As the BG riot tradition gradually transformed itself into civil disobedi-ence, and a former crime became a legal mode of expression, the students had to figure out how they might use their new voices and discover what they needed to say. Over the years the issues had always been a mixture of lifestyle matters, such as cars, alcohol, and expressions of affection, and such civil-liberty questions as a free student press, democratic student government, privacy from university police searches of student apartments, and the right to complain publicly and in print about the university.

One development in the processing of the lifestyle questions was to gradu-ally reinterpret these as civil-liberty issues. Automobiles were freedom to travel, alcohol was a matter of privacy, expressions of affection were merely normal and healthy modes of communication or free speech between men and women. These developments transformed issues that could easily have been trivialized as student hedonism and excess into matters of rights and freedoms. This re-framing of issues was, as we will show more fully in Chapter 8, a pivot on which the fifties became the sixties at Bowling Green.

But more important was the renewed emphasis on free communication itself. Bowling Green had few black students, but the university was definitely not set up for minorities to speak out and pursue their rights. Had there been enough black students to form a black students' association of some kind, they would have found all channels of protest closed. If women had become similarly organized, or gays and lesbians or Latinos or the disabled, they too would have found protest criminalized. At this time, protest got one expelled on this campus. And the eight or more students who were expelled during the early days of the 1961 demonstration were dismissed for what would later be redefined as ordinary, fully legal expressions of protest.

So the issue became one of civil liberties, or voice. The students wanted the normal freedoms that were, in fact, available on other public campuses. And they wanted these freedoms expanded to fit the movement toward increased civil rights and civil liberties that was afoot in American society. The student issues, then, during the three months of shadowboxing at BGSU, became more and more dignified, adult, and legalistic. They became exactly what the state legislature was trained to understand, and it was the legislature that eventually sided over-whelmingly with the students, thereby embarrassing McDonald into resigning.

ADMINISTRATION VOICE

At the same time that the students were expanding their voice, both in form and content, the administration was sliding into a crisis of voice. It was encountering fewer channels of communication and fewer safe things to say in the remaining channels. Before the 1961 demonstrations, the administration had had a smooth and highly functioning voice system. It communicated with the students in the ordinary administrative and academic channels. The Student Handbook was crucial, and it was revised every year. The dean of students, Elden Smith, would enforce these rules when necessary with warnings and expulsions. The campus police, who were widely referred to by the students as the Gestapo, also enforced the rules.

The academic system of deans, departments, and professors supervised the teaching, though this system included the unusually harsh rule against missing any classes. When necessary, the administration would send warning letters to students and parents. This communication was primarily one-way: the students had no voice, and no channels to the administration except those concerning minor administrative matters.

The university's communication with the public was also smooth and routinized. The five members of the board of trustees considered themselves the actual policymakers of the university, but they gave McDonald a free hand, and were regarded as a rubber-stamp board. The purpose of the bill to enlarge the board of trustees from five to seven was to give power back to the board and take it away from the administration. This presumably would be done by appointing new trustees with distinctly independent minds in university matters, who would force (or embarrass) the existing trustees into a more active role. Actually, during the three months of maneuvering, between the March demonstrations and McDonald's resignation in June, the trustees were beginning to drift away from McDonald's control. But during McDonald's actual administration (1951 to 1961), he had working control over the board. This meant the board's official communications to the governor, the legislature, and the press were pretty much what McDonald wanted them to be.

The administration's communication to the faculty was also smooth and one-way. Messages came down through deans and department heads, who were tightly regulated in what they could do or say. At one point in the fall of 1960, the vice president's wife, Mrs. McFall, toured South Hall and observed, through windows in the doors, the interiors of the professors' offices. She told her husband she thought the offices were too messy. He told the relevant department heads. And the professors in these offices were told to make their offices less messy. This was an unusual case of close supervision, but it suggests the controlling attitude the administrators had toward the professors. Another example is that "McDonald would make his rounds at University Hall to check the faculty doorknobs at 8 each morning, to make sure his profs were punctual" (James Gordon, *Bowling Green Sentinel-Tribune,* June 24, 2010).

When there was something exceptional to communicate, President McDonald held a faculty meeting. As mentioned earlier, he was the only one who would speak at these meetings, and professors had no approved way of meeting on their own. The system of voice at the official faculty meetings was monological and one-way. There were informal and unauthorized meetings of groups of professors, increasingly so after the March demonstrations, but these were conducted outside the normal university channels. On one occasion in April of 1961, in an incident that was widely discussed among the faculty, a group of about four professors was chatting in the hallway of the administration building. As it turned out President McDonald was walking through the hall just as this informal confab was going on. When McDonald saw the group he stopped and glared at the professors, saying, "Is this an unauthorized faculty meeting?" Using the word *unauthorized* for an informal chat among a few professors suggests how unwelcome actual faculty meetings were to the administration.

The university, then, had a smooth and highly restrictive system of communication between itself, on the one hand, and the students, faculty, state government, press, and general public on the other. When the student system of voices enlarged as the demonstration began, the administration's system of voices at the same time contracted and became less effective. It took a while for the administration's loss of voice to reach its low point, but it deteriorated, week by week, during the three months. Perhaps the most important and most dramatic sign of this collapse was when Professor Stanage actually spoke at a faculty meeting and rebutted everything President McDonald had just said. This astonished all parties concerned, but it gradually became recognized as a sign that the administration could no longer rely on its time-worn system of communication. Stanage too had had to change from a bleating sheep into roaring lion, and he did this with amazing self-confidence and aplomb.

One of the administration's voices that was quickly seized by the students was access to the legislature. The administration had no formal lobbyist, although it did have informal channels to the legislature. But these proved inadequate in the battle with the students. The demonstrations occurred on Sunday, Monday, and Tuesday, March 26, 27, and 28. On the next day, Wednesday, March 29, the president held the famous faculty meeting. And on the following Monday, April 3, the delegation of about nine students met with the education committees of the House and Senate. In other words, while the administration was still trying to formulate its explanation of why the demonstrations occurred in the first place, the demonstrators were giving their version of the story to the legislature. And the legislators were listening with great interest. When this occurred, the administration's channel to the legislature was rendered somewhat closed because the students had seized it.

A second administrative voice that was gradually shut down by the students was access to the press. For a long time the university had enjoyed favorable press throughout the state of Ohio. Students were forbidden to complain to the press about conditions at BGSU, and they were effectively intimidated from doing it. So the press got little information from the students' point of view, and they had no choice but to print the administration's press releases. But, as mentioned earlier, on the second day of the three days of demonstration some students had already left campus to return to their hometowns and were out talking to their local newspapers. Students had never talked to the press about their complaints before, so the speed with which this occurred was remarkable. This, along with the delegation to the legislature, must have taken the administration by complete surprise. The administration may have underrated these initiatives for a while, but as the spring wore on it became clear that the students had found new voices, new ways of conceptualizing what they had to say with these voices, and a degree of political skill and courage they had never shown before. In effect, they took the riot tradition and regularized it into normal, institutional channels.

The *Toledo Blade* was the most important newspaper as far as the BGSU administration was concerned. It was twenty miles from Bowling Green, it had a large circulation, and it was regarded as one of the best newspapers in the country. The owners, the Block family, were Jewish and liberal—in fact, very liberal—Republicans. When the demonstrations broke out, the *Blade* began by reporting on them in a cautious, impartial manner. But by April 2, 1961, the paper was already beginning to suggest that the administration was at least in part at fault. One of its editorialists wrote,

> It is also becoming apparent that the impetus behind the student body demonstrations comes from something of far more substance than that transitory thing called spring fever.
>
> [Singling out two of the letters that had come in, the editorial continues:]
>
> Among them are two of particular interest—one from 44 BGSU students who obviously are in no position to sign their names, and one from a BGSU employee whose tenure on the staff might be in equal jeopardy if his identity were publicized. Both of these missives present calm, well-organized explanations of conditions at the university that contributed to this continuation of ill feeling among segments of the campus community. Both letters also abound in examples of the way the rights of the student body, faculty members and school organizations appear—at least to those immediately involved—to be getting short shift from an administration that rules with a heavy fist.

This editorial writer was especially impressed by the letter from forty-four students. The editorial piece appeared four days after the students had gone home. For forty-four students to get together in some way and agree to sign this letter shows singular organization. Students on spring break are usually out having fun the whole time, possibly in some vacation spot. But these students were obviously in a concerned and serious state of mind. The *Blade* was aware that the students would be expelled if the paper printed their names. And the editorial comes out and says the university is ruled with a "heavy fist." But perhaps the larger significance of this editorial is that it would have been read by the editors of all the other Ohio newspapers, as well as by the members of the state legislature. It was a strong signal that the press could reasonably side with the students and the dissident faculty. If the *Toledo Blade,* the major reportorial organ concerning BGSU, could question the campus administration this soon after the demonstration, then other newspapers could question it too, at least eventually.

In this same April 2 1961, editorial, the *Blade* repeats something it had said four years earlier, during the 1957 demonstration: "But [Dr. McDonald's] abilities do not give him license to ignore the rights of others. And if Bowling Green is to be the university its president clearly wants it to be, someone had better tell him he cannot make it so without the help of other groups who must be just as eager as he is to work toward the goals he wants to achieve." This 1957 editorial was a warning shot, meant, in effect, to tell McDonald he'd better mend his ways. Then, four years later, when it was clear that things may even have gotten worse on this campus, the *Blade* took another shot, but this time to actually hit the target.

Other Ohio newspapers were slower to move toward the students' side than the *Blade.* Initially they were mostly in favor of the administration. But gradually they began to recognize the students' complaints. In addition to the power of the *Blade*'s lead, this was probably due to the presence of disgruntled Bowling Green alumni on the staff of Ohio newspapers, the continuous complaints of students to the press, the news of the legislature's hearing student complaints, and the shaky and ineffective way the administration defended itself. By early June, after some ten weeks of student lobbying, some newspapers were suggesting that it might be good if McDonald resigned.

Ohio was full of alumni from McDonald's decade of tenure. Many of them had bad memories of the current Bowling Green administration. William Day, who wrote for the *Toledo Blade,* was perhaps the clearest example. He had edited the school paper during his time at Bowling Green, and censorship of the paper had become an issue with the 1949 demonstration. Day reappeared in university politics during the 1961 demonstration, influencing the *Blade*'s critical pieces on the BGSU administration. After his resignation McDonald blamed Day and the *Blade* for his downfall.

The problem of unhappy alumni was evidenced again, as mentioned earlier, when the trustee James C. Donnell assembled the Bowling Green alumni in his company. Once they realized their honest opinions were being asked for, they spoke quite disparagingly of McDonald and his administration. This meeting seems to have had a lot to do with the turning of this trustee from a pro-McDonald to an anti-McDonald position. The Bowling Green alumni in various other institutional sectors, including the civil service and the legislature, probably added to the general turn of opinion.

A related problem of the administration's voice was that it had trouble giving a credible explanation for the demonstrations. Recall that the main fight was not over the conduct of the demonstrations themselves; in any case, the students conducted themselves in a relatively creditable manner. The fight was over the why of the demonstrations. And the administration was immediately expected to give a believable explanation for why they had happened. Initially the administration used time-worn clichés as explanations. These ran from spring fever and beer riots, to the work of outside agitators, to the combined presence of a few bad apples and inexperienced freshman. Then when these relatively self-serving explanations stopped working and students began refuting them in the press, the administration seemed unable to find any revised account for what had happened. In fact, McDonald began mentioning negotiation and the softening of some rules, suggesting, without quite saying it, that the students may have been right all along. This was the only position McDonald could take, once he had used up the student-blaming ones. But generous as it may have sounded, it played right into the students' hands. Now the administration was beginning to admit that the rules were too harsh, and that this may have had something to do with the demonstrations. If the administration had continued to meet the students halfway and suggest negotiations, it may have ridden out the storm and stayed in power. McDonald's rule would have been weakened and it may not have lasted many more years, but he could perhaps have used what voice he had left to redefine his administration in a way that was tolerable to the students.

But when he fired Stanage, he lost all the negotiating momentum he had been gathering and went right back to the dominating voice of the previous ten years. He no longer had enough support to use this now obsolete voice, so his administration again became wobbly. Perhaps, as previously discussed, McDonald had promised Father Ollivier that he would fire Stanage in June—perhaps he felt he had to keep this promise.

This is speculation, though Father Ollivier's later comments seem to confirm this interpretation. Still, the situation had changed, and McDonald could have easily backed out of any promise, particularly if it was secret and off the record. As it looked, the move against Stanage was simply retaliatory, or even vindictive. But whatever the reason, firing Stanage evoked what was now an out-of-date and delegitimized voice. And it was the one lethally bad move in a series of otherwise fairly workable moves in McDonald's final spring.

McDonald made another communications error, however, which evidently caused him a lot of trouble. This was the four-page letter he sent to the Ohio Senate Rules Committee on May 12, 1961. In it he argued strongly against the passage of the Senate bill that would increase the number of BGSU trustees. The House later voted 31 to 1 to pass this bill, and the Senate voted 112 to nothing for its passage. These votes were more than a mere rebuke. In effect the legislature fired McDonald on the spot—that is, they gave him no choice but to resign. It may be that no university president was ever handled this roughly by a state legislature. In his letter McDonald had argued in such scolding tones that he probably was perceived as attempting to bully the legislature. And the legislators may well have said to themselves, "This is how he treats his students." Here are some selections from the letter:

> McDonald said that the bill had been introduced "immediately following student demonstrations on our campus that were widely publicized as mob riots. . . .
>
> "I predict that there will be demonstrations of unruly students on other campuses if the General Assembly does not take firm action to defeat the Pepple Bill and thus demonstrate that legislators believe in having an orderly campus."
>
> If the Pepple Bill should be passed by the General Assembly, the damage to the University would be irreparable. Everyone close to the University, whether friend or critic, would know that it has resulted from the demonstrations plus the fervent support of those who have tried for many years unsuccessfully to pressure the university trustees and administration into doing things that would have been injurious to or would have weakened the University. We still find it impossible to believe that a responsible committee of the Ohio Senate would have approved a bill under these circumstances. (*Toledo Blade,* June 9, 1961)

We will not quote further from this lengthy letter, although it continues to be reckless and demanding. One serious mistake was to suggest that the Senate education committee, which had approved the trustee bill in committee, was not acting in a "responsible" manner. This must have infuriated this committee's members, not to mention their colleagues.

Normally one would expect a legislature to vote perhaps two to one in such a situation, which kind of result would have given McDonald a workable way of retreating and saving face. But the House's vote of 112 to nothing was to repay McDonald's bossy letter with a considerably more bossy response.

McDonald also revealed something about his state of mind when he said to the legislature that the demonstrations were "widely publicized as mob riots." By May 12, the date of this letter, McDonald had been backpedaling from his initially harsh interpretation of the demonstrations, gradually seeing them as more responsible. But then he broadly hinted to the legislature that these were mob riots. This suggests that he was insincere in his increasingly appreciative comments about the students' motives, and that his true feelings were that they were an irrational mob. So in this letter, which the *Blade* made public, McDonald spoke in a manner offensive both to the legislature and to the students.

In the three months after the demonstrations, then, we see a remarkable transformation in the communication structure of the university. The students found new voices and new ways of expressing their issues. Their power grew enormously and they now had a significant influence over how people viewed the BGSU campus. The administration had the opposite experience. It lost voice in all respects. Established and reliable channels became suddenly closed, and long-accepted themes were no longer convincing. The administration had to get along with fewer modes of communication and the loss of previously reliable forms of self-justification. The students' position was opened, and their voices became more convincing and louder. The administration's outlets were closed and its voices more muted and confused. This suggests that the students were winning the contest of ideas. And this is exactly what happened. The students won the battle, and the McDonald administration capitulated in defeat.

FACULTY VOICE

Where does this leave the faculty and its voice? During the period of the demonstrations it was frequently said that the students were doing the faculty's job. It was the faculty that was present at BGSU for decades, not just years, and it was the faculty that had the institutional memory. Also, the faculty probably had the most to gain from a liberalization of the McDonald regime, at least in terms of ordinary rewards.

The students had a deeper psychological desire for liberalization, however, for they were doing developmental tasks, matters of psychological growth, at the same time that they were going to college. The college experience should be a bridge from adolescence to adulthood, building on those teenage qualities that can be formed into adult capabilities. Perhaps the main task is the building of a value system and an identity—one that will serve the student as a base for moving into and through adulthood. This transition, while not without its own stresses, should still be one that can move the student reasonably smoothly into adulthood.

By contrast, at Bowling Green the students felt themselves being infantilized. They were kept in a high school level of constraint and they did not see themselves becoming prepared for adulthood. The rules of this college made it harder for them to construct an identity. In particular, the dating and courtship system was being blatantly interfered with by the administration.

So perhaps we should say the faculty had more at stake in terms of routine adult rewards (such as class, status, and power) while the students had more at stake in terms of building psychologically healthy selves. In any case the students acted much more aggressively than the faculty did, suggesting that the stakes in this drama were at least different if not higher for the students.

During the fall of 1960 there were rumors about the coming spring demonstrations, and occasional graffiti on that topic appeared on campus walls. The liberal faculty, though aware that these rumors could come and go, were interested in the idea of some kind of student voicing to slow down the highly confident, and to them oppressive, administration of Ralph McDonald. The faculty were fully aware that McDonald's strict regime, strict both for the students and for them, was out of date and against their interests, but university governments are a bit like monarchies, with top-down control. So the faculty could not just walk over to the levers of power and change McDonald's policy mix. With only modest countervailing powers, the faculty pretty much had to just sit there and accept what came down to them. Unlike the students, they had no explosive riot tradition. That is why Stanage's rebuttal of McDonald at the post-demonstration faculty meeting was so electrifying. It had been, or had been thought to be, impossible for a professor to stand up after McDonald spoke and dispute him. No one had walked it through in his or her mind, that is, tried to figure out what might happen if one did this, but it was assumed that something bad would nevertheless happen. If the offending person was not disciplined right on the spot, he or she would be severely punished soon after. So when Stanage did the impossible, it took a long time for the stunned faculty to even admit that it had happened, much less figure out and process the impact of the event. When the expected punishment is extreme enough, some acts become unthinkable. This means we become so afraid of them that even allowing them into our thoughts is terrifying. Repressive regimes create and rely on huge numbers of unthinkable actions. This is an efficient way to rule, and it is, in a way, tidy, or psychologically clean. In this sense, standing up publicly and denouncing President McDonald was unthinkable.

What the faculty did not do was participate in the student demonstrations. There may have been a few younger professors who observed them from a distance, but for the most part the faculty stayed away from the demonstrations and just read about them in the next day's newspapers. But they were keenly aware of the actions, and a few faculty were talking to and probably encouraging some of the more vocal student leaders. This was not easy, for there were no actual leaders. There was no one like Mark Rudd of Columbia or Mario Savio of Berkeley[1] to speak charismatically and give meaning to the students' hopes and desires. In fact there was almost no rhetoric at all in the three days of demonstrations. The demonstration started with what was, to some extent, an accident, when the fraternity pledge hit the dean with a water bag. This act was the equivalent of Mario Savio's impassioned rhetoric. And when someone in the crowd yelled "Founders!" another crystallization occurred. But this person too was anonymous. And his speech was a single word, not a rounded set of paragraphs.

What the faculty was doing during this period was meeting privately in small, informal groups, raising their own consciousness by talking to each other and exchanging information. These meetings resembled the later practice by feminist women in the seventies of consciousness-raising sessions. In both cases, the gatherings were an exploration of a new voice. The major BG faculty leaders were relatively senior people, and they would occasionally get their names in the local newspaper. Perhaps the most visible thing they did during the post-demonstration spring was visit with the trustee James C. Donnell and give him their side of the story.

The faculty always had two professional orientations: toward their own university and toward their colleagues and professional societies on other campuses. An aspect of their national professional orientation was their contributing scholarly papers and monographs to technical publications in their field. This gave them an avenue of expression quite distinct from any on their own campus, and a second source of professional prestige and authority. One reason the faculty were so uncomfortable at BGSU was that their national statuses in their fields were higher than their local statuses on an administration-dominated midwestern campus. On most campuses, the leading, most famous faculty pretty much stick to their work and avoid campus politics. An unusual feature of Bowling Green was that the leading faculty were also the most politically engaged. This was because the repressive regime prevented these professors from fully taking on the roles of leading faculty members. They were not allowed the power and dignity that should have come with their position. They were treated like teachers college employees. This was a status inconsistency, and it created massive discontent among this faculty. The combination of disgruntled students and a simmering faculty inevitably had to coalesce at some point and bring down the house.

McDonald had engaged in a long-term effort to raise the number of faculty members that had PhD degrees. He was successful at this, and it raised the academic standing of the university. However, it also raised the aspirations of the faculty in question. It made them want a university atmosphere more suitable for academic freedom and unrestrained scholarship. A good scholar wants to be in a reasonably democratic setting; a tightly controlled, top-down authority system is inimical to creativity and successful scholarship. For this reason the faculty had been restive for some years, in a process that ran parallel to the students' increasing dissatisfaction.

It was also the case that the top administrators, particularly President McDonald and Vice President McFall, had no significant scholarly records. They both had PhDs, but their dissertations had not been on important topics. McDonald's had been "An Investigation of the Study Processes Employed by High School Pupils in American History" (Duke, 1933), and McFall's had been "From Normal College to State University—The Development of Bowling

Green State University" (Case Western Reserve, 1947). Neither administrator was published in a scholarly manner after receiving his PhD. It is not uncommon for university administrators to have modest scholarly records, but in this case, where the administration was pressuring the faculty to go from a teaching to a scholarly emphasis, the discrepancy may have made it difficult for these administrators to understand the mind-set of active scholars.

Just as the students were stuck in a prolonged adolescence, so the faculty were stuck in a prolonged lack of social mobility. The students wanted to go up the psychological or developmental ladder, and the professors wanted to go up the professional ladder. These were quite distinct sources of unhappiness, but each had the same cause: the dominating style of the McDonald administration. This meant the faculty-student alliance, like many coalitions, was quite complex. It was not like the later alliance at University of California, Berkeley, in which both components were concerned with student freedom (Blauner 2009). The Bowling Green alliance had to straddle the differences in their causes of stress and find similarity in relief of stress. In other words, the faculty-student alliance at Bowling Green was based on the fact that the two groups had the same source of dissatisfaction. McDonald made the faculty and the students unhappy in different ways and for different reasons, but in both cases McDonald was the cause. So striking out against McDonald was in the interests of both segments of the coalition. The two sides could agree on acting against him.

The Stanage issue stood in complicated relation to the student-faculty coalition. On the surface, the Stanage situation was a faculty issue, for he was a faculty member and he had stuck his neck out for the faculty at a faculty meeting. But the substance of his rebuttal of President McDonald did not address faculty interests. It had to do with the students' concerns. He cut across the faculty-student difference by introducing a student issue in a faculty-administration venue. Thus he tended to be a uniting symbol for both the faculty and the students.

Despite these complex student-faculty connections, the faculty did not have a clear course of action between the three days of demonstrations and the firing of Stanage. But once Stanage was fired, they had what was clearly a faculty issue: defending him. Technically, that is, legally, Stanage was fired, and there was no way of doing anything about this. But McDonald's administration was now so shaky that some sort of direct move against him looked like it might fit the situation. This move turned out to be a petition defending Stanage. As mentioned above, the liberal faculty produced a pro-Stanage petition with sixty names on it. And shortly afterward a pro-McDonald counter-petition was produced with 115 names on it. The press gave more attention to the first petition, the second evidently looking less authentic (and certainly less dramatic).

During the three months, then, the faculty developed an enlargement of voice. The main action was Stanage's speaking out at a faculty meeting, but the rest of the faculty also began talking to newspaper reporters, to the American Civil Liberties Union, to their colleagues on other campuses, to their professional societies, to the trustees, and above all to each other. Informal faculty meetings were becoming more frequent, and plans for strengthening the faculty senate were afoot.

In the contention of voices, the administration lost voice in both where to speak and what to say. It lost the press and the legislature and it gradually got more distant from the trustees. By contrast, the students gained in these areas. They gradually became the main source for the press, and the legislature turned toward them and away from the administration. The faculty also gained voice, but the most obvious change was in the students' seizing the administration's publicity outlets and communication venues.

In a sense the university community began developing a dialogue—that is, a back-and-forth conversation. This was not Bakhtin's pure dialogue, but it was a step in that direction. Earlier there had been a pretty dominating monologue, with the administration doing all the talking and the students and faculty doing all the listening. Now the administration was gradually learning how to listen to the students. It took a while, but early dismissals of the protestors and their issues did not work, and the university had to begin treating the students as serious partners. This dialogical process was moving along steadily and looked as though it would move toward a cooperative form of government. But then, to everyone's surprise, McDonald fired Stanage and reversed what moderate progress he had been making. If McDonald had not made other mistakes before firing Stanage he might have weathered this crisis too, but he was already losing credibility with all of the main audiences: the press, the legislature, the trustees, the faculty, the students, and the general public. Firing Stanage was the creation of a new crisis when his administration did not have enough strength for another one. McDonald soon lost the test vote in the House and Senate and, because of this resounding defeat, was forced, given the politics of the situation, to resign.

NOTES

1. In the undergraduate library of the University of California, Berkeley, there is now a cafeteria named after Mario Savio. The walls are adorned with mementos from the Free Speech Movement, including Savio's famous oratorical statements. The twenty or so tables all have laminated into their polished tops sheets of newspaper reporting the main issues of the Free Speech Movement. There is an enlarged photo of Savio giving a speech. The overall impression of this room is that the university itself thought up the Free Speech Movement, and that it is one of the many great accomplishments of this fine educational institution. This may be an extreme in embracing the sixties student movement, but perhaps it is erring in the right direction.

By contrast, Bowling Green State University has yet to honor its 1960–1961 student demonstrators. The eight or more students who were expelled for civil disobedience are still expelled. The expulsions have never been withdrawn. And the two female leaders, Suzanne Ericksen and Margorie Levin, who are among the bravest of the early sixties feminists, have never been formally thanked by the university.

**Students on Strike: A Limbo Dancing Contest
(Bowling Green State University—Center for Archival Collections)**

**Student Protest Enters the American Reform Tradition
(*Sentinel-Tribune*, Bowling Green, Ohio)**

**Professor Sherman Stanage: Ex-Army Paratrooper and Catalyst for the Sixties
(Bowling Green State University—Center for Archival Collections)**

**President Ralph McDonald: Pride Before the Fall
(Bowling Green State University—Center for Archival Collections)**

Chapter 6

Ripple Effects at BGSU

Important social events often have effects that reverberate through their environments, bringing about changes in neighboring groups and organizations. Wars are disruptive to all social institutions, often even in countries that were not in the war. Economic recessions affect politics, families, schools, etc. And social movements, especially successful ones, can create waves of change throughout an entire social structure. These waves are ripple events, sometimes referred to as domino effects. They are much like the transmitting of a hydraulic force, such as an underwater explosion, through a large body of water. Sometimes the effects are slight, and sometimes, as with some tsunamis, they are quite powerful.

The student movement of the sixties had all sorts of ripple effects, especially in universities themselves. More minorities were drawn into higher education, students were added to faculty committees, and the in loco parentis system was thoroughly dismantled, giving students significant new rights. Ripple effects are caused by dissonance or tension in the social fabric. Societies and social organizations seem to need a certain amount of consistency, and if this consistency is disrupted, integrating forces often appear. These changes are not automatic and inevitable. People see their need and bring them about. Sometimes people talk about finishing the job, striking while the iron is hot, and so on. But we can still speak loosely as though the social system were an organic unity.

These effects were quite visible at Bowling Green after the uprising. The student rebellion and the resignation of President McDonald had consequences over the entire next decade. The strict regime had permeated all features of the university, and the dismantling of that regime would also have to spread, step by step, throughout the entire institution. The ripple effects were evident in the polarization of the faculty, in the faculty's taking control of the governance process, in student expressions of discontent, in faculty-student relationships, and in virtually all aspects of campus life (Givens 1986, 23–48). The uprising produced a political context and a vacuum of control that resulted in a campus atmosphere favorable for creativity.

To show the effects of the 1961 rebellion we will describe how this emancipating spirit spread through the university for the next ten years. To make this description we will have to fall back on bureaucratic jargon at times, since universities operate, even when they change for the better, through bureaucratic channels. But within these channels the excitement and solidarity of the student uprising provided the basic energy that made things happen.

The faculty had been sharply divided over the McDonald issues and over the rights of students to engage in organized protest. To a large extent the disagreement was between conservative and liberal educational values. The students' protest was regarded by some as praiseworthy. It called attention to neglected issues that needed to be faced. But other faculty, and with them many of the residents of the city of Bowling Green, regarded student protest as a form of criminal behavior that should be dealt with in an expeditious and harsh manner. The personal animosities and hostilities within the faculty persisted over the ensuing years. These conflicts have obvious implications for, and could be described in terms of, Bakhtin's theory of voice. The voices were clashing, but some were getting stronger and others less dominating.

The dean of the College of Business Administration, Ralph G. Harshman, served as the interim president for two years, while a search committee screened applicants for McDonald's replacement. McDonald took a year-long sabbatical so that events could transpire peacefully, without people looking over their shoulder at the toppled monarch. Special concern was directed toward finding a new president who would initiate a more liberal atmosphere on campus while promoting an innovative approach to the development of the university. Institutional continuity was assured by retaining the central administrative leadership. This included Paul Leedy as provost, Kenneth McFall as vice president, Donald V. Smith as dean of students, and Erwin J. Kreisher as treasurer and business manager. These four, all of whom McDonald originally selected, had tended to be yes-men during the McDonald years. But perhaps this same quality allowed them to again become yes-men after the turn to liberalism. At any rate they pretty much went along with the U-turn the student rebellion brought about.

The administration building that had been designed and approved during McDonald's regime was completed at about the time the new president arrived on campus. The building was ten stories tall and was, to mention a modest distinction, the tallest man-made structure between Toledo and Columbus. The tenth floor was designed to be the president's office. The windows to the east provided a comprehensive view of activities on campus. The windows to the west permitted an overview of the town. The building was described by some of the faculty and students in jest as "McDonald's last erection" and was regarded as a monument to a big ego.

This was a Bakhtinian reading of the meaning or voice of this structure. The building, had McDonald lasted long enough to rule from it, might have functioned as the Panopticon in Foucault, a building designed with a point from which an entire population—a prison population in Foucault's example—can be surveilled. The new president in 1963, William Jerome, gave out a strong signal that "the times they were a-changing" when he did not like the building and re-designed the less pretentious McFall Center as the offices of the central administration.

FACULTY GOVERNANCE

To curb the arbitrary exercise of authority by a future president, a group of faculty created a new Academic Charter. This was more or less the same group that had encouraged student dissent, backed Sherman Stanage after he was fired, urged the trustees to withdraw support from McDonald, and called for a liberalized university after McDonald was forced from office. The group also included many of the top scholars on campus.

This political move, then, was a far cry from the cowed faculty's inaction under McDonald. The charter was in the nature of a Magna Carta, to maintain, to the extent that it can exist, academic democracy. It would become a legal document for fixing responsibility and limiting authority. The duties and responsibilities of administrators at all levels were specified and limited. The creation of a new faculty senate gave broad powers to the faculty. This faculty senate became a representative form of government with the authority to make decisions on academic issues and to make recommendations to the president. The board of trustees approved the Academic Charter the same year that a new president was selected. These seemingly legalistic changes actually did something akin to cleansing the soul of the university.

In response to the power vacuum created by the removal of an authoritarian president, the faculty also made extensive and creative use of the self-appointed Committee of Concerned Faculty. This power vacuum was in an institutional space that had been occupied by the administration but would now be controlled by the faculty. The committee permitted those who identified some neglected issue to bring forward policy recommendations for official action. It lacked any official authority other than an organized capacity to initiate remedial action. Initiatives at the grassroots level may generate newsworthy events and provide innovation at many levels within a university.

This committee was dominated by the university's top scholars, particularly those in the social sciences and humanities. Usually the leading scholars of a university just stick to their knitting, do their research, and let someone else do the administrative chores. They want to be left alone. But at Bowling Green, as mentioned earlier, the best scholars had been leading activists throughout the rebellious years. They had learned that just sticking to their research might mean losing control to administrators who had dubious academic values. So now they were more than willing to give up some of their precious time to keep the university favorable to their collegial values, the foremost of which being lots of academic freedom. And the fact that the leaders of this committee were top scholars gave the committee enormous prestige and power.

All of the academic councils were in favorable positions to undertake reme-dial action. For example, the Social Science Divisional Council initiated a study of the university's recruitment procedures. As a result of the market for faculty in the early 1960s, universities were in stiff competition for well-qualified faculty. The concern of the council was what faculty candidates liked and disliked in their recruitment experiences. To find out, they sent all faculty members hired during the previous three years a questionnaire for tapping campus experiences. Nearly all of the questionnaires were filled out and returned.

The results indicated that the positive aspects for job candidates came from interactions within academic departments: from opportunities to discuss their dissertations with potential colleagues, and to reflect on their own career aspira-tions. The major negatives came from interviews with the central administrators, who were largely the old McDonald yes-men. The dissatisfaction stemmed from being asked about religious beliefs, marital status, and lifestyle preferences. Such questions were seen as intrusions into personal life having no relevance to a ques-tion of professional qualifications. It will be remembered that McDonald had a sly way of trying to keep out atheists. He would ask, in a seemingly informal way, what church the candidate might be attending. Then, if the answer was "none" or seemed shaky, he would blackball that candidate. The separation between academic qualifications and personal values, which had already been recognized on most American campuses, was still only in the process of getting accepted in the minds of some Bowling Green administrators. In other words, even though McDonald had been deposed, there was a substantial cultural lag left over from his years of micromanagement—an Augean stables that had to be cleaned up.

To offset this leftover intrusiveness, the Social Science Divisional Council recommended that departments be given the freedom to work out individual recruitment processes with their academic deans. During the debate in the faculty senate the proposal was strongly opposed by the provost, Paul Leedy. According to Leedy, it was a primary responsibility of the central administration to maintain quality control over the qualifications of university personnel. Still, the faculty senate approved the recommendations of the council over the objections of Provost Leedy. Overruling a provost was a distinct sign that times had changed.

At the time of McDonald's administration, the faculty teaching load was uniform across campus and consisted of twelve semester hours (four courses).

Occasionally, a faculty member would even be required to have four separate preparations. It was the relatively high teaching load that generated the funds for the high salaries of the faculty. But the pressure on the faculty for research and publications was incompatible with the heavy teaching load. For this reason a committee was set up in 1964 on Long-Range Planning for Faculty Personnel.

After examining the academic aims of the university, the committee's recommendations placed considerable weight on research and on upper-division and graduate teaching. Their recommendation that the university take steps to reduce the average teaching load to nine semester hours (three courses) generated a great deal of controversy. Those professors who were primarily teachers and did little publishing would still have four courses. This kind of distinction among faculty is a brawling issue on most campuses—that is, the publish-or-perish ethic seemed bound to displease a significant proportion of any faculty, particularly in the early 1960s. The faculty members who had built their identities around teaching resented having four courses while the publishers had lighter loads.

The committee structure was used at Bowling Green, but not all committees were successful. For example, a faculty committee was appointed to address the cost of the university's intercollegiate athletics program. The committee did find that the cost was considerable and that the money could be used for academic programs. However, there was no constituency in favor of doing away with intercollegiate athletics. These programs are a sacred cow on most campuses. Also, the committee found that intercollegiate athletics was one of the few sources of unity for the university. Sports provided a link to the university for many of the alumni, and encouraged some degree of unity for a faculty fragmented by departments and separate programs. One can certainly question whether these contributions were worth the financial expense, but at Bowling Green, intercollegiate athletics remained untouchable.

The 1960s were a favorable time for the development of new academic programs on campus. The Ohio Board of Regents made the decision that only Ohio State and the University of Cincinnati would be permitted to develop comprehensive PhD programs. All other state universities would be required to develop programs that would not duplicate the offerings at those two institutions. This turned out to be an advantage to some extent for the other state universities, for it rewarded innovation.

During the 1960s the view was widely held that universities in the United States would not be able to produce PhDs fast enough to keep up with the growing demand. Eventually this mind-set produced too many PhDs, but at the time this possibility was ignored. Several of the departments at Bowling Green had developed strong master's degree programs and had hopes for developing programs at the doctoral level. The psychology department was one of the early programs to seize the opportunities. They succeeded in developing one of the strongest programs in the country in organizational psychology, and became successful in obtaining funding for a new psychology building. With the endorsement of other departments, and strong support from the administration, the psychology department obtained funding from the National Science Foundation for departmental development. It is significant that psychology was one of the departments that contributed the most liberal faculty, both during the protest year and later.

The sociology department had developed a strong MA program and was pushing for an innovative doctoral program. Their ultimate decision was to develop a new doctoral program in the sociology of conflict. During the student uprising, the sociologists were heavily represented among the activist faculty, so, in a way, the program was a timely one. The need for specialists in the study of conflict was evident in the 1960s, when the country was awash with protest and conflict. All the sociology graduate departments and relevant agencies in the state readily approved the proposed doctoral program. It was the first, and for many years the only, PhD program in the sociology of conflict in the United States. Of course, the purpose of the program was not to promote conflict, but to understand it. But it was not opposed to the use of conflict.

The biology department also took an innovative approach to new programs. A marine biology lab was created under the leadership of Professor Cynthia Stong. A successful program was developed in genetics, and the lab at Bowling Green supplied the fruit flies that were used for testing genetic effects in outer space.

Virtually all departments of the university, from the humanities to the College of Business Administration, were caught up in an emphasis on growth and innovative programs. Substantial funds were allocated to the newly created Faculty Research Committee, as well as to a newly created sabbatical leave program and a Committee for Faculty Development. The argument we are making is that the student rebellion and the liberalization of the university allowed improvements in academic quality. In other words, democratizing the university made it better.

Many of the faculty members hired in the late 1950s and early 1960s initially did not intend to stay at Bowling Green. It was a time in which mobility was relatively easy because of the national increases in student enrollments. Many came to Bowling Green because of the high salaries. But the excitement of their experiences and the newfound openness of the university led most of them to decide to stay and carry out the rest of their academic careers at BGSU.

THE EXECUTIVE CATALYST

In September 1963, William Travers Jerome III assumed the presidency of the university. The tensions of the spring of 1961 had temporarily subsided under the interim administration of President Harshman. The youthfulness and idealism of the new president, William Jerome, offered a great deal of promise for a new style of leadership on campus. In his doctoral dissertation, *The Executive Catalyst,* Jerome established a philosophy of administration that he intended to implement. In his view, effective leadership was to be derived from maximizing the use of talent within the organization. Uninterested in a top-down type of administration, he was more concerned with promoting an innovative approach at all levels. He had an unusually democratic leadership style, setting him at the opposite extreme from Ralph McDonald.

The events surrounding his inauguration were focused on the theme "The State University: Creator or Conformist?" The title was somewhat tongue-in-cheek, since Jerome was in the camp of emphasizing creativity and innovation. As a part of his inaugural event, several public figures and intellectuals were brought to campus to address the role of the university in modern society. Among them were R. Sargent Shriver, director of the Peace Corps, Lauris Norstad, president of Owens-Corning Fiberglass, William R. Tolley, chancellor of Syracuse University, and Anthony J. Celebrese, secretary of the Department of Health, Education, and Welfare. The idealistic values of higher education were being tuned up for application to the BGSU campus.

President Jerome did not like the president's home, which was located across the highway from campus. The blocking of the highway during the 1950s and 1960s had been frequently accompanied by building a bonfire on U.S. Route 6 as a way of sending a message to the president about student discontent. With his personal money, Jerome bought an old mansion to the west of Bowling Green to serve as the home of the university's chief executive officer. Upon his retirement, he gave his home to the university, along with a personal tennis court and a heated swimming pool. What all this means is that Jerome's lifestyle was just the opposite of McDonald's. Jerome believed in a maximally egalitarian organization, and he designed his life that way.

In contrast to the micromanagement of the McDonald administration, Jerome delegated a great deal of authority to the grassroots level of the university. Departments were given a high degree of autonomy. For example, it was up to the departments to decide how to allocate any additional money that was available for increases in salary, and to make decisions on the assignment of faculty members to courses being taught and in their recruitment and evaluation. The administrative staff, which included the deans of the colleges, was also given a greater degree of autonomy in their areas of expertise and responsibility.

Many departments turned their attention inward in their quest to develop new PhD programs. In this process, the notion of the university as a community of scholars lost some ground. It was for this reason that under Jerome's leadership an emphasis came to be placed on the development of interdisciplinary research centers. This idea grew out of the recognition that the more innovative ideas came from the periphery, the part closest to neighboring disciplines, than from the center of academic disciplines. Unfortunately, there is a built-in conflict between interdisciplinary ideas and the core of disciplines. The core has the history and the money, whereas the periphery, regardless of how vital its ideas are, has to struggle for recognition and budgeting. But this is merely the way organization works, requiring that a new idea be quite powerful if it is to elbow its way into acceptance.

It was during the 1960s that the faculty and administration recognized the importance of a greater degree of cultural diversity in the education of BGSU students. Several study-abroad programs were established, in such places as Austria, England, Spain, and Japan. A new international affairs office was developed under the leadership of Edward Shuck as its first director. This office was involved in recruiting international students, providing housing for them, and working to facilitate the meeting of their special needs. Efforts were also directed toward recruiting a larger number of minority students, as well as a larger number of non-traditional students.

STUDENT ACTIVISM

At about the time of Jerome's inauguration, student rebellions were affecting colleges and universities throughout the United States. Following the Port Huron Statement of 1962, a chapter of the Students for a Democratic Society was formed on the BGSU campus. Elaborating on the doctrine of "participatory democracy," students maintained that they should have the right to participate in making the decisions that had an effect on them. These ideas had an obvious connection to the 1961 rebellion, but that rebellion had never actually had any organization. It was a decentralized social movement. So even though the rebellion had caused a complete reconstruction of the university, it had no tangible organization when the SDS came to campus. The students had to reinvent the wheel.

As we pointed out earlier, the Port Huron Statement, and the Free Speech Movement at Berkeley, elaborated some of the themes that were contained in the statement of grievances at BGSU in 1961. All of these included critiques of universities for restricting freedom of speech and depriving students of other civil liberties that are guaranteed to adult citizens by the U.S. Constitution. Universities were seen as dehumanizing and alienating institutions that were organized along the lines of a factory model, a metaphor that Clark Kerr, then the president of UC Berkeley, actually thought was flattering to a university. In reflecting the values of other basic institutions, universities were seen as promoting inequality at home and imperialism abroad. In effect, dissatisfaction was expressed with the intellectual, social, and political functioning of universities. Some Bowling Green students became so disillusioned with the university system that they dropped out and joined the countercultural movement in San Francisco. Others went to Chicago and other cities to engage in such direct-action programs as organizing consumer cooperatives among the poor.

According to SDS, the challenge of making the world a better place was the responsibility of those who matured in the postwar years. Because universities have a large proportion of the youth of the nation, so ran the argument, higher education must be the beginning point for a radical transformation of society. Those over thirty had been socialized into political apathy and conformity to the status quo. The ideal university was seen as a community of controversy. To achieve the objectives of a democratic society it was necessary to wrest control of the educational process from a bureaucratic administration (Cohen and Hale 1967).

In contrast to Ohio State, there was never a speakers rule at Bowling Green for keeping controversial speakers off campus. It may well be that the conservatism of northwest Ohio was so well entrenched that controversial speakers were not seen as posing a threat. Departments had a high degree of freedom in inviting speakers to campus, and students had control over the selection of speakers whose visits were funded through student fees. As a result, a large number of outside speakers came to Bowling Green, including most leading presidential candidates at some time or another. It was generally recognized that students were not that readily persuaded by what controversial speakers had to say. The speakers rule at Ohio State and many other universities grew out of an exaggeration of the extraordinary impact controversial speakers have on their audiences.

In the idealism of the 1960s, student activists saw it as their mission to address the problems of poverty, environmental deterioration, militarism, nationalism, alienation, and political apathy. Accordingly, speakers were invited to campus to address basic social problems: Michael Harrington to address the issue of poverty; Stuart Udall to address environmental issues; active student participants in the civil rights movement to address the issues of race. Norman Thomas, a previous candidate for president on the Socialist Party ticket, gave one of his last public addresses at Bowling Green. The next day, he rode to Columbus with students and faculty to participate in the first statewide protest against the war in Vietnam. Drawing on the principles of nonviolent resistance, he marched around the statehouse with the Bowling Green delegates while being exposed to threats and name-calling on the part of militants in support of the war.

Men and women who had participated in the civil rights movement orchestrated the marches in Bowling Green from campus to the Wood County courthouse. The theme of nonviolent resistance had been clearly established. The defects and injustices of the system could be dramatized through deliberately disturbing the tranquility of everyday life. The news media reported on these marches, and the Bowling Green police provided protection for orderly demonstrations.

The leadership of SDS on the Bowling Green campus came disproportionately from students in the social sciences and the humanities. Faculty offices were used for storing their microphones and other electronic equipment and the placards they used in demonstrations. The front porch of Williams Hall became the focal point for student rallies and protest. While there were frequently large gatherings of students in the inner campus, most of these were spectators rather than active participants in social protest. But although the vast majority of students were observers, those who played an active leadership role were articulating the sentiments of students in general.

This was an unusual generation of students, with an active interest in politics and the political process (Lipset and Wolin 1965). They developed a high degree of sensitivity to social issues and were articulate in their expression of social discontent. Through emphasis on critical thinking, universities promote a style of thought that weakens tradition and diminishes conformity to the status quo, even though this might not always be their intention. Within the context of a modern society, universities became primary agencies of creativity and innovation. Through an emphasis on the ideal of objectivity, the analysis of society came to be distinguished from conformity to it.

Student dissatisfaction at Bowling Green was only partly related to the internal organization of the university. The 1961 demonstrations were aimed primarily at issues inside the university, but as time went on students shifted to larger problems. Extensive changes were occurring in the social order, but they were not occurring fast enough.

The greater sources of dissatisfaction were with such contradictions as being a member of a society organized along democratic lines while that same society enforced Jim Crow policies of discrimination. The sympathies of college students were with the demonstrators and active participants in the civil rights movement. The students at Bowling Green were a part of the nation that watched in shock and sadness as peaceful demonstrators at Selma, Alabama, were met with violent brutality from the sheriff's department and from the state police. They were, in effect, a part of a mass judiciary that sat in judgment on the issue of racial discrimination in the public sector.

The assassination of President John F. Kennedy on November 22, 1963, had a dramatic effect on the Bowling Green campus. All ordinary activities were halted as students and faculty gathered in small groups to discuss what had happened, how it had happened, why it had happened, and what the implications would be for personal lives and for their society. Students turned to faculty members, family, and close friends for support. Phone lines out of Bowling Green were jammed with the extremely large number of calls students made to their parents. Over the next three days, the campus joined the nation in mourning the slain leader.

A survey of students conducted the day after Kennedy's funeral suggested that the responses were highly emotional and varied (Abcarian, Groat, Neal, and Stanage 1964). For some students, the assassination tapped into perceptions of evil and the many defects of our social system, while for others, the emphasis was on regarding Kennedy's existence as a special gift and a source of inspiration. Kennedy's unique gift was that of promoting a sense of idealism, dedication, and hope for making the world a better place. Several students responded to the survey by making a vow to become better informed about political events and to become more highly dedicated to public service and political action.

The student activists were among those who experienced more intensely the contradictions that were deeply embedded in modern social life. Rather than remain indifferent, they felt compelled to act on the basis of their convictions. Several Bowling Green students interrupted their college education to spend one or two years with the Peace Corps. A sense of social responsibility was also reflected in the actions of a small group of demography students that decided to stage an attention-getting activity to dramatize the problem of world hunger. They notified the press of their plans, and scheduled a Thanksgiving dinner to be held in front of the Alpo dog-food factory in Cleveland. Newspapers reported on the students opening cans and eating dog food for their Thanksgiving dinner. The event was picked up by the wire services and responses came in from all over the world from people who wanted to know more about their non-existent organization and how to join their campaign.

Latterday Bowling Green demonstrations were particularly geared toward expressing opposition to the Vietnam War. When compulsory military service was initiated to meet the manpower needs of the military, the opposition intensified on college campuses. Many of the Bowling Green students appealed to their draft boards for exemption on the grounds of moral opposition to the war. These were uniformly denied because of the lack of affiliation with a pacifist religious group, and the ruling that an exemption could be permitted on the grounds of opposition to a specific war but not to war in general.

Students considered it an absurdity to be required to sacrifice their lives for a war they believed to be unjust. The war was a further absurdity considering that the majority of men dying in combat were only eighteen, nineteen, or twenty years old—old enough to die for their country, but not old enough to vote in elections or have a drink of whiskey in a public bar. By the time the war was over the voting age in all parts of the country had been lowered from twenty-one to eighteen.

The initial opposition to the Vietnam War originated on college campuses. The opposition was based largely on a condemnation of the war on moral grounds.

Many college students perceived the United States to be intervening in what was seen as a civil war, to be supporting a corrupt and unpopular government, and to be using sophisticated military technology against an underdeveloped country and a peasant population. Several BGSU students expressed their discontent by crossing the border into Canada and renouncing their citizenship. It was not that the students were unwilling to make personal sacrifices for their country, but that they perceived as absurd the risk of having to make an ultimate sacrifice for a cause they believed to be unjust. Renouncing one's citizenship and going to live permanently in some other country is not a step most Americans would be able to take lightly.

The trauma of Vietnam intensified as deep divisions surfaced within the nation over our foreign policy, over perceptions of the immorality of the war, and over the frustrations of being involved in a war we could not win. In Vietnam we had a tiger by the tail, and there seemed to be no reasonable way to let go. Students on the Bowling Green campus followed the pattern of opposition to the war that played out at Berkeley, Wisconsin, Michigan, Columbia, and many other places. "Teach-ins" were held as a way of arousing opposition to our conduct of the war. Marches and demonstrations were held throughout the country; petitions were sent to representatives in Congress; a series of publications emerged to question the legitimacy of public authorities and the military emphasis in American life.

The Bowling Green veterans of World War II were appalled at reports of American youth burning their draft cards and burning the American flag. Their generation had not questioned the legitimacy of being required to serve in the armed forces during times of war. The atmosphere was pretty tense at Bowling Green when marches and demonstrations against the war were conducted around the football stadium before football games. The conservatives among the veterans frequently expressed their anger, particularly at faculty who joined the students in the protest.

Opposition to the war on college campuses mounted in intensity with the Tonkin Gulf Resolution and President Lyndon Johnson's announcement that bombing raids would be conducted against North Vietnam. Many college students saw the loss of civilian lives in the bombing raids as further evidence of the immorality of the war. The opposition reached a peak in early May 1970 when President Nixon announced plans for conducting bombing raids on Cambodia. The concentration of Viet Cong forces in Cambodia permitted them to strike targets in South Vietnam and then retreat to the safety of "a neutral country." Those who opposed the war regarded Nixon's announcement as a statement of intent to broaden the war in Southeast Asia, rather than to contain it. Following the announcement, demonstrations erupted on college campuses all across the country.

THE KENT STATE CRISIS

At Kent State University, students had burned down a World War II–era Quonset hut that had housed the ROTC unit on campus. When the demonstrations spilled over into the town of Kent, the Ohio National Guard was called in to maintain order. The national guard unit was armed, and in response to a tense situation started firing indiscriminately into the crowd of students on campus. Four students were killed, and several others were wounded. As the news of this spread, campuses were disrupted throughout the country. Many colleges and universities were required to suspend normal operations for several days. The responses on campuses were now not only to the moral issues of the war, but also to the actions of the police and the national guard on college campuses. Many of those who opposed the war saw the actions of the Ohio National Guard as a form of criminal conduct. The resources of the state were drawn upon to deny individuals their constitutional rights.

BGSU was the only state university in Ohio that remained open during the Kent State crisis. President Jerome and a group of his advisers came to an early conclusion that a concerted effort should be made to keep city and state law-enforcement personnel off of the Bowling Green campus. And yet, it was recognized that under the circumstances it was important for students to be able to express their concerns and to openly debate the issues they saw as being of relevance. Accordingly, faculty took turns meeting with students in campus dormitories to lead discussions on whatever topics were of concern to them. Students were also permitted by the administration to change their class enrollments to a pass/fail basis in order to keep their grade point averages from being affected by what was happening on and off campus.

The ideals of a "free university" were also drawn upon to permit students and faculty to meet in a seminar setting to discuss a wide variety of social issues. Under this rubric, seminars were organized for discussion on war and peace, poverty, race relations, women's rights, and any other topic of interest. Faculty assisted in setting up these seminars, selected appropriate readings, and guided discussions. There were no formal enrollment requirements, there were no grades assigned, and attendance was fluid and open. Many Bowling Green students took advantage of these seminars to engage in an exchange of ideas on topics of immediate concern.

Several residents in the city of Bowling Green claimed that the academic integrity of the university had been compromised. Instead of seeing the BG administration's decisions as effective leadership of the university in a time of crisis, the townspeople more nearly favored a forceful suppression of student dissent and an emphasis on "law and order." Nationally, the Kent State tragedy was followed by the largest strike in American history. Thousands of faculty members accompanied the millions of college students who joined in the national strike. The number of army desertions increased during the month of May, and the Vietnam Veterans Against the War nearly doubled their membership.

The BGSU response to Kent State was probably about as enlightened as that of any university in the country. President Jerome's liberal leadership was extremely rare among university administrators, and the behavior of the faculty was a creative combination of education and protest. And the students combined a clear protest message with scholastic activities. Before the 1961 rebellion, Bowling Green had had none of these capabilities. It was clearly the uprising that allowed this highly sophisticated combination of dissent and positive educational practices. In other words, you could not ask for any stronger proof that the uprising had good effects than the way this school responded to a national crisis.

Following the Kent State tragedy, the idealism of the student movement diminished very rapidly. The students had not recognized how difficult it is to bring about basic changes in the institutions of a society. Particularly, they had not taken into account the coercive powers of the state that may be brought to bear on a direct confrontation. In their disillusionment, levels of alienation increased rapidly within student populations. As many had during the 1950s, students came to believe that "this world is run by the few people in power and there's nothing the little guy can do about it." Instead of seeking to make the world a better place, students became increasingly career-oriented, in a quest to attain personal goals and objectives.

In retrospect, the 1960s was one of the more turbulent decades in the history of the country. The threat of nuclear war with the Soviet Union and the quagmire in Vietnam had traumatic effects on the nation. The escalation of military expenditures and the development of increasingly sophisticated weapons of war did not diminish the sense of national insecurity. The epic struggle of the civil rights movement eliminated some of the more blatant forms of discrimination in the public sphere, but it did not solve the problem of racism in our society.

Before the decade was over, students did win a large number of concessions from the university. They were now permitted to select representatives to serve in the faculty senate, as well as on all major university and college committees. Students were also permitted to play several roles at the departmental level, including having representatives in departmental meetings and on committees relating to recruitment and curriculum. While there was extensive debate over the qualifications of students for evaluating the faculty, the students eventually won out with the initiation of a university-wide requirement of student evaluation of all classes. Students were also permitted to select a representative to the university's powerful board of trustees.

Chapter 7

Explanations of the Crisis

Most complex problems have multiple meanings, and this truth becomes evident in the many interpretations of the student uprising at BGSU. How did it happen, why did it happen, and what was its significance? These are among the questions that emerge in response to national traumas, such as the Japanese attack on Pearl Harbor, the Kennedy assassination, and the terrorist attack on the World Trade Center (Neal 2006). They are also among the questions asked at the local level when something unusual has occurred, when an event is surrounded by a high degree of emotionality, and when people are unable to remain indifferent.

In reflecting on our case, which took place over fifty years ago, those who experienced it often still have vivid memories. It was a conflict that struck the university community like a bolt out of the blue. The series of events were sufficiently dramatic and emotionally charged to become imprinted memories, memories that remain vivid and persistent. However, we found that people's memories were divided between seeing the event as unique and seeing it as similar to what happened on campuses across the country. One purpose of this book is to clarify the uniqueness and theoretical importance of this event.

We have already mentioned solidarity as a key process. In addition we have drawn on the recent literature on social movements that emphasizes framing. Framing is the process of interpreting an important event. The key question is what does it mean? What are its implications? Why does it matter? While all of the explanations that we looked at have plausibility, we think the students' combination of solidarity and framing provides the most viable explanation of how they won and how the university became changed in the process.

MULTIPLE INTERPRETATIONS

We will briefly consider three interpretations that have initial plausibility.

These three are preliminary and by way of giving context to the explanation we will choose. After discussing them, we will take a closer look at what we think is the most plausible interpretation of why the students won: their attaining powerful solidarity and then applying this energy to the task of giving meaning to and framing the demonstrations.

1. *Chance.* To some extent this case is a chance event or fluke with serendipitous qualities, and hence of little generality. This argument draws on the unusual personality of the president, Ralph McDonald. He was a good administrator in some respects but he made serious blunders. He consistently made errors with power, always in the direction of excessively strict rules or holding on too tightly. Most people who were worthy of getting his job would be too smart to make such mistakes. Which is to say, most people with his clumsy hand for power would never have gotten a job of this importance in the first place. The fact that he was so awkward with power and still held this high-placed job might be called a matter of chance.

But everything has a cause. "Chance" merely means that the causes are unusual or infrequent in occurrence or difficult to specify. First McDonald got the job, and then he started showing a shaky hand with power. When he had been in office as university president for two years, in 1953, he made his first bad decision. This was to tighten up the alcohol rules, at a time when most universities were loosening them. He forbade all drinking of alcohol, no matter what the student's age, unless the student was drinking at home. This created a sea of trouble in policing the rule, leading eventually to McDonald's forced resignation. We will look more closely at the alcohol issue later. At this distance we can only guess why McDonald was drawn to this decision (or why his advisors let him get away with it). Yes, his story was in some respects a fluke or a phenomenon defying ordinary explanation, but the larger question of why the students revolted and how they forced the president to resign still needs to be explained.

2. *Personalities.* In a way, this story is about a war between Ralph McDonald and Sherman Stanage. Both were powerful personalities and both had crusading mentalities. McDonald was a Bible-thumping conservative Methodist and Stanage was a Kierkegaard-quoting liberal Methodist. Both were driven by intense ideals, albeit drawn from opposite ends of the spectrum. When McDonald, at the faculty meeting, faced Stanage and denounced the students, he was expressing one kind of crusade. When Stanage stood up and defied McDonald, he

was articulating another. McDonald was committed to a declining crusade and Stanage to one that was rising.

This battle of personalities explains a lot. In particular, the fight between liberal and conservative Protestantism draws on how institutions have internal conflicts and how they change. On this religious battleground Father Ollivier also weighed in with his version of conservative Catholicism to ally with McDonald. But this was all going on at a state institution financed with tax money. None of these religious viewpoints had any reason to claim authority in a government facility. And the powerful personalities, the towering egos, were all occupying positions in a bureaucratic apparatus. Bureaucracies are supposed to be controlled by offices or roles, not by the particular people who occupy these roles at any point in time.

The explanation of how a medium-size university, dead set on its course, made a 180-degree turn in a matter of a few months requires more than an explanation based on personalities. Some kind of systematic, historical forces must also have been operating.

3. *Modernizing Teachers-College Syndrome.* Still another interpretive theme is the idea that American teachers colleges, given the impending rise in enrollments, had to become universities after World War II. And when they did so there were inevitably severe growing pains. The old student rules would lag behind before changing, and the students would become restive over this. Administrations would be slow to become more collegial and democratic. Faculties would face problems in improving the opportunities for research, publication, and intellectual cosmopolitanism. Students would inevitably push administrations to hurry up the liberalization process. These were built-in problems for the American higher-education system during the difficult 1945–1961 years at Bowling Green. The difference is that Bowling Green was slower and more halting than most in making this transition. In fact, it had to be pushed.

In other words, something other than the teachers-college syndrome was going on at Bowling Green. There were dozens of these schools, but the student revolution occurred at BGSU. The school couldn't get past this modernizing hump. In fact, McDonald got tough when it was time to be tender. There had to be additional reasons why Bowling Green, of all the teachers colleges, had the most trouble becoming an ordinary university.

OUR THEORY: SOLIDARITY AND FRAMING

In Chapter 1 we showed how the Bowling Green demonstration was a deviant case, the sort of unexpected and unpredictable event that often leads an observer to uncover some unnoticed and novel causal process. We will now show how the highly regulated nature of the university led to a demonstration that was so explosive and successful that it created unusually high solidarity in the student body. It was this intense solidarity that produced a major demonstration where no one would have expected it. After an analysis of how the students became a cohesive crowd, possessed of enormous political energy, we will turn to the second part of the explanation. This concerns the way the students used their solidarity to frame the issues as they saw them and to conduct a public communications battle with the university.

The concept of solidarity was central to the classical work of the French social theorist Emile Durkheim (Bierstedt 1966). It refers to cohesion, bondedness, social unity, shared morale, and identification with a social group. For Durkheim, a group can achieve solidarity if it has three qualities: assembly, shared and focused attention, and a symbolization of the group's values and beliefs. We will refer to Durkheim's general treatment of these three processes and then show how they applied to the Bowling Green demonstration.

1. *Assembly.* All the members of the group or collection must assemble in one place, so that they are in physical proximity. This can be a crowd getting together to make a public statement, and the statement can be one of support or protest, positive or negative. It can also be a group of like-minded people attending, let us say, a political rally or a religious affirmation. Or it can even be an extended family or clan, as it was in Durkheim's case (Durkheim 1995/1912), getting together for some kind of kinship celebration.

To fit Durkheim's scheme, the gathering must be a self-aware collection, people who know that they all share some characteristic. This shared characteristic is the reason for the assembly. The mere getting together to see a movie or hear a concert is not enough. To pay attention to and be conscious of itself, the group needs to be reflexive. This distinction resembles the one previously made in Chapter 2 between a crowd as a mere audience and a crowd for itself, thrilled by its own pulsations and power. If a self-aware group assembles in Durkheim's sense, it acquires an identity as though it were a single, acting individual. The separate identities of the component individuals lose salience, and the personhood of the group comes to the fore. This is not to say the individual identities cease to exist, merely that they become temporarily subordinate to the group identity.

Assembly is thus both a physical and a psychological coming together. Physically it is the gathering of the group in close proximity, as in a hall, on a field, in a stadium, or, in the case of kinship groups, over a meal. The psychological closeness is the sense of all being part of the group, as well as the group's knowledge of itself as a cohesive group. Beyond that, everyone knows that everyone knows it's a cohesive group. When the pulsation is strongest there's a touch of the "group mind" here, because everyone knows what is in everyone else's mind.

The task of assembling is sometimes quite difficult, and when it happens it may itself be a momentous achievement. Far-flung families and kinship groupings are a case in point. Getting everyone from the communities in which they live to the location where they are assembling can be time consuming, expensive, and psychologically problematic. When dispersed groups such as this assemble, the mere fact of being together can be intensely dramatic. In these cases the remaining Durkheimian tasks of sharing attention and symbolizing the group's values are easy. In the case of Bowling Green students, assembly was difficult because the university would not allow it, at least not unless the administration fully controlled the conditions of assembly and the behavior that would ensue. Getting assembled at the water fight with around five hundred people and without any university authorities controlling the assembly was itself a major achievement for these closely watched students.

2. *The Focusing of Attention.* In the Durkheim model, the group members must all pay attention to the group activities at the same time. This means everyone must be physically present in the assembly. They cannot be wandering off, taking side trips, or going away from the actual group. They must cut down on or stop the chitchat and interpersonal conversation. There is a corporate or public face that the group must attend to. When this really catches hold, there is an air of expectancy, and, people sometimes say, "You could hear a pin drop."

This concentration of attention should go further than merely stopping talking. People should also stop their daydreaming or thought processes to the extent that they can, and pay heed to the overall activity of the group. In other words, they should control their private consciousness and enter fully into the public consciousness of the gathering. Actually, most if not all of them will do this automatically, because it is in line with the purpose of having gathered together in the first place. The group is assembled to affirm and intensify its identity. The mental unity, it should be noted, is both cognitive and emotional. The assembly needs to think about the same thing and also to experience the same "crowd thrill," or expanded self, as an emotion.

3. *The Declaration of Values and Meaning.* When the group is together and everyone's attention is concentrated on the gathering, there should be some kind of group action or performance. This performance will express the meaning and values of the group. We are not using the term *value* in the exclusively ethical sense but in the sense of cultural meanings. The values are the beliefs, feelings, hopes, moral orientations, etc., that characterize the identity of the group. They are the traits that define the group. If the group is political, the symbols will be

political; if it is religious, the symbols will be religious; and if it is a personal group, such as a kinship community, the symbols will be those that are meaningful to the particular history and hopes of the kinship group.

The group can even be a two-person relationship, such as that between two lovers. In this case the assembly will be these two in a private setting. The central meaning of this group will be the love relationship itself, and the symbolism might be words, gifts, or even sex. The closeness and intimacy of this dyad can be symbolized in a wide variety of ways (Collins 1982, 42–47).

According to Durkheim the solidarity that this social process brings about will strengthen the identity of the group. The statement of the values will not only represent the values but also create and intensify the values. For a political group to jointly say, in some symbolic manner, that it is committed to a particular ideology or set of political goals will actually create and strengthen this commitment. In linguistics, this kind of utterance, one that not only declaims but also creates something, is called a performative. Examples are promises, including that of the marriage ceremony. To say "I do" in a marriage is not only to accept the marital bond but also to construct this bond. The bond exists if and when we say it exists. Promises in general are like this (Austin 1962).

Durkheim's notion of reality construction in a ritual ceremony is merely an elaboration or extension of the linguistic notion of a performative. When groups assemble, focus attention, and utter symbols that enunciate their values, these enunciations are performatives in the sense that they create as well as affirm the shared values. And when groups reassemble at some later date and restate their sacred symbols, recharging their batteries so to speak, these values are brought back to the fore and intensified. Groups feel more strongly defined and possessed of a firmer character after they get together and express their identities.

The actual way in which these values are expressed can vary. The expression can be open, explicit, and possibly performed by some individual or sub-group that represents the group. A political speech by some charismatic leader can be such an expression. Or a group of some kind, say a choir at church, can express the symbols together (Heider and Warner 2010). Sometimes the entire group can, in unison, express the identity. Singing can do this. Cheering can. And even whooping and hollering. There are a variety of ways in which a group can express its performatives. The actual signifiers or tokens of expression can also vary. They can be straightforward linguistic sentences. Or the important meanings can be in the overtones or feelings that are carried by the sentences. Even the gestures and body language of whoever is doing the expressing can carry the meaning. Of course, singing and other music are often powerful expressions of a group's culture. In American history, the Battle Hymn of the Republic was used over and over again by different political groups, each group changing the words of the song to fit its beliefs while still taking advantage of the stirring music.

Having now sketched Durkheim's solidarity model, we will show how it applies to the Bowling Green case. Even before the 1961 demonstration the students had a moderate amount of solidarity. Most students lived on campus or in nearby private housing, so clusters of them were in physical proximity all the time. And of course they were together in classes. The opposite case would be a large urban university that had few or no dormitories: this kind of institution is closer to the other extreme of an atomized student body with almost no solidarity.

The students also had a certain togetherness in their dissatisfaction with the strictness of the lifestyle rules. Without doubt a majority if not all of the students would have preferred a more relaxed interpretation of in loco parentis. There was also a constant vigilance about getting caught (for example by the campus police) breaking one of the rules. We can assume that both the consumption of alcohol and expressions of affection would be a constant source of worry for the students. But this "them and us" stance, while it provided a moderate amount of solidarity, would have had its limits. In particular, expressions of dissent against the rules and the administration would be kept under wraps. Students who made individual expressions of protest were regularly punished, and this punishment successfully deterred almost all the students from publicly complaining about the school. Dissent was largely a matter of inner speech or imagination and comments made privately among small groups of students.

The strictness of the rules and the vagueness of some of them (e.g., where you could drink and where you could express affection) also created a lot of uncertainty for the students. It would not be going too far to call this a mild state of paranoia or a persecution complex. Paranoia has two characteristic elements of thought disorder: one is seeing more enemies and danger than there actually are, and the other, functionally related to the first, is believing that you are special or "grand" in some way. Delusions of grandeur feed the delusions of persecution, even in mild, non-clinical cases such as the one we are talking about. Delusions of grandeur, however, can also feed solidarity, for it is something that a group has in common, and it is something, vague as it is, that they can be proud of.

In other words, for the university to create a situation that might instill feelings of persecution in the students meant that it was also creating the possibility of self-aggrandizement. When the students began their demonstration, and when all the signs, even in the first three days, were of having successfully checkmated the administration, their grandeur started coming true. All of a sudden and completely unexpectedly, they had the upper hand in a historical confrontation with the administration and the campus police, and this degree of success was in fact a confirmation of their feelings of grandeur. In fact, to stay on the theme of paranoia, Ralph McDonald also exhibited signs of a persecution complex throughout the three-month-long demonstration, and this weakness was a powerful stimulus to the students' feelings of potency and importance.

This peak experience and solidarity were why they left campus for Easter vacation after the three days of civil disobedience and immediately went to the state legislature and their local newspapers.

Everyone had assumed that they would go home, seek pleasure as students always did on break, and forget the demonstration. The fact that they kept right on with the demonstration, so to speak, by politicking in their hometowns, suggests that the degree of solidarity was unusually intense. When McDonald was making his major move, delivering an impassioned speech at a faculty assembly and getting neutralized by Sherman Stanage's rebuttal, the students were out publicizing their grievances in the public institutions of the state of Ohio. This was a foreshadowing of the fusion of intense solidarity and skillful framing that would gradually follow.

But to return to the initial growth in student solidarity, this process was first visible during the first day of the demonstration—at the time of the water fight. Solidarity, as stated, is created when a group assembles, focuses its attention on its situation, and then enunciates, in some way, its beliefs and values. This is exactly what happened during the water fight, and it was Dean Taylor who inadvertently created the student solidarity.

Initially it was a nonpolitical crowd that had assembled to watch the water fight. People in the crowd were calling to the twenty or so water fighters, things like "Hit him back" or "Get another bucket" or "Soak him good." These were the sort of crowd calls you might get at a football or basketball game, mere exuberant expressions of audience enthusiasm. They probably gave the audience a sense of participating in the water fight itself. But they had no political significance, and they did not raise the crowd solidarity to any extent.

As the afternoon began coming to a close and it was obvious the fight would eventually have to end, the crowd got a bit more rowdy and the water fighters got more daring and theatrical. This was still within the bounds of a "first warm day" event, but it may have been pushing the boundaries. In any case, these activities were still contained within the parameters of a lively water fight. And the crowd wanted nothing but an intensely entertaining splash party.

But when the campus police came to stop the fight and disperse the crowd, the political meaning of the event began to change. As we said earlier, the students began to experience the heightening of consciousness that transforms a crowd of entertained audience members into a political crowd. The active water fight slowed down and almost stopped, but the crowd did not obey the police order to disperse. The half dozen or so police had now become the entertainment, and members of the crowd began yelling epithets at them. It should be recalled that the campus police represented and often enforced the strict rules of the university. And their presence could only heighten the entire, ever-present issue of chafing rules and student dissatisfaction.

After about ten minutes of police-versus-crowd tension, Dean Taylor arrived to take over. It should be recalled that Dean Elden Smith had successfully dispersed a crowd in the 1957 demonstration. Undoubtedly Dean Taylor was assuming it could be done again. When he began addressing the crowd and attempting to push them away from the still-present water fighters, the crowd began the noose-tightening action we referred to earlier.

This tightening of the circle was a highly defiant act, but it was done under the cover of crowd anonymity. No doubt this anonymity, along with the gradually rising excitement of the situation, was what emboldened these students to disobey the dean. Still, the action was a crowd statement or gesture, a significant, that is, a meaningful, gesture. The meaning of this gesture was "We do not accept the legitimacy of your authority at this time; you do not have the right to break up this highly entertaining water fight." This was a direct and, to the dean, infuriating act of dissent.

Recalling again the three-part Durkheimian model of how solidarity is created, this gesture can be interpreted as the ritual utterance of an assembled crowd. The symbolization (crowding the dean) was nonverbal, but it still had meaning. Nevertheless it was not enough. It did not yet have the full ritual power of a defiant act. The dean concentrated all of the crowd's attention onto his person and his pushing. The assembly and the focus were already present to an extreme, waiting for the match to strike, for the crowd to engage in some stronger act of value-laden symbolization. This symbolization came little by little. Yelling at the police was the beginning of it. Then defying the dean intensified it. And finally, the fraternity pledge's hitting the dean on the back of the head with a large rubber bag—actually a contraceptive—filled with water was what might be called an explosive ritual utterance. The crowd solidarity shot up at this point.

But when the offending fraternity pledge ran, when the police chased him and the crowd chased the police, the ritual expression intensified and the solidarity rose even more. As mentioned before, when people in the crowd yelled "Founders" to divert the crowd to the women's dorms, the solidaristic, political crowd was in full swing. This was a textbook case of how a political crowd is created, and it goes a long way toward explaining this demonstration as a deviant case.

Notice that the solidarity preceded the demonstration. That is why we can say it caused it. The cause should come before the effect in the temporal order. If the demonstration had somehow started without a water-fight crowd to start it off, we could not say the solidarity caused the demonstration. In that case the solidarity would have *been* the demonstration. It is important for our argument that the solidarity came into existence before the demonstration began. First we had audience solidarity, engendered, as we pointed out, by the unwise actions of an over-confident dean. Then we had demonstrator solidarity, which was merely a natural transformation from audience to participant solidarity. The two phases of the solidarity, audience and demonstrator, had somewhat different qualities, in terms of Durkheim's three ingredients.

The university's strict rules worked well up to a point. They channeled the students' behavior and controlled their motivation rather effectively. But even at their most successful, these rules were already risking being stretched too far. The annual (and mythical) spring riot was no joke. It may have acted as a safety valve for the university, blowing off student steam, but this mythology also kept the students on edge and in a disobedient frame of mind. It kept them imagining themselves in a defiant crowd. This imagining was itself a political resource for the students, even if an incomplete and limited one.

The students could talk and intrigue and fantasize, but they could never transform themselves from a disgruntled mass into a truly acting, political crowd. Getting into a legitimate nonpolitical crowd, and not just an audience at some school-sponsored event, was already difficult. But changing a legitimate crowd into a defiant one was much harder. The students had no idea how to do this. In fact, it was done for them when the university's strict rules went just a step too far—when an unusual, spring-fever kind of crowd was handled so ineptly that it became a political, intensely activated crowd. In other words it was a case of a repressive regime going so far that it created its enemy through the repression itself. As the saying goes, oppression can be its own enemy. The students were now on the march.

The occasion of the original crowd, a gathering at a fraternity event, is also significant. The fraternities (and sororities) and the administration had a love-hate relationship. The fraternity members were the future supportive alumni, the someday professionals and businesspeople who would bring both loyalty and money to the university for the rest of their lives. They were a precious university resource. But while they were at the university they were also a problem. The Greeks were the hardest student group to keep from alcohol. They were always tempted to sneak alcohol into their parties, and the university saw them as the biggest threat to the alcohol rules.

The obsession with alcohol at this university cannot but suggest that alcohol symbolized sex to the administration. God knows what was in President McDonald's unconscious when he tightened the booze rules just as the rest of academia was loosening them. And well might his decision have had this underlying meaning, since alcohol, given its interdiction on this campus, was given a mystique and power that looked suspiciously like a displacement of sex.

The Greeks had also been quite active in the hedonistic "riots" in earlier years at the university. To some extent, these could be called beer riots and delegitimized in that manner. But these lifestyle riots always had an edge of civil disobedience to them. For instance, the censoring of the student newspaper was a more elevated issue in these earlier demonstrations. It is also true that upperclass students regularly led college riots of a much earlier period, around the turn of the century (DeMartini 1976). They thought they were entitled to their pleasures, and college was then defined as a place where student pleasures should be given their due. This earlier tradition of upperclass student riots was now buried in the past, but the unruly character of college fraternity life, including the way it was at Bowling Green, harkened back to these riots.

Another morally confusing feature of the Greek system was that students believed they could kiss their dates goodnight at the entrance to sorority houses even though they believed they could not do so at the residence of non-sorority women, that is, at the Founders Hall complex. How students may have made sense out of this is unknown. As we mentioned earlier, it is now impossible to check on the origin or significance of the many unwritten rules at BGSU. Even the faculty believed there were rules that applied to them that were not written down or formally communicated. Unwritten rules are a standard feature of repressive regimes, though some of these may be products of the subjects' paranoia. The point is that, at Bowling Green, the Greek neighborhood seemed somewhat "safer" from rule enforcement than the independents' part of campus. And if you could kiss there, and sneak alcohol more easily, then maybe this was a place where you could get away with other things as well. If this reasoning is correct it would help explain why a crowd in the Greek part of campus might think it could get away with more.

In other words, the Greeks' part of the campus and their activities were in a morally (or at least regulatory) ambiguous zone. For a crowd to assemble in the Greek area was fully legal in terms of campus rules, even though it was also something to be watched. On Greek turf, the independents had some of the same relaxed rights that the Greeks had. This is what allowed the independent students to gather in a crowd that was unsupervised but still fully in accord with the rules. Rule-wise this crowd fell through the cracks, and therefore it was allowed to assemble and enjoy unusual freedom. Perhaps this was the only way a crowd of students could have assembled on campus and begun to create the conditions of Durkheim's political model. Of course, the full development of the model would not have occurred had the administration not made the mistakes it made. Still, the location of the gathering in the lightly policed fraternity part of campus was part of the perfect storm that produced the demonstration.

This does not mean the water-fight crowd in question was initially a political one. It was just as it appeared—there to watch a harmless entertainment. But it was still a crowd, and it had the potential of turning into a self-conscious crowd that the audience at a school-sponsored sporting event, stuck in its chairs, would not. So, to elaborate on the "perfect storm" metaphor, a very unlikely concatenation of circumstances conspired on this Sunday afternoon. To begin with, the first warm day of the year was on a Sunday, not a school day. This meant there were no classes, and people had nothing in particular to do. The fraternity-versus-pledge water fight was held in the midafternoon on a field in fraternity row. A large, unsupervised, but still legitimate crowd assembled to watch the fight. The crowd, possibly feeling the thrill of its freedom, grew from a few dozen to several hundred. The afternoon began cooling down, and the fight should also have begun cooling down. But the crowd egged on the water fighters and their antics (exaggerated "Indian dancing" and so on) and got even more florid. This would have stopped, and the festivities would have ceased on their own within minutes. But the campus police came to break up the fun, creating a resentful and mildly unruly crowd. Then the dean appeared, adding to the crowd's defiance. And when the dean was soaked with water, the demonstration (and the gradual destruction of President McDonald) began.

THE USE OF SOLIDARITY FOR COMMUNICATION AND FRAMING

The construction of a political crowd, with its intense solidarity, is the first part of the model. The use of this solidarity to frame the issues of the demonstration and conduct a public communications fight is the second part. Solidarity was maintained throughout the three months of student lobbying, even though the actual assembly process had only gone on for three days.

Normally, group solidarity becomes strong when the group has an emotional assembly. Then, after the assembly, it slowly declines. It takes another assembly to build it back up again. But in this case the excitement and solidarity stayed high, even without any further assemblies or demonstrations. The three days of crowd intensity ended with the spring vacation, but the sense of unity, self-confidence, and pride never ended at all. It seemed to grow. This was a case of solidarity that seemed to create not an ordinary physical assembly but a psychological assembly, which in turn kept the solidarity at a high pitch. The students became so close and so committed during the initial three days of demonstration that they maintained this stance and these social resources for the entire three months of what might be called the dispersed or decentralized demonstration. The students' hunger for solidarity and a sense of moral rightness was so strong that they broke all the sociological rules of what produces solidarity and kept maintaining it with only the slightest hints of togetherness and assembly. In other words, the sociological magic of the three days of demonstration was so strong that it kept the students in a highly cohesive state for the remainder of the semester. A factor was probably the better sense of self that the demonstration created. Before this action the students were continuously belabored by guilty consciences and cognitive dissonance. Now the insides of their minds were clean and happy for the first time at this university.

It is probably going too far to say there was no assembly at all for three months. Small groups of the more politically active students were undoubtedly getting together during that time. There were also natural crowds throughout that spring, groups sunning themselves on the lawn, for example, or dining in the cafeteria or the dorms. On these occasions, protest symbols, such as making a *V* with one's fingers or clenching one's fist, or even exchanging significant smiles, kept the spirit alive. Durkheim wrote of how, under certain circumstances, solidarity and confidence can be maintained in ordinary, everyday social life. He was thinking of morality and religiosity, but the mood of the students in the middle of their successful social movement was both moral and quasi-religious. Recall that on the second day, two preachers (not simply professors or athletic coaches) addressed the students—using plenty of religious language. As Durkheim says,

> In all kinds of acts that express the understanding, esteem and affection of his neighbor, there is a lift that the man who does his duty feels, usually without being aware of it. But that lift sustains him; the feeling society has for him uplifts the feeling he has for himself. Because he is in moral harmony with his neighbor, he gains new confidence, courage and boldness in action—quite like the man of faith who believes he feels the eyes of his god turned benevolently toward him. Thus is produced what amounts to a perpetual uplift of our moral being. (Durkheim 1995, 213)

In addition to this kind of internalization, solidarity can be stored in the protest symbols of a social movement (Collins 2004, 81–87). The production of these symbols, even in small groups, will amp up solidarity. For the BG students, victories in the press, such as favorable coverage in the *Toledo Blade,* also kept the solidarity alive. Our point is that even though there were no large assemblies all spring, student solidarity managed to remain high, even increasing in amplitude, despite the absence of overt assembly.

Framing

We will now shift to the framing process, which is the second part of the explanation. In the recent social-movements literature there is an emphasis on the interpretation or framing of a movement's goals and meanings (Snow 2004). The framing process flows through communications media, both formally and informally. Sometimes a social movement is won not on the barricades but in its ripple effect through institutions. In the Bowling Green case the students and their faculty allies seemed much more effective in framing and interpreting the three days of demonstrations than was the university administration. It will become apparent that solidarity gave the students not only the energy and the nerve to press their case with the Ohio newspapers and legislature but also a sense of how to pitch a credible argument. They did not exaggerate the administration's mistakes, nor did they show any fear of calling a spade a spade. They spoke out directly and bluntly in ways that made sense to the Ohio newspaper readers and general population. This was a sharp change from the way the university had dominated the institutional voices for as long as anyone could remember.

Another remarkable feature of the students' actions was the lack of anything they could be criticized for. There was no destruction of school property, no graffiti on the walls of buildings, no vulgar handouts, no anonymous letters to key administration personnel, no excessive cutting of classes, nor any other expression of antisocial activity. Of course, such actions would have been publicly criticized by the administration, and this would have hurt the students' cause. The students acted as though they knew this, although Sherman Stanage had exhorted them to make it a clean fight all the way.

Before the 1961 demonstrations, the university's administration had routinely enjoyed favorable press coverage. The 1957 demonstration had been led by fraternities and was over the use of alcohol at off-campus parties. This was a serious demonstration with national coverage, but the university had looked entirely reasonable in the press reports. And from 1957 to 1961 the university continued to look good in the media and enjoy favorable public opinion. The students and, increasingly, the faculty grumbled about McDonald's paternalistic administrative style, but they seemed to have no way of making their case. There were no specific rules forbidding them to go to the press, but there were the above-discussed general rules about following "moral and ethical standards." The university interpreted these rules with wide latitude, and both students and faculty believed that they would be punished if they went to the media.

The situation immediately prior to the 1961 demonstrations, then, was one in which the students and faculty were effectively prevented from influencing public opinion. Of course, most faculty were university loyalists, but the approximately one-third who were in the dissident camp were a significant minority. The students, meanwhile, felt that their only means of telling their story would be to stage a demonstration, and the rumors about the expected demonstration on April 9 were to that end.

By contrast, the university's administration had smooth-working communication channels. They had an efficient press bureau, and they also had friends at many of the Ohio newspapers and TV stations. There were a fair number of BGSU alumni working in the Ohio media, however, and, as we said earlier, some of these had unfavorable memories of their years at the university.

The pre-demonstration communication situation may have seemed stable, but the threat of a demonstration showed how tension-riddled it was. In fact the situation was its own enemy, for it produced forces that would eventually cause its demise. These forces were disgruntled students, a restive faculty, unhappy alumni in important positions, and an increasingly concerned state legislature.

Once the demonstrations began, the communication pattern was opened up quite quickly. There was immediate and extensive coverage in the Ohio papers and also some notice in the national press. Many Ohio papers initially accepted the administration's diagnosis of spring fever, but the *Toledo Blade* did not. It expressed concern for whatever underlying problems might be operating at Bowling Green. And the *Bowling Green Sentinel-Tribune,* the town of Bowling Green's local newspaper, was highly influenced by the *Blade.*

In other words, even though one might expect that the major local newspaper would, in the usual boosterish fashion, side with the university administration, it tended to be critical. The people in the town of Bowling Green themselves, along with their local institutions, tended to support the administration, but the local newspaper was President McDonald's enemy. Still, this newspaper could do very little before the students got up the nerve and the solidarity to become vocal and deliver their grievances to the press.

In McDonald's speech to the faculty immediately after the demonstrations, he blamed the press for amplifying and dignifying the demonstrations. The press did not cover this speech, but the word still went out, informally, that McDonald was blaming the press. His behavior contrasts with the students' seeking out and embracing the press. McDonald's challenge to the young instructor who was taking notes during his address also suggests his fear of the press. This display of weakness may have been another factor in emboldening Stanage to make his unprecedented rebuttal statement, although he told people he had planned it ahead of time. In any case, the balance of power, communication-wise, between the administration and the students changed radically once the window had been opened.

Let us put this argument more formally:

a. The public meaning or frame of Bowling Green State University was positive before the demonstrations. There were disgruntled students, alumni, and faculty, but these groupings had no voice. The public opinion of Bowling Green was that it was a somewhat strict but trustworthy administration taking good care of Ohio's college-age youth.

b. The demonstration changed the public meaning or semiotic representation of BGSU. Now something was clearly wrong, although it would take a while for any public definition of the problem to set in.

c. On the second day, the speeches by Reverend Trautwein and Sherman Stanage began to frame the demonstrations as a matter of civil liberties and civil disobedience.

d. On the third day, the demonstration was stopped when McDonald read the riot act. This looked like it outflanked the students, but it just made them angrier.

e. On the fourth day, when President McDonald addressed the faculty, and Stanage made his response, there was an intensification of the rival interpretations. McDonald gave what had become the standard administrative interpretation. Stanage, by contrast, stated the position of the students in existentialist phrases and biblical cadences.

f. The students began going to the media as soon as possible, during the days of demonstration themselves. Because the administration was saying little, the voluble students must have been welcome to the press, if for no other reason than to get the story.

g. As discussed earlier, on April 3, eight days after the demonstrations began, about nine BGSU students appeared before the House Education Committee, asking for an investigation of their grievances. This was fast and hard-hitting political action. The students were going back and forth from the press to the legislature in whipsaw fashion, and doing so with a public-relations skill that is rarely found in a barely organized dissenting population.

h. The spring continued with steady student advances in the fight for public opinion and for concessions on the part of the administration. Still, for a while it looked as if McDonald would be able to ride this one out. Instead, on June 2 he dismissed Stanage. This firing played right into the hands of the students and the increasingly concerned press. It also intensified the faculty's solidarity, making them major players in the dismantling of the McDonald administration.

i. The final scene was over the trustee-packing bill in the Ohio state legislature. This bill was a mild rebuke to McDonald and to the existing board of trustees. But the liberal faculty had already met with trustee Donnell. After that meeting, Donnell, who was influential with the other trustees, gradually removed his support from President McDonald. Thus it was primarily McDonald who was hostile to the bill. The trustees had a mixture of opinions.

McDonald should have welcomed the bill and also the new trustees. The students and the press had already convinced the legislature that something was wrong at Bowling Green. The legislature could either conduct an investigation themselves or strengthen the board of trustees so that they would do it. Favoring university autonomy, the legislature took the latter option. But with McDonald standing in the way of this option, it would have to be a "come what may" vote. When the Senate voted 31 to 1 for the bill and then the House voted 112 to nothing, McDonald lost so much face he had no alternative but to resign. And right to the end he blamed the press for his defeat.

The passage of this law concluded the brilliant framing fight the students had staged against the university. When communication was tightly controlled in the pre-demonstration period, the university had a free hand to interpret the students' actions as it wanted. The students and dissident faculty could do little but grumble ineffectually. But when the demonstrators tore away the veil that had covered the university, the media could make their own interpretations, and the students were quick to sense their opportunity. This entailed a shift in leadership from fraternities and sororities to students with a civil-libertarian outlook. The issues also shifted from hedonistic and lifestyle matters to those of civil rights and political liberties. This political transition would become a standard pattern as student demonstrations continued through the sixties.

An additional point should be added. In most social movements, the protestors have to prove that something is wrong, that they are being treated unjustly, that serious issues are at stake. The minority protests of recent decades—those of African Americans, women, and gays and lesbians, to mention just the biggest ones—have required pretty strong arguments that the minorities are being mistreated. This has entailed something along the lines of legal briefs, dramatization, incessant publicity, and solid arguments concerning the mistreatment. This framing and advertising of issues is usually required to change the public's mind about the rights of the minority group.

In the Bowling Green case, though, the problem was an entirely different one. The evidence of out-of-date rules and heavy-handed treatment was itself overwhelming. It did not have to be proved. The problem was that it was secret. The public did not really know what was happening on that campus. If students had been allowed to publicly complain, the word would have long been out, and the public would have inevitably, if gradually, sided with the students. As one legislator told the petitioning students, "They are making their own laws on that campus." But the window was closed, because students thought they would be expelled if they complained publicly. When the forty-four students wrote the *Toledo Blade* a list of grievances, and when the *Blade* editor took this letter seriously, the word was out. Of course, the students told the *Blade* it could not print their names or they might be expelled, and the *Blade* went along with this request. Then the fear of expulsion gradually subsided and the student letters to the press became a tidal wave.

Once the veil had been lifted and the students started going public, it became obvious that the situation at Bowling Green was outdated and unacceptable on a tax-supported campus. The framing problem in the case of this social movement was not in making a plausible argument that wrongs were being committed. It was simply one of getting the truth out to the public. On other campuses in the later sixties the framing problem was much greater. Students were considered a privileged group of Americans and it was a mighty task for them to convince the public that their civil liberties—primarily their freedom of speech—were being curtailed. And when they spoke, they talked about quite controversial issues: minorities, war, and colonialism, to name a few. Their best asset was often that they were being beaten up by the police.

But at Bowling Green the issues were much more glaring, once they became known to the people of Ohio. Not only were these students not being given the adult rights to free speech—they were not being given the right to speak at all. They were being treated so like children that their education, in the broad sense of the development of one's human capacities, was being held back. And the public's money was being badly spent. In addition, the administration was careless about the separation of church and state.

For this reason the Bowling Green case was an exceptional one. It was a deviant case, as we mentioned in Chapter 1. The mistreatment was so severe and extreme that once the window was opened the place exploded. And the citizens of Ohio gradually realized that this school needed some housecleaning. That was why the legislature was only one vote shy of unanimous in demanding a change on this campus.

The combination of solidarity (i.e., energy) and framing in this case was the most powerful of any student movement or any other social movement of the period. This was a polar case in the sixties and it shows how social movements work. Normally, aggrieved groups have to work hard at solidarity, framing, and the other social-movement processes. But if unaddressed issues accumulate and frustration becomes acute enough, all it takes is one incident—one that carries out Durkheim's ritual processes—to make the whole thing explode. Then the social-movement process proceeds almost automatically, the aggrieved minority wins a victory, and the situation gets remedied.

We have now considered a series of interpretations, dwelling at greatest length on the solidarity and framing processes. There was a fight over defining the situation, in which the students gradually and decisively overcame the administration. This framing process, even more than the events of the demonstration themselves, best explains how the students won this prologue to the sixties, and how the university benefited from the ripple effects that were set in motion.

EPILOGUE: SOME THOUGHTS ON POLICY

After the military and hospitals, universities may rank next as the most bureaucratic and power-oriented institutions in our society. But even so, in an open society it is possible for ideas and initiatives to originate at any level of organization. Self-appointed committees of concerned faculty can have a major impact on the course of events within a university. Such committees may not have the capacity to implement their deliberations, but they can move beyond the atomized weakness of single individuals. The attention-getting capacity of such committees and their ability to initiate recommendations to those in positions of authority may be quite consequential.

In an organization composed of highly knowledgeable men and women, there is no single administrator who knows enough to arbitrarily exercise effective governance. Successful leadership is dependent on mobilizing talent at all levels of the organization. It is for this reason that within universities the faculty must be given the power to initiate whatever contribution they have to make. If a university is to grow academically, departments should be given substantial autonomy within their spheres. In this way they can maximize the use of talent in achieving their research, teaching, and service agendas. The primary responsibility of the chair of a department should be to represent the interests of that department's faculty to the administration, rather than to implement top-down decisions from the higher administration.

The Bowling Green case indicates rather clearly the importance of coalitions within a university. While the coalition of students and faculty in the uprising of 1961 included only a moderate portion of students and faculty, through their mobilization they were able to topple a very powerful and authoritarian president. However, removing the president from office was never an objective of anyone throughout the disturbance. It was heat from the state legislature that ousted the president. The students were only requesting that excessively harsh rules be lifted. The faculty was only coming to the rescue of a colleague who had been arbitrarily denied a renewal of contract.

If McDonald had been more sensitive to what was happening at the grassroots level, he might have attempted to use cooptation for quelling the discontent. For example, if he had appointed a committee composed of both students and faculty to study the basis for the student uprising and to make a set of policy recommendations, the students might have been satisfied and might even have regarded their efforts as victorious. As the sociologist Sam Kaplan, one of our interviewees, suggested, if McDonald had called Stanage into his office, listened to what he had to say, and then asked him if he would like to be considered as dean of students or as a vice president of university relations, the outcome of events would have been quite different. The most effective way for administrators to exercise power and control is not through the use of coercive methods, but through a variety of cooptation techniques.

A comparison of the administrative styles of McDonald and Jerome reveals an important distinction between authoritarian and democratic leadership. Instead of closing down the university during the Kent State crisis, President Jerome recruited faculty members to stay in touch with the students, to listen to what they had to say, and to organize them into seminars for discussions on the topics of interest to them. It is probable that McDonald would have declared a state of emergency and called in law-enforcement personnel, as most university administrators did across the country. Jerome's approach was not a compromise of integrity, as some of the residents of Bowling Green maintained, but a demonstration of effective university leadership under conditions of crisis.

The coverage of uprisings by the news media often has a major bearing on the outcomes. In the Bowling Green case, the role of the press was decisive. One of the special problems of the media is that of presenting objective information under conditions of uncertainty. Journalists usually attempt to be objective even when the facts are still in the process of emerging. In order to sustain at least the appearance of objectivity, journalists frequently draw on interviews as sources of information. We know from the Bowling Green episode, as well as from the civil rights movement, that coverage of news events frequently has a framing or shaping effect. There were many constituencies making judgments of the events on campus based on the news media reports. These included citizens of Bowling Green, the parents of the students, former graduates, and, most crucial of all, the university's board of trustees. In combination, these groups constituted a collective judiciary.

Prior to 1961, many student demonstrations could have been described in Gary Marx's terms (1972) as "issueless riots." They frequently were characterized by a carnival atmosphere, expressive behavior—a time for fun and games. Such demonstrations provide a source of pleasure through the blatant disregard of the rules. However, it is important for those in authority to recognize the difference between inconsequential "spring fever" and the expression of deep-seated frustrations, resentments, and social discontent.

If there are no demands or list of grievances, the call for help in social disturbances is typically too quiet to be heard. Moral appeals alone are unusually ineffective as attention-getting devices. They take on a greater degree of urgency if they are accompanied by threats and if some degree of fear can be generated. The successful forms of social protest are those in which there is a balance between appeals and threats. If the threat is too great, it has a tendency to drown out the appeal and to evoke a punitive response. If the appeal for remedial action is too soft, it is likely to be ignored.

Ralph Turner (1969) observed that the credibility of a protest is dependent on the conviction that unfair treatment has occurred and that those affected cannot correct the situation through their actions alone. That is, an appeal must be made to a level of morality and justice higher than that held by their oppressors. Further, the protestors' list of grievances must be suitable for remedial action.

Encounters with authority are among the basic consequences of social life and group living. We experience authority as a social force that resides outside of ourselves and as a set of legitimate claims on our conduct. Other people have control over the resources and services we desire, and to get what we want out of life we must learn to cope with authority relationships. It is by means of authority that rules are established, interpreted, and enforced. It is by means of authority that binding decisions are made and moral judgments are imposed on conduct. Authority is legitimate power; this implies that the orders, commands, directives, and requests that are issued by selected others become binding on our own conduct.

One of the major ways of identifying the presence of legitimate power in any given situation is to raise questions about the decision-making process. How are decisions to be made? Who has the right to decide? Under what circumstances are decisions binding on conduct? How are available resources to be allocated? If decisions are made, can we count on them to be backed up by an official line of action? These questions are answerable in any given case through awareness of the social drama embedded in authoritative acts.

If we cannot answer the above questions with confidence, the social world becomes chaotic and lacking in coherence. Systems of authority contribute to stable and predictable social relationships. Only certain individuals are permitted to do certain things, and this has the effect of fixing responsibilities. The predictability of events and a person's sense of mastery and control are closely related to judgments about how to cope effectively with authority. We incur responsibilities in the pursuit of goals, and the cost of noncompliance may be very great indeed. Compliance "with the system," "working within the system," and "beating the system" are popular expressions that originate from the necessity of coming to terms with the conditions of authority.

Authority involves more than issuing commands and insisting on obedience. It also involves the rights of specific individuals to engage in certain kinds of performances. If certain individuals are granted the power to issue requests, directives, or mandates, others necessarily have grounds for making fairness judgments and assessing leadership effectiveness. For example, students have the right to expect professors to be competent in their areas of specialization and to be fair in grading practices. For this reason, the authority of the professor is controlled to some degree by the responses of students, by academic standards, and by a professional code of ethics. Authority is limited to the legitimate exercise of power, and the test for legitimacy is the compatibility of decisions with group values and norms. Consequently, authority relationships are properties of social groups and are encompassed within normative boundaries and limits.

The character of power relationships constitutes one of the basic sources of conflict in modern society (Dahrendorf 1959). Authority relationships often emphasize rational values at the expense of tradition, enhance selfish interests at the expense of the common good, and draw on claims of legitimacy as a basis for manipulation and control. The accountability of authority figures frequently places a heavy set of demands on them, while subordinates often feel coerced into serving interests other than their own. Such conditions lend themselves to a great deal of controversy and debate, and the outcomes of social relationships are often based on negotiation and compromise.

The connection between authority and status is a major part of everyday understandings about the organization of social life. In our patterns of interaction we necessarily make assumptions about the attributes of those who have had a particular status conferred upon them. These attributes are an outgrowth of notions about the manner by which individuals are recruited for status positions. We necessarily assume that those in positions of authority are trained and certified and competent to carry out the tasks that are delegated to them. Such assumptions about status and authority are necessary for maintaining stable social relationships, for making norms binding on conduct, and for predicting future events. By being socialized into a particular organization, the individual learns to accept numerous aspects of authority as being normal, natural, and the preferred state of affairs.

While it is important for us to recognize the importance of authority in the modern world, it is also important that abuses of power in society be recognized and dealt with. Over time, leaders sometimes see themselves as being above accountability, as they place their own personal interests above those of the organizations they represent. In order to present a positive public image, there is a tendency to cover up harmful and destructive patterns of leadership. The high crimes and misdemeanors of President Nixon's administration, the My Lai massacre by Lt. William Calley's platoon during the Vietnam War, and the misappropriation of corporate funds by Exxon executives are among the egregious abuses of leadership positions that are remembered, forgotten, and reconstructed in our collective memory (Schudson 1992). The Bowling Green case study merits a place in our consciousness of what may or may not be done by those who hold positions of trusteeship in higher education.

Chapter 8

How the Fifties
Changed into the Sixties
at Bowling Green

Decades do not usually have much cultural coherence or unity, but some do, such as the decade of the Great Depression. And the twenties too have a distinctive, sandwiched-in quality between World War I and the Depression. But the 1970s, '80s, and '90s have little internal unity. And even though the civil rights movement started in the mid-fifties, what are usually thought of as the distinctive sixties do not begin until about 1963 or '64. The central issue of the '50s was anti-Communism, both against the Soviet Union and, in its McCarthyist version, against American citizens who leaned in a liberal or radical direction. But anti-Communism started tapering off with the censure of McCarthy by the Senate in 1954.

So there is an amorphous period as the fifties come to a close and the sixties find their student-protest character. The movement from the fifties to the sixties is hard to spot, and anything but crisp. That is why the transition was so striking during the Bowling Green demonstration, for you could see the fifties becoming the sixties as the demonstration moved from stage to stage and ran its course. This could be noticed especially in the way the issues were gradually defined and redefined. But you could also see it to some extent in the development of tactics and the flow of leadership. And it was noticeable in the way the students came to define themselves as a class.

In the study of social revolution it is a commonplace that revolutions tend to begin moderately and move gradually leftward. The Bowling Green case did not move leftward though. It moved to what might be called the future, to a posture that fit into the new and emergent tendencies of the period. It evolved from an old-fashioned, hedonistic sort of demonstration into a vanguard and principled social movement. This arc can be seen in all features of the rebellion. As we describe this transition, we will be drawing on materials already presented, but we will be organizing them in a new way, a way that we think will capture the pulse of the event.

The Issues. We will discuss the evolution of the issues at some length and give shorter treatment to the tactics and leadership. The issues began as a list of rather familiar student complaints. One batch was of a hedonistic or lifestyle variety, extending from use of alcoholic beverages to expressions of affection on campus. The other batch had to do with such things as autonomy in the student newspaper and the student senate. These issues had been around for decades, and all campuses, particularly the former teachers colleges in the Midwest, had them to some extent. At Bowling Green the complaints were given new life when the recently hired President McDonald made the prohibitions on alcoholic beverages, already strict when he took office, considerably stricter in 1953.

Even though the students had some reasonable arguments concerning the lifestyle rules, they always knew that these issues looked selfish and peripheral to the main purpose of getting an education. They were in college to get a degree, not to have fun, and they should be grateful they were given this chance. For this reason, the students, starting with William Day in the 1949 demonstration, always tried to argue that the censorship rules were the major concern. What was considered to be the riot tradition at Bowling Green was a general discontent with the power relations between the students and the administration, a discontent distinct from the exact character of the rules at any given time. In other words, the discontent was a somewhat amorphous and unstructured force, the nature of which at any given moment would have to be carefully examined, should the politics of the moment make it necessary.

The mythology of "the day" of the next rebellion did not require a list of grievances. It was merely a feeling that another demonstration could, and should, come with the warm weather, quite apart from whether it would or not, and also apart from specific issues. This feeling was like Karl Marx's concept of utopia, in being a goal without any attached notion of what means were needed to reach it. In this respect no one knew just what the issues were in any particular spring, and there was probably always a tension between the more selfish and the more principled, mature grievances.

When the 1961 rebellion began at the water fight, the shouted word "Founders" was the catalyst. All this shout meant was that the crowd should move to the women's dorms, at Founders quad, before the authorities locked the doors and prevented the coeds from joining the crowd. It was a tactic, not an issue, although it did evoke the idea of turning the crowd into a protest. Also, feminism itself was an underground or "preconscious" issue at this time; it started rumbling around 1960, but it would not achieve clear language or consciousness until later in the decade. So the message "Founders," which was an instruction to free the women physically, also resonated with the idea of freeing the women politically, legally, socially, and culturally. Although nobody quite knew this yet.

Through the three days of the rebellion there was never any agreed-upon list of issues. A committee of student elites, on the second day, began to try to hammer out such a list, but they failed to reach agreement. The first list that actually surfaced was the one the student delegation presented to the legislature's committees on education, six days after the conclusion of the actual demonstration. This list of issues, which was reported in the press, was as follows:

> Lack of student expression in the school newspaper, the *B-G News.*
> Ineffective student government.
> Strict rules on class attendance.
> Not enough sections of popular courses.
> Lack of student representation on governing organizations.
> Poor system of academic counseling.
> Double jeopardy in the student court.

The news story goes on to say, "The students denied that off-campus beer drinking and kissing in front of women's dormitories were major issues in the demonstrations, but did say they felt these were matters that should be at the discretion of the students and not the administration" (*Bowling Green Sentinel-Tribune,* April 4, 1961, front page).

But as the three days of demonstration, and then the three-month framing battle, progressed, the word *freedom* began to appear as a common denominator for the issues. This term encompassed both the lifestyle and the censorship issues. In particular, the word took its meaning from the Bill of Rights in the U.S. Constitution. In other words, the notion of civil liberties as an expression of freedom began to be the overarching issue of the rebellion. Full access to civil liberties is something that adults have in the United States. Children and teenagers have not usually been included under these rights, at least not without limitations. To say these students wanted freedom is to say they wanted to be treated as adults, not as wards of the school. The in loco parentis rule collided with being free, so this subordinate status was excluded under the word freedom.

As we mentioned earlier, however, freedom also had clear implications for the lifestyle issues. Kissing after a date is a way of expressing feelings, a form of free speech. The varieties of intimate behavior in a close emotional relationship, particularly among adults, are considered legally private matters. And among near adults, those of college age, such actions as kissing and petting are also legal. In fact, the age of consent to sexual intercourse is sixteen in Ohio and was so at the time of the BG demonstration. Therefore the prohibition of kissing on the BG campus was an infringement on the rights of the students, a violation of their civil liberties.

The fact that the no-kissing rule was unwritten did not help things. The student handbook of 1960–1961, on page 30, read, "A student found guilty of violating or dishonoring University regulations, or of being involved in moral or ethical misconduct, may be dismissed." "Dishonoring" and "being involved" are loophole words, which could be—and were—used quite comprehensively to interdict a loosely defined category of behaviors. This ambiguity increased the feeling of being violated, because the rule infringed in two ways. Overtly it contradicted freedoms of expression and speech. But covertly, in its imprecision and shadowy status, it created a second violation by allowing for the poorly spelled out "moral or ethical" rules. These were vague rules, against which there can be no secure defense. The more general rule (also unwritten) against any complaining about the university or publicly criticizing the rules merely compounded the feeling of danger on this campus.

Until 1953, the only rule concerning alcohol stated that a student legally convicted of drunkenness was eligible for dismissal from the university. In 1953 President McDonald, then in his second year of office, changed the rule to forbid not just drunkenness but any drinking at all. This rule underwent some subsequent transformations, eventually forbidding all drinking by students of any age. The rule came up, as mentioned earlier, when the student delegation went to the statehouse, and one of the legislators said they are usurping the legislature's authority on that campus. If a certain behavior (e.g., the drinking of alcohol by those twenty-one or over, or the drinking of near beer by those between eighteen and twenty-one) is permitted by law and a university forbids it, that university is obviously violating the rights of the students.

Turning to censorship and self-government, the BG students had quite limited freedom of speech and of self-regulation. The censorship rules were partly written and partly unwritten, a mix that was more oppressive because of its uncertainty. Of course students cannot completely run the university, but they have a right to a moderate amount of self-regulation, including expression in the student newspaper and any other media.

It is clear then that both bundles of rules, those concerning lifestyle and those concerning self-expression, were covered by the general concept of freedom, including freedom of speech. The students were always at least implicitly aware that the university was restricting their legal freedoms, but the appropriate language (and consciousness) was not readily available. When the demonstrations began, the students were still using the old legalist and regulatory categories. Historical memory favored this frame of mind. But as time went on the argument went up a notch and the students realized it was their overall legal status that was being restricted. When Rev. Trautwein and Professor Stanage addressed the protesting students on the second night they emphasized the dignity and even the morality of the students' position. Trautwein used the language of the civil rights movement and Stanage used the language of authenticity and existentialism. But both were addressing the students as an adult audience with legitimate grievances and a voice of which they should be proud.

Initially the students were defensive and a bit sheepish about some of their issues. But as the emotions churned and the moral climate evolved, the students lost all their feelings of shame, realizing it was an inappropriate emotion. In fact, the sloughing off of shame was probably one of the reasons the students felt such a surge of emotional growth. They now had a clear conscience, and the sneaking around was over. In fact they deflected this shame onto the administration, making their opponents look petty and a bit prurient. Pride in one's moral position is a powerful force, and the two preachers helped the students to understand and harness this force.

The Catholic chaplain, Father Ollivier, privately condemned the demonstration in the strongest terms, but he chose not to speak along with the other two preachers when invited. Evidently he thought that addressing the students at all would be to recognize the legitimacy of the demonstration. So even though Ollivier had a strong voice, was a powerful speaker, and would have issued a rebuttal to the other two speakers, the politics of the situation boxed him in and prevented him from exercising his voice. As a result, his disapproval was rendered silent and ineffective. The students ended the second night, then, with a clean slate, morally speaking, and with the injunction to define their issues with all the dignity and principle they could find in them.

The demonstration was being transformed from the airing of a batch of tentative, somewhat whiny-sounding complaints into an altruistic and resounding appeal to American values. The strongest of the new themes was freedom of speech, the same value that would pervade the later student movement of the sixties. The issues had shifted from a shopworn list of fifties grumbles to the liberationist voice of the sixties, the call for freedom. This transformation, while partially vocalized, had to travel through the student unconscious (i.e., their ruminations) before it could be given formation. But by the time the student delegation went to the legislature, the issues—as listed a few pages back—had a strong sixties resonance. Perhaps this is why they were taken so seriously, seriously enough to generate a sympathetic new law, by the initially skeptical members of the legislature.

The Tactics. During the long, multi-year period of mythological demonstrations (i.e., the "dream on" period), there were few tactics. These can be expressed in the two names, Founders and Route 6. Founders meant "Get the girls out," and Route 6 meant "Let's block traffic on Wooster Street." There were no other tactics, except for milling around the campus and maybe standing in front of the president's house, itself situated on Route 6. Burning an effigy of the president was another stock play. No one suggested the sixties idea of lying down on the street when the trucks were rolled out to clear the road. Actually, the limited tactics used were not bad for getting attention and raising the social costs for the university. But like Marx's utopias, they did not lead anywhere. And they were subject to being publicly defined to the press, and thereby deflected, by the university. The two-hour, early-morning demonstration of 1957, led by the fraternities, was the classic. It was also the only one remembered by the students, even though almost none of them in 1961 would have actually participated in it. The torchlight parade was a dramatic stunt, but there was no next step. And the 1957 demonstration was essentially exhausted about an hour after the action of Don McFadden, the Pi Kappa Alpha leader who hosed the city fire chief. We might note in passing that the dousing of Dean Taylor during the 1961 water fight bore a close resemblance to McFadden's watering the fire chief.

In fact, the 1961 demonstration initially looked as if it would go the way of the short-lived 1957 demonstration, for no one knew what to do with the energy, with the crowd, and so it seemed destined for exhaustion. But on this latter occasion, unlike the earlier one, the liberal faculty was more or less in cahoots with the student demonstrators, even though they were not participating themselves. This faction of the faculty did approve of the demonstration, and individual members were informally talking to and encouraging the students.

Also, President McDonald did talk to one group of demonstrators the first night. This dialogue turned the crowd into an audience and gave it a definition and a partial legitimation that encouraged the students to keep going. Assembling again the second day made the 1961 demonstration completely different from the one in 1957, for it raised the question "What do we do next?" that is, "What new tactics can we try?"

The talks by the two preachers on the second night were mostly about tactics. Rev. Trautwein outlined three tactical routes the students might take next—that is, on the third day. Trautwein's talk was soaked with the language of civil rights and, to a mild extent, civil disobedience. Stanage disapproved of outright civil disobedience, such as the aimless blocking of traffic on Route 6, but he did encourage the students to continue the demonstration and to aim it toward freedom of speech. These two speakers then moved things toward the exploration of what new moves to make, including those created by Martin Luther King and the civil rights movement.

By the second day some students had already left town, getting an early start on the spring break of two days hence, and some of these students were out talking to their local newspapers. Staging what were in effect press conferences was a brand new tactic for the riot tradition. This posture obviously assumed that the students had legitimate issues, arguments they wanted the public to hear. This cockiness was a bold new action. Other groups of students were already composing the lengthy letter, signed by forty-four students, that would impress the editors of the *Toledo Blade*. Remember, it was the *Blade*'s editorials that, as much as anything, impressed the public, caught the attention of the legislature, and eventually toppled McDonald. And a third group of students was planning the trip to the already somewhat sympathetic chair of the Senate Committee on Education, Ross Pepple. In other words, there was a burst of tactical creativity moving through channels that would eventually give complete justification to the student rebellion. The fifties bundle of boisterous and semi-adolescent tactics was being abandoned in favor of a distinctly adult, highly measured batch of political moves, carefully designed to meet their mark. Tactically as well as ideologically, the BG demonstration was shifting to the sixties, and in some respect inventing the sixties. And again we see, in midair, so to speak, the transition from the fifties to the sixties.

The Leaders. The 1961 demonstration began spontaneously when the water fight audience was turned into a political crowd. This happened when one of the Sigma Chi pledges hit Dean Taylor with a bag full of water. This pledge might be considered a leader, but his leadership was short lived and a matter of chance. Because he was not caught, his name was not publicly recorded or remembered. And the people who shifted the running crowd to the Founders dorms are also not remembered. Crowd actions in demonstrations are often leaderless. This does not mean there is no leadership at all; there might be someone starting a chant or changing the direction of a march, for example. But this kind of leadership is embedded, more or less anonymous, and of short duration. More formal spokespersons appear only later (if then) to interpret the demonstration and state some version of the issues.

There is also often a reluctance among demonstrating groups to talk about their leadership. Protesting groups usually veer toward an egalitarian stance, and the existence of leaders tends to weaken this stance. Also, the opponents of social movements sometimes try to identify leaders in order to neutralize them in some way, hoping to disorient or decapitate the movement with this tactic. But a demonstrating group still usually needs some way, beyond shouted slogans or placards, of communicating their concerns. They may need a voice, one with enough precision and force to state their grievances.

Earlier demonstrations at Bowling Green were led by fraternities and other elites. On the second day of the 1961 demonstration, student government set up a microphone in front of the student union and speakers appeared. These included the two preachers, as previously mentioned, and such student dignitaries as Bernie Casey, the football star, Clark Tibbits, student body president-elect, and Murray Ferderber, student-newspaper columnist. The three students were in the kind of elite positions that, in the past, would have fit them to be leaders of the protest. But in this case they did not know quite what to say, they spoke in vague language, and they did not assume leadership roles. Trautwein and Stanage had already moved into a kind of faculty advisory role by discussing tactics. The three students, by contrast, spoke in generalities. We can assume that there were also less visible, embedded leaders, whose leadership centered on small clusters or "affinity groups" (Snow and Soule 2010, 157), but this is a matter of speculation, and it does not refer to leaders in any ordinary sense.

On the third day, a committee of fraternity leaders and dorm representatives spent the day trying to produce a list of grievances. But they were unable to agree. Whatever disagreement or split it was that held them back, it is clear that these elite students were unable to step into a leadership role. Students would soon be talking to their local newspaper editors, though. These students were self-appointed spokespersons, although the press seemed glad to get whatever information they could about the demonstrations, and printed stories that included increasingly high-sounding lists of grievances. These spokespersons were taking a leadership role of a kind by moving the consciousness of the demonstration into the public eye. What little leadership there was seems to have been quite dispersed and to have come from the ranks of ordinary students.

The delegation that went to the legislators in Columbus seems to have been as close to a leadership group as there was, and they too were self-appointed. The legislators asked which student was the leader, and the group spontaneously chose Tom Brundrett, for he had actually organized the trip. Brundrett, a freshman, then spoke for the nine—and for the student body generally—by presenting the issues. Brundrett had been an activist from the moment he hit the campus. According to the BGSU news director at the time, James Gordon, "I remember Tom because he was such a pain in the neck for McDonald, led the charge to the House and Senate" (e-mail, January 23, 2008).

The group was composed primarily of freshmen and was decidedly not of elite student status. In other words, these were leaders from below, decentralized, self-selected, and, although this campus tended to be run by the Greeks, non-Greek. The fact that the delegation was primarily underclassmen, with a leader who was a freshman, also shows how striking this change in leadership was.

Another notable feature of the delegation was that five of the nine students were women (*Toledo Blade,* April 4, 1961). This hearkens back to our earlier point, that the McDonald administration was met by an early wave of feminism. Margorie Levin and Susan Ericksen both spoke freely to the press, but the identities of the other three women are unknown.

As the sixties progressed this leadership pattern continued. Mark Rudd of Columbia University and Mario Savio of Berkeley were the best-known leaders of the student sixties. These two, Rudd a junior and Savio a sophomore, were also of non-elite student status and spontaneously generated from below.

The new Bowling Green leadership pattern, then, was a sharp break from the one that had preceded it. The fifties style was leadership by elite students from fraternities and sororities, student government, or the student press. The 1961 demonstration started the same way, with students from fraternities defying campus authorities and leading the way. But as the demonstration actually got underway the fraternities shifted into the background and the leadership was slowly transformed into that of ordinary students of non-elite if not outright "nerd" status. The shift in leadership then parallels the shift in issues and tactics already mentioned. And it is again an example of how this demonstration shifted mid-course from a fifties to a sixties style.

Students as a Class. We are not using *class* in the Marxian sense of workers and owners. Instead, we mean an interest group united by moral goals and energized by self-consciousness. The traditional goals of students were to get an education and to have some fun while doing it. When the then-president of UC Berkeley, Clark Kerr, lectured on the nature of the university in 1959, he compared it to a factory. The product was educated students and the knowledge that would give them an education. When Kerr used this industrial metaphor he struck a raw nerve with the Berkeley students, for they resented being defined in such mechanistic terms. And it made them conscious of the impersonal way in which they were treated at Cal. They did not regard themselves as raw material to be processed into products. They thought of themselves as having the moral role, in fact the mission, of steering the social order in the direction of justice. Initially, racial justice and anti-colonialism were the major orientations of this role. This meant that the students did not want to be an economic or bureaucratic status group, worked on during their years in college so that they could meet the economic needs of society. That was the Clark Kerr model. Instead, they insisted they were a moral class, leading the way for society toward a just community.

Kerr sensed that students were beginning to think of themselves as a "class," in something akin to the Marxian sense of lumpen proletariat. This seems like a misperception. Students did think of themselves as a united group with a common or defining attribute. But this attribute was not some position in the social arrangement, comparable to a Marxian class—or a niche in some kind of functional apparatus. Instead it was more of a prophetic or moral class. Students were in a better position in the social structure to see the totality than people who were already ensconced in jobs, and that included educators such as Clark Kerr.

Students, it is true, were being trained for and were on the verge of entering the functional arrangement. Being incorporated into society would require that they accept the moral status quo as something they were buying into.

But their role as students, gazing at the whole array of knowledge, and as "new blood," entering the business of a society, had sensitized them to the morality of the culture they were entering. School had encouraged them to think for themselves, at least during the period of their schooling, and this temporary moratorium on commitment, this opportunity to look before they leaped, made them look at the values as well as the functions of their host society. And when they stopped to look at the values, they saw that there was a lot of inconsistency, and even hypocrisy, in the social order. Gunnar Myrdal (1944) studied American race relations and concluded that there was a massive conflict between the egalitarian values of the American system and the actual set of inegalitarian practices in the racial arrangement.

The Bowling Green students began the 1961 demonstration in the old model: here to get an education and to have some fun while doing it. But as they pondered the issues in the discussion from week to week, they realized they needed to secure their rights and move the university toward becoming an institution of and for justice. They did not go as far as students in the mid-sixties would in defining their moral position. But they went most of the way. They wanted an administration that would not resort to questionable and, in their eyes, unjust measures. They wanted a university that practiced fairness and that treated the student body as a moral entity, one endowed with liberties and rights. Education would come from these values just as much as from information and experience.

The definition of the students as a moral class rather than as a dependent, fun-seeking, non-adult population was somewhat implicit in the activities of the demonstration—but also somewhat explicit. For example, the existential statement of student grievances in Appendix A has strongly moral overtones. This statement, written by one of Stanage's students and read by Stanage when he defied President McDonald at the faculty meeting, is the expression of Stanage's circle of students. But it is also close to the way Mario Savio would speak three years later.

In light of the way students were defining themselves as a new class, going to the press, to the legislature, and to the people of Ohio was a proud activity. It expressed their newly found moral status. And it came not from their traditional leaders, the wealthy and the high-achievers, but from the ordinary guy and girl.

We have now shown how the 1961 rebellion was a transition between the fifties and the sixties. And this link was made in process, in midair, as the demonstration gradually changed character. The change was most clear in the issues, but it was also visible in the tactics and leadership. It resulted in a new self-awareness for these students. Now they represented the best American values, and it was their mission to make these values a reality.

Chapter 9

How the Fifties Produced the Sixties Nationally

The previous chapter, on how the fifties glided into the sixties at Bowling Green, was not about an isolated event. This transition grew out of national trends. We might say that although pressures were building throughout the system of higher education in the late fifties, Bowling Green may have been the weakest link in the chain. It is where the system first broke. It was, as we mentioned earlier, a deviant case according to ordinary expectations, but it had some odd peculiarities that also made it a highly volatile case. Student discontent was high, the contradictions between students and administration were glaring, and the students had an intense desire to "kick ass." In particular, as we will discuss in the next chapter, women were the most oppressed students on this campus. They were experiencing a mixture of shame and outrage. Also, female demographic changes throughout the country were beginning to nudge the consciousness of women upward. Throughout this book we have been showing how outdated rules, carefully wrought secrecy, and the threat of reprisal kept the lid on this university a lot longer than was natural. Every autumn, the new freshman, with their more current expectations, increased the tension. For all these reasons, when it blew, it *really* blew.

The Bowling Green uprising was an advance indicator of the turbulence that would follow in the decade of the 1960s. The uprising was symbolic of the student discontent that would subsequently develop throughout the country, indeed throughout the world (Feuer 1969). After the BGSU uprising, student expressions of discontent and demonstrations erupted at Berkeley, the University of Wisconsin, the University of Michigan, Columbia, and numerous other campuses. Before the decade was over, students organized and demonstrated at colleges and universities throughout the country. While special circumstances

141

prevailed on each campus, the episode at Bowling Green was an early stage of what became a powerful trend.

In this chapter we will look at the campus fifties to see which problems and issues grew to generate the massive discontent of the sixties. This will be social history, and it will not have the narrative drive that most of the chapters have. It might come as a break in the story. Still, it will be a break that should shed light on the story itself. This chapter will also go into more detail concerning issues mentioned only briefly in earlier chapters.

It might seem as though the sixties came out of nowhere, with a decade of calm and apathy followed abruptly by a decade of disturbance and discontent. There *was* a turn from relative calm to relative turbulence, but there was also a broad continuity as issues smoldered and became more intense. The discontent was directed toward the internal governance of universities, toward irrational forms of authority, and toward repressive attempts to control the non-academic lives of students. The anger was directed toward the many contradictions and forms of social injustice, as we discussed in Chapter 3, that were deeply embedded in the social system. This anger was expressed in several forms of protest. The view of students as apolitical during the 1950s was soon to be replaced by the student activism directed toward making the world a better place.

During the academic year of 1960–1961, the majority of undergraduate students at BGSU were between the ages of eighteen and twenty-two. Most students lived in dormitories on campus. Older and nontraditional students accounted for only a small proportion of the student body. This generation of students was born during the later years of the Great Depression (1938–1939) and the early years of World War II (1940–1943). Their parents were of the generation that personally experienced the hardships of the Great Depression and the intense patriotism that emerged following the Japanese bombing of Pearl Harbor. Their fathers were among the 15 million Americans who were in uniform by the time the war was over. Many of their parents were separated by the war, wives embracing their husbands in bus and train stations, the men departing for a war from which they might never return.

Their parents were a part of what Tom Brokaw (1998) called the Greatest Generation, and they participated in what Studs Terkel (1984) called the Last Good War. Some of the husbands returned from the war to wives who had learned to manage without them and to children they had never seen. In a country with a low divorce rate by modern standards, the divorce rate of veterans was relatively high. Although the term *post-traumatic stress syndrome* had not yet been coined, we now know that combat veterans of all wars suffer some degree of traumatic stress (Shay 1994).

In the very early lives of the college students of 1960, the world's first atomic bombs were exploded over the Japanese cities of Hiroshima and Nagasaki. Before these students had completed elementary school, the Russians had exploded their first atomic bomb, and the Cold War was growing. The Republic of China came under Communist control, and the United States became deeply involved in the Korean War. The Russians launched Sputnik, and the race was underway for the control of outer space.

In contrast to the hardships of their parents, 1960s college students' teenage years occurred during the economic prosperity of the postwar years. Many of these students were the first of their families to attend college. Drawing on family values and personal memories of the hardship and deprivation of the Great Depression, their parents had high aspirations for their children. Achieving a college education was seen as the avenue for upward mobility and realizing the American Dream. Postwar parents wanted to provide opportunities for their children that they themselves had never had.

The college students of the late 1950s were seen by many academics as conformist and lacking in serious social and political commitments (Keniston 1960; Dean 1961). Surrounded by the economic prosperity of the country, they took the good life for granted and sought to find their place within the broader scheme of human affairs. They presumably lacked the idealism that developed in the next decade. The overall assessments of college students in the late 1950s were soon to be altered by the widespread shift from conformity and political apathy to extreme political activism. Some observers at the time noted that when the alienated become involved in the political process, they tend to take extremist positions. Political apathy and political extremism are not opposite ends of the same continuum but alternative reactions to conditions of alienation. The student rebellions of the 1960s did indeed have shocking implications for the defenders of the status quo and for those who thought that all was well in the social realm.

A great deal of literature in the 1950s emphasized the theme of conformity. After the tumultuous decade of World War II, the decade of the fifties is remembered as a quiet time, a period of stability and normality. To meet the housing needs and preferences of returning veterans, suburbs were greatly expanded. Family values were emphasized, and millions of babies were added to the nation's population. But amidst this conformity was the emergence of rock and roll; the music of Elvis Presley blared from the radios of hot rod cars throughout America. Television came into its own, and the programming placed a premium on situation comedies, westerns, drama, and depictions of normal families.

Social scientists were inclined to see the conformity of the age as problematic. In William H. Whyte's (1956) *The Organization Man,* concern is directed toward the psychic costs of loyalty and dedication to the corporate world at the expense of all other concerns and values. Sloan Wilson's 1955 novel *The Man in the Gray Flannel Suit* draws upon a similar theme in symbolically depicting uniformity in dress code for the corporate world. In C. Wright Mills's (1956) analysis of the new middle class, he describes the white-collar man as "more piti-ful than tragic as he lives out in slow misery his yearning for the quick American climb." The themes of normality and tranquility stood in contrast to the deep fears and anxieties that simmered below the surface. It was during the next decade that some of the contradictions of American life were to become major sources of rancorous conflicts.

Images of the 1950s as a decade of peace and tranquility are misleading. It is true that the carnage of World War II was over, and the veterans had returned to a nation grateful for the sacrifices they had made. The veterans had idealized social life in their communities while they were gone and had returned home to promote the importance of family values. They also desired their own homes on their own lots. It was a time in which a high reward value was placed on children—the more children the better. The economy was booming and images of the Great Depression had receded into the background of collective memory.

Many students of American culture have seen the movie *Pleasantville* as capturing the essence of a decade. But the idyllic images were only a part of those times. There was also the fear generated by the Russians' launching of the first space satellite. As Sputnik circled the globe, levels of anxiety intensified. The Russians' development of atomic capability caught the nation by surprise, and the threat of nuclear war shattered the sense of tranquility.

Within the United States, the active protest against Jim Crow policies and racial discrimination by the civil rights movement highlighted the presence of serious contradictions in American life and suggested that not all was well in the social realm. The emerging pluralism and complexity of American life precludes any thought of uniform lifestyles and cultural patterns of the 1950s (Thompson 2007).

THE CRISIS OF AUTHORITY

By 1960, traditional, conservative values were clearly in conflict with the changes that were occurring in the larger society. Previously, with the large increase in veterans who had served during World War II, conventional morality and tradi-tional norms had lost a great deal of their hold over individual conduct. In the quest for a college education, many veterans came to feel that the regimented values and restrictions on behavior they had experienced in the military had no place on the college campus. Most campuses, including Bowling Green, found that the vets resented rules that had been designed for younger students. But more generally, fundamental changes in student attitudes toward authority were occurring.

In several academic courses in the late 1950s, questions were raised about the crises of authority growing out of World War II. Foremost among them was the academic struggle with the Nazi Holocaust. Why did the German people follow the mandates of the Nazi Party when it was not in their own best interests to do so? How was it possible for a country that had produced some of the world's finest music, philosophy, and literature to also produce Adolph Hitler? The proceedings of the Nuremberg Trials of Nazi war criminals were widely publicized. The defendants, who had participated in the atrocities of the Holocaust, consistently defended themselves on the grounds that they had "just followed orders." This argument held, in effect, that obedience to authority was a form of virtue in all modern bureaucratic and military organizations. The Nuremberg tribunals saw such arguments as inadequate and rejected them (Taylor 1992). Then as now, it was generally recognized that subordinates are obligated to disobey orders if the orders are unethical (Hamilton 1978).

A part of the academic debate at that time was whether the evil of Nazi Germany was of such a magnitude that it was a unique event in the human experience. While some argued uniqueness, others maintained that it was an atrocity of the type that had occurred in many times and places. Following the prosecution of Nazi war criminals and the enactment by the United Nations of the Universal Declaration of Human Rights, Americans were being asked to take a look at the ugliness of their own historical past. This involved particular reference to the atrocities of the institution of slavery and the policy of genocide toward Native Americans in the confiscation of their tribal lands (Barkan 2000).

The crises stemming from obedience to authority were widely discussed in undergraduate classes during the late 1950s and early 1960s. Special emphasis was placed on the study by Theodor Adorno and his associates (1950) called *The Authoritarian Personality.* The Adorno study indicated that an emphasis on conventional morality and authoritarian values was clearly implicated in negative stereotypes and hostilities toward minorities. The policies of racial segregation, discrimination, and Jim Crow were foremost in the consciousness of Bowling Green students at the time of the 1961 uprising. People in positions of power and authority were violating the rights accorded to all citizens by the U.S. Constitution. In some localities, African Americans with college degrees were denied the right to vote for having failed "literacy tests." Lynchings were recent memories.

Following new reflection on totalitarian examples, tyrannical and authoritarian styles of leadership fell by the wayside in all major social institutions. In government, business, education, and other institutional areas, democratic leadership and participatory democracy came to be emphasized. Even the command-obedience structure of the Catholic Church was called into question (Neal 1965). In addition, under the guidance of the influential Dr. Spock, childrearing practices became more permissive and less punitive.

The news reports of the early 1950s were filled with frightening reports of treachery, spies, the advances of Communism, and the development of new atomic weapons. The influence of Senator Joseph McCarthy was in full force during the early part of the 1950s. His game became what we will call a Ponzi Scheme in the next chapter. Charges had been made that Communists had infiltrated the state department, the army, and virtually all of America's basic institutions. While little evidence was found to back these claims, the fear of Communism played an important role in the life of the nation.

The notion that some American citizens had formed a personal allegiance to the Soviet Union to promote international Communism developed into mass hysteria. The international situation seemed so complex that many individuals were uncertain about what they should believe. The jolting experience of World War II had generated a predisposition to believe that anything or everything was a realistic possibility. Political demagogues seized the opportunity to promote their own careers through making outrageous claims about treachery and subversion in American life (Neal 1998).

Levels of anxiety intensified in the early 1950s when President Truman initiated a crash program to develop a hydrogen bomb. He saw this as necessary for keeping ahead of the Russians in the Cold War. However, instead of generating an increased sense of national security, the announcement only intensified awareness of the new forms of destruction. Some of the scientists who worked on the Manhattan Project had had second thoughts about their contribution to the development of the weapons of mass destruction. J. Robert Oppenheimer, the father of the atomic bomb, for example, was strongly opposed to the development of any weapons with increased explosive capability (Bird and Sherwin 2005). Many of the scientists who worked on the making of the atomic bomb suffered intense guilt from their contribution to a project resulting in more than 100,000 civilian deaths at Hiroshima and Nagasaki. They had become brutally aware of the distinction between scientists who developed technology and the government officials who decided what to do with it. Inspired by their concern, the *Bulletin of the Atomic Scientists* created the image of the Doomsday Clock to inform the world what time it was (McCrea and Markle 1989). When the Soviet Union exploded their first atomic bomb, the hands on the clock were moved to three minutes to midnight. When the United States and the Soviet Union in 1953 tested new thermonuclear devices within nine months of each other, the Doomsday Clock's time was moved to two minutes to midnight.

The crisis of authority had become a widespread concern among the younger generation, in their perceptions of the inevitability of a nuclear holocaust, in the nation's fear of international Communism, and in the perceived absurdity of young people's preparing for careers that they might never be able to have. The crisis of authority was expressed in the distrust of government. This distrust grew out of perceptions of politically misplaced priorities, candidates making campaign promises they did not intend to keep, and government officials serving only their own special interests. The protest against authority grew out of the failure of those in positions of power to address the basic problems that surfaced. Attitudes of benign neglect were seen as prominent among those authority figures representing the establishment. Within this context, college students gradually developed their idealism and took it upon themselves to initiate the changes needed to make the world a better place.

In undergraduate education, analyses of society came to be separated from conformity to the status quo. The crisis of authority evident in the Holocaust of Nazi Germany, the massive slaughter of civilians during World War II, and the social injustices of American race relations were among the macro issues that called for new forms of consciousness. Many students developed an interest in revising collective morality and responsibility. Unquestioned obedience to authority was discarded.

TENSIONS FROM THE THREAT OF NUCLEAR WAR

Following World War II, there was initial hope for the international control of nuclear weapons. Such control could take the form of negotiating an agreement to ban nuclear weapons from future warfare, or to ban the proliferation of nuclear weapons among the nations of the world. This possibility quickly receded into the background. The United States was the only nation that had nuclear weapons, and these weapons were seen as trump cards for preventing the Soviet Union from overrunning Western Europe. There seemed to be no feasible mechanism for banning the use of nuclear weapons as instruments of war. The United States had demonstrated not only its capability for making nuclear weapons, but also its willingness to use them when it thought necessary. Following the Soviet detonation of a nuclear device in 1949, the race was on for the development of nuclear capability with increased explosive potential.

The tensions stemming from the threat of nuclear war grew out of a series of questions that could not be answered with confidence: Is nuclear war inevitable? How will a nuclear war start? What is the probability that a nuclear war will start in the next few years? Will there be any advanced warning, or will it start suddenly and unexpectedly? Will it be possible to survive a nuclear war? The uncertainty of the answers to these questions precluded determining the seriousness of the nuclear threat. For most people, the threat of nuclear war was gradually muted as forms of denial and repression were developed. Some Americans downplayed the threat of nuclear war by developing attitudes of fatalism. "Since there is nothing we can do about the world situation, why worry about it?"

Others took a more direct, active approach and were concerned with surviving nuclear war. Rather than succumb to a fatalistic resignation in the face of atomic war, these people believed that individuals could take matters into their own hands (Popkess 1980). Accordingly, during the 1950s a small number of Americans constructed fall-out shelters in their backyards. The shelters were bunker-like constructions covered with several feet of dirt and stocked with a supply of food and water sufficient to survive several days after a nuclear attack. When shelter builders were asked what they would do if neighbors attempted to force their way into the shelter, the response was frequently, "We would have to shoot them."

Several scientists elaborated on the concept of a "nuclear winter" and maintained that there would be no survivors of an all-out nuclear war. The debris released into the atmosphere from the explosions would alter the earth's climate by blocking out rays from the sun. The rapid drop in temperature would soon result in heavy snowfall covering the millions of burned bodies. Drastic environmental changes would occur as temperatures dropped to severely low levels. The plant and animal life upon which humans depend for food would be extinguished (Ehrlich et al. 1984). The disappearance of the dinosaurs after a drastic change in climatic conditions was drawn upon as a precedent.

Appraisals of the aftermath of nuclear war suggested that the planet would become engulfed in a "long darkness" devoid of life forms (Grinspoon 1986). If this ever occurred, the result would be a human absurdity. The technology designed to increase the sense of national security would result in the ultimate insecurity and vulnerability. The nuclear holocaust came to be perceived as a form of self-destruction. The bumper sticker "Better Dead than Red" reflected the desperation growing out of the awareness of the potential for human annihilation. The destruction of civilization, or living under Communism: It was a tragic choice that few Americans were willing to make.

With the many crises that surfaced during the 1950s, latent fears were recurrently brought to the surface. Anxiety levels intensified with the news that the Russians had developed the bomb, with the Russians' launching Sputnik as the first man-made satellite, and with the tensions mounting during the Berlin Airlift. By the end of the decade, we had detonated hydrogen bombs with several times the explosive capability of the bombs dropped on Hiroshima and Nagasaki (Teller 1987). With the doctrine of "mutually assured destruction," the race was on not only for developing increasingly effective weapons but also for increasing the efficiency of the delivery systems. From a military standpoint, history had demonstrated that wars were won by the technologically more efficient war machines. But there was nothing in historical precedent to demonstrate the need for increasing the "overkill capacity" for eliminating every man, woman, and child on this planet.

The research of John E. Mack and Roberta Snow (1986) reported on the anxieties among children and adolescents to do with the threat of nuclear war. The civil defense program in the public schools that called for "duck and cover" exercises had unexpected psychological consequences for children. Many children concluded that because of their school exercises they would survive a nuclear attack but their parents would not. Fears were directed toward "being stuck" and not having anyone to take care of them. While a few adolescents were fascinated with the idea of nuclear weapons, most were strongly anti-nuclear, angry with the older generation for playing with their future and perhaps depriving them of the opportunity to live out normal lives. Typical responses of adolescents reflected a mixture of anger, hopelessness, and helplessness. The majority were doubtful that either they or their country could survive a nuclear war. Very few adolescents expressed an interest in personally making plans for surviving a nuclear war. The mushroom cloud over Hiroshima had become a major symbol of the challenges and dangers of the world in which they lived. The symbolism of the bomb went far beyond its function as a weapon. It had become a device for destroying the world. Nothing humans had ever made before had such tremendous power and destructive ability. In their more solitary moments, students in 1960 who were working on a degree and making long-range plans for a career sometimes became concerned about what they were doing. Why defer immediate gratification in favor of long-range plans if it is all to be ended in the futility of nuclear destruction? Resentments by youth were subsequently translated into attitudes of distrust of established institutions and of those in positions of authority.

CONFRONTING SOCIAL INJUSTICE

Gunnar Myrdal (1944), an eminent Swedish economist, was commissioned by the Carnegie Foundation to make a definitive study of American race relations. His book *An American Dilemma* clarified many of the contradictions inherent in American society. He especially noted violations of the principles of personal liberty and social equality that were deeply embedded in the social heritage of the nation. Such documents as the Declaration of Independence, the Bill of Rights, and the Emancipation Proclamation affirmed the guiding principles of the United States as an egalitarian society, at least in its official self-definitions.

These ideals and guiding principles were blatantly violated in the many facets of deep-seated racism. These violations included the terroristic burning of crosses, churches, and homes, the lynchings initiated by the Ku Klux Klan, and Jim Crow legislation and the many other forms of racial discrimination. Segregated schools, buses, lunch counters, swimming pools, restrooms, and drinking fountains were among the numerous spheres of public life in which the freedom of movement for those of African ancestry was restricted. Such policies were designed to keep blacks in their place and to relegate them to an inferior status in American life.

During the formative years of the college students of the 1960s, the many contradictions in American race relations were brought to the surface. Recognizing the imperative of political action, Harry Truman issued a presidential proclamation on July 26, 1948, mandating the integration of all of the armed forces. Previously, all military units were segregated, and African Americans were either assigned to the most menial of tasks or given unusually dangerous assignments. Through Executive Order 9981, the president established a Committee on Equality of Treatment and Opportunity in the Armed Forces. The president's directive put the armed forces at the forefront of the growing movement to put an end to discriminatory practices in the institutional sectors of public life. The integration of the armed forces was a momentous event in military history and national development.

The blatant forms of discrimination in the public sector of American life were dramatically documented in the landmark Supreme Court decision of 1954. In *Brown v. the Board of Education of Topeka,* the Warren Court overturned the previous ruling on "separate but equal" facilities in the public schools. The Court ruled that all public schools must move with deliberate speed toward integration. Evidence presented to the Court clearly indicated that black schools were not adequately funded and that opportunities for obtaining a quality education were much better in white schools.

At the time of the Court's decision, there were seventeen Southern and border states that enforced laws mandating school segregation. The racism ingrained in institutional practices constituted a major form of resistance to school integration. In defiance of federal orders, Governor Orval Faubus of Arkansas in 1957 called out the National Guard to block black students from entering Little Rock Central High School. After President Eisenhower federalized the National Guard, Little Rock policemen surrounded the school. It was only after 1,200 members of the 101st Airborne Division were assigned to Little Rock to provide protection for black students that the school was integrated.

National awareness of the contradictions and injustices of American race relations was enhanced by the very rapid escalation of television sales during the 1950s. Before the decade was over, ownership or access to television was nearly universal. Visual images were thus added to news reports, and major advances were made in programming and news reporting. An important new dimension was added to informing the nation about itself. On the nightly news, viewers were able to see dramatic depictions of the abuse of authority by law-enforcement officials.

The college students of 1960 were well aware of the news coverage of the resistance to school integration. Public schools in several counties of Virginia were closed rather than integrated, a move that was defined by the federal courts as illegal. Attempts were made to boycott the schools that were integrated in New Orleans. News of resistance to school integration was reported from Alabama, Georgia, Mississippi, and many other places. The abuses of authority in the resistance to school integration received extensive publicity on a worldwide basis.

One of the critical events in triggering the civil rights movement occurred on December 1, 1955, when a Montgomery woman named Rosa Parks was ordered by a bus driver to relinquish her seat to a white man. Rosa Parks had spent a hard day at work and was tired. Attempts by the bus driver to intimidate her were unsuccessful, and she was arrested. The arrest became a focused event that tapped into the resentments over preferential treatment of whites and the requirement that blacks sit only in the back seats of buses (Powledge 1991). Few practices evoked such bitter resentment among blacks as the humiliation of legally sanctioned segregation in public transportation. Jim Crow trains, buses, and streetcars served as a grim reminder to blacks of their inferior status.

The arrest, imprisonment, and conviction of Rosa Parks resulted in meetings of the Montgomery Improvement Association to plan a line of action within the black community. Rather than comply with racial injustice, the association decided to seek remedial action through a bus boycott. The local chapter of the NAACP selected Martin Luther King to provide leadership for the organized protest. During the Montgomery bus boycott, more than 40,000 blacks stayed off the buses for more than a year, vowing not to return until they were desegregated. Boycott carpooling and walking made good television footage, as did the reports on random acts of violence from the white community (Wilkinson 1970). It was this news coverage that thrust Martin Luther King into the spotlight and dramatized the terrorist and repressive measures that were used to deny American citizens their constitutional rights. When the Supreme Court declared racial segregation of buses to be illegal, nonviolent resistance as a viable strategy for social change was confirmed. Students, along with the rest of the nation, followed with interest the unfolding of one of the greatest humanitarian movements of all time. Undoubtedly the Bowling Green student demonstration drew a lot of its moral energy from the bus boycott.

The militancy of the civil rights movement forced Americans to recognize the injustice that had emerged and persisted in a fragmented society. Oppression, exploitation, and physical abuse had promoted routine conditions of fear and anger among African Americans. The central message of the civil rights movement was that the oppressed are not required to silently endure the indignities of their oppression. Through taking direct action and mobilizing group support at the grassroots level, social change is possible.

GENERATIONAL EFFECTS

In the socialization process, those who are most dramatically affected by the changes in their society are those in the formative years. While we cannot say precisely what those years are, they are generally recognized to include the years of late adolescence and early adulthood. The formative years represent the time period in which personal identities are being formed, social norms and values are being internalized, and hopes and aspirations are being shaped for the future.

Among college students in the early 1960s, the three historical developments reviewed in this chapter had dramatic effects on their views of the social world. One consisted of the crisis of authority growing out of the contradictions within the society and the residual effects of World War II. The second consisted of the tensions stemming from the threat of nuclear war and the possibility that social life as it was known and understood would be annihilated. The third was the dramatic effect of the civil rights movement in documenting the injustices and contradictions in the deep-seated racism in American life. These aspects of the moral crisis had the effect of producing in students some degree of estrangement from their own society and the culture it manifested.

The macro changes that were occurring in the larger society had significant implications for the conservatism of northwest Ohio. For example, congressmen from the Bowling Green and Findlay area were consistently rated among the top conservatives in the House of Representatives in terms of both party standing and voting record. The area was conservative in its religious beliefs as well. Both President McDonald and his predecessor, Frank Prout, believed in the importance of religion and conventional morality in turning graduates of the university into educated persons. The rule of compulsory student attendance at chapel was not dropped from the university handbook until after 1938. The regulations built into the student code were highly conservative for a modern and rapidly developing university. Many of the rules on student conduct had lost their appropriateness in view of the dramatic secular changes that were occurring in the larger society.

The emphasis on rules and regulations seemed to reflect a desire to promote uniformity and standardization among students. This stood in contrast to later models on university campuses advocating heterogeneity and diversity within the faculty and in student populations. The value placed on uniformity in behavior, values, and lifestyles was supplemented by a student body composed primarily of students from upper-middle-class families residing in northwest Ohio. What was missing from the uniformity model was the very kind of diversity that serves to encourage creativity and novelty. There was no attempt on the part of the university to recruit minorities, international students, or nontraditional students.

The new generation of students entering the university, however, had been socialized into a different set of values. For example, Dr. Benjamin Spock's (1960) advice on childrearing had been widely read and applied by the parents of the college students of 1960. Spock's book *Baby and Child Care,* initially published in 1946, sold more than 50 million copies and was one of the bestselling nonfiction books ever published. Dr. Spock's book focused on the emotional and physical development of the child. Parents were advised to be flexible and affectionate with their children and to treat them as individuals, rather than to emphasize discipline and obedience to authority. Spock advised parents to take pleasure in watching their children grow and develop and to appreciate a child's spontaneity. The values instilled in childhood for this generation were antithetical to the emphasis on traditionalism, conventional morality, and obedience to an oppressive set of rules and regulations.

Faculty members who had received their graduate education at Ohio State or at other universities throughout the country were surprised at the homogeneity they noted on campus in terms of social class, race, and ethnicity but not gender. The selective admissions policy of the university assured that the freshman class would be composed of an equal number of men and women. This policy was subsequently declared unconstitutional because women with higher test scores were being denied admission in favor of men.

The attempt of McDonald's regime to promote religious fundamentalism stood in opposition to an academic emphasis on critical inquiry, rationality, and the scientific method. Notions about collective morality and responsibility were superseding concepts of personal morality. Outmoded forms of personal morality were being replaced by a growing social consciousness that morality concerned such collective issues as racism, poverty, and nuclear war (Lance 1966).

Other problems developed among students from Catholic backgrounds. According to the demographics of northwest Ohio, a substantial percent of the students at BGSU were from Catholic families. They were products of the baby boom generation and were keenly aware of the pressure on their parents from the mandates of the Church on birth-control issues. The consequences of having to live with an exceedingly large number of siblings and the observation of the strain on their parents to raise a large number of unplanned children were central to their social consciousness. A crisis of authority surfaced when the Church refused to bend its position on birth control, even after the introduction of the birth control pill. By 1960, many younger Catholics had already resolved to disobey the authority of the Church on the issues of sexuality, birth control, and family planning (Groat, Kniseley, and Neal 1975). They had decided to make major life decisions on the basis of what they saw as being in their own best interests. Many of the rules of a fundamentalist Christian tradition were regarded as out of place in the modem world. Local Catholic religious leaders waged a vendetta against the presumed atheism of the philosophy department and the evils of the secular approach in the sociology department. Yet the philosophy and sociology departments were attracting an increasing number of Catholic students, and the verbal assaults by local priests fell on deaf ears.

The generalized sense of discontent among students led some to be sympathetic to the early phases of the counterculture that emerged during the 1950s. The Beat Generation, the movies of the decade, and the new forms of music provided important referents for young people searching for a personal identity in an age of discontent. For example, the troubled life of James Dean struck a chord among many young people. His image was summed up in his famous movie *Rebel Without a Cause.* The youth of the nation were able to identify with this sensitive adolescent who was struggling with self-discovery and the pressures of living in a world promoting conformity. The anxieties growing out of the larger society were added to the stress of the large number of life decisions young people are always required to make. While late adolescence and early adulthood is a time of increasing independence and freedom of movement, it is also one of the more stressful stages of life. A large number of consequential life decisions must be made within a compressed time frame. These include decisions relating to becoming sexually active or remaining a virgin, continuing or terminating one's formal education, selecting a career, entering the labor force, getting married, and becoming a parent. While these decisions are compressed into only a few years in early adulthood, they have consequences that extend throughout a lifetime. A failure to make these decisions is not an option. If these choices are not consciously and deliberately made, they will be made by default through a process of social drift.

The stress implicit in a large number of vital choices is also accompanied by special problems associated with early adulthood in our society. The weakening of tradition and the crisis of authority that goes along with psychological modernity have thrown the individual back on his or her own resources in times of critical decision-making. Attempts to clarify these special problems have been the focus of several classical writings in the social sciences. For example, Erich Fromm's (1951) *Escape from Freedom* addressed the historical increase of loneliness and isolation within the general population. While an increase in personal freedom is an overall development of the modern world, it is of special relevance for late adolescence and early adulthood. Elaborating an adult identity calls for breaking away from the family of origin, having a place of residence separate from one's parents, and becoming financially independent. While such freedom is associated with expanding opportunities, for many young adults it results in intense feelings of loneliness and isolation. Humans are indeed social animals, and they require some degree of membership and belonging for a sense of well-being.

David Riesman and his associates (1950) used the metaphor of "the lonely crowd" to describe the conditions of modernity. His thesis held that during the nineteenth century, children were socialized to have internalized values that would serve to guide and direct their behavior in adult life. In coining the concept of "other-directedness," Riesman maintained that in the twentieth century individuals developed much more flexible personality types and oriented their behavior toward the cues that were available in their immediate environment. "The lonely crowd" notion referred to the sense of homelessness that derived from the lack of a clear identity or commitment to a clear set of values.

In the writings of Ruth Benedict, an emphasis was placed on the lack of continuity between the norms and behavior patterns emphasized in childhood and those required for success in adult life. For example, family and religious values frequently focus on the importance of asexuality and sexual abstinence, while success in intimate relationships as adults requires sexual responsiveness; children are valued for obedience and dependency, while adults are expected to be skilled in exercising independent and critical judgment. Thus, Benedict maintained, the transition to adulthood is stressful because of the contradictions and inconsistencies experienced by young adults (Mead 1974).

A major challenge to normative authority grew out of the publications by Alfred Kinsey and his associates (1948; 1953) of the results of their empirical studies on human sexuality. Prior to the Kinsey studies, sexual matters were primarily covert and unmentionable in public discourse. The authority of the normative order held that sexual intercourse was to be limited to married heterosexual couples. All other overt expressions of sexuality were taboo. The responses to the Kinsey studies, particularly among college students, brought the many aspects of sexuality out into the public arena for reflection and discussion.

The Kinsey studies documented several aspects of human sexuality that were not generally known. Among them was the finding that masturbation was widespread among both males and females, that bisexuality was more widespread than was generally recognized, and that a substantial number of both males and females had had homosexual experiences to orgasm. While there has been criticism of Kinsey's methods and of the specific percentages he reports, it is clear that what was previously defined as deviant, extraordinary, and abnormal was in reality widespread and a part of the normal differences in human behavior and experience. In the recognizing of the many forms of sexual expression, sex came to be no longer thought of primarily in terms of marriage and reproduction. Instead, sexuality was recognized as a variable and natural physiological process, part of our biological heritage as animals.

The different human expressions of sexual behavior became topics of conversation in college dormitories as students concentrated on developing their personal sexual identities. While the Kinsey studies had an impact on social awareness among college students, it was the subsequent development of the youthful counterculture and the introduction of the birth control pill that had a primary impact on their sexual behavior patterns.

This crisis of authority had emerged from religious and ethical mandates that were out of alignment with physiological predispositions and urges. Changes in the rules had left many people at a loss to know the boundaries of acceptable sexual conduct in everyday life (Michael et al. 1994). All societies are required to regulate sexual behavior in some way. It was through developments in popular culture, mass entertainment, and commercial advertising that traditional sexual values were replaced by the emerging rights of individuals.

Each generation is required to take the social heritage from the past and rework it to fit the needs of their own time and place. The emergence of a particular type of youth culture was one of the reactions of young people to the events of a turbulent decade. Aspects of the counterculture were centered in the sexual revolution and in perspectives from the Beat Generation that surfaced in San Francisco. Some of the basic norms and values of society were turned upside down. A positive value was placed on extramarital and premarital sex, taking illegal drugs, and rejecting the lifestyles of the American middle class. Before the counterculture ran its course, it circled the globe and embraced many members of the generation (Feuer 1969).

The Beat Generation was a relatively small group of writers during the late 1950s whose novels and poetry stood in sharp contrast to what they saw as the emphasis on conformity in the society around them. Prominent in the group were Jack Kerouac, Alan Ginsberg, and William S. Burroughs. In contrast to Erich Fromm's emphasis on escape from freedom, John H. Schaar (1961) described this group as characterized by an escape from authority. Their lifestyles were bohemian and epicurean. Their literary work emphasized spontaneity, open emotion, visceral engagement, and gritty, worldly experiences. The controversy surrounding their lifestyles and written work grew out of their advocacy of nonconformity and the positive value they placed on socially disapproved behavior. In effect, they advocated what some regarded as criminal behavior, questioned the legitimacy of authority, and sought to promote lifestyles of experimentation with sex and drugs.

STUDENT IDEALISM

In response to the crisis of authority that developed during the 1950s, students became actively involved in the political process. Reflecting on the unique character of their time and place, they became dissatisfied with what they saw. Congruent with the views of C. Wright Mills (1956), students were disenchanted with the defining characteristics of their time and place, with the men who held key positions of power, and with the direction in which history was moving. Personal lives were being linked with historical circumstances.

Students developed what Gwynn Nettler (1957) described as "a sense of estrangement from their society and the culture it manifested." The future as an extension of the past and the present was regarded as unacceptable. The liberal idealism of Michael Harrington (1962), John F. Kennedy, and Martin Luther King provided a clear focus to their concerns. Kennedy and Harrington were among the forward-looking idealists invited to deliver addresses at Bowling Green. The idealism of the liberal Left offered persuasive appeals to the youth of the nation (Neal 1970). Its emphasis on democratic values were accompanied by direct plans for remedial action.

The rhetoric of the 1960 presidential campaign included the theme of a new frontier, of being on the threshold of a bright new era. The youth of the nation had seen Eisenhower as symbolic of the establishment and as a representative of the status quo. By way of contrast, Kennedy, as the first president to be born in the twentieth century, conveyed the image of the ideal man with the ideal family. In his inaugural address, Kennedy declared, "The torch has been passed to a new generation." The youth of the nation were caught up in his idealism and his emphasis on making the world a better place. Kennedy's inauguration symbolized a new beginning and suggested the prospect of an American future that would be compatible with the personal aspirations of students.

The inspiration for political activism also came from the leadership of Martin Luther King in the civil rights movement. In mobilizing a constituency, Martin Luther King drew upon the Constitution and the Declaration of Independence to document the default on democratic values and the basic rights of all citizens. He elaborated an effective set of tactics and strategies for bringing about social change. Through deliberately violating Jim Crow laws and discriminatory practices, the tranquility of everyday life could be disturbed, and glaring injustices could be demonstrated. Such strategies were drawn upon by students in other social protests and efforts to bring about social change.

In the late fifties and early sixties, students from Bowling Green, as well as from campuses across the country, went to the segregated areas of the South to participate in freedom rides, lunch-counter sit-ins, and voter registration programs. They were willing to take chances with their personal safety to make a contribution toward the attainment of their ideals. The nation became indignant watching events portrayed on television, as mob action was directed toward peaceful demonstrators with the police looking passively on. The excessive use of force by law-enforcement officials became symbolic of oppression and injustice.

With the many divisive issues of the late fifties and early sixties, the nation became highly fragmented. The liberal ideologies of students, the Kennedy administration, and the civil rights movement clashed with the emerging repression of counterinsurgency groups on the radical Right.

We have now shown how the fifties produced the sixties. Social problems which were "babies" in the fifties grew into fully grown issues in the sixties. We singled out the problems of understanding Nazi Germany, coping with the Cold War, and appreciating the African American rebellion as major sources for what became the consciousness of the sixties. In some ways the fifties were passive and choked by anti-Communism. But in other ways the fifties produced a rising concern for a moral transformation; this ache for a moral revolution was first seen in the Bowling Green rebellion, and it continued to infuse the protest currents of the sixties.

Chapter 10

An Overdetermined Conclusion

Some possibilities get so ripe and ready they become over-caused or overdetermined. Hitler started World War II looking like a winner. Defeating France and kicking the British off the Continent at Dunkirk seemed like the beginning of the end for his opponents. But when the Brits bounced back, stopping the German air force in the Blitz of summer 1940 (Korda 2009), just weeks after the Dunkirk debacle, the momentum was broken and the handwriting was on the wall. "Hitler will lose," it said. And by spring of 1945 there were so many forces coming at the Germans they could have been defeated ten times over. Their loss was drastically overdetermined.

History is full of these unexpected routs, and the case we are looking at is one of them. As soon as the dean squared off with the crowd at the water fight, McDonald was doomed. You could feel it in the air as the fraternity boys fought their hearts out, entertaining the buoyant crowd of onlookers. Crowds were not allowed on this campus, but once one formed you could tell something would happen. As McDonald pointed out in his speech to the faculty, he would call the Ohio State Patrol when a questionable crowd had gathered. This time he sent a dean to do the dispersing, after the crowd had defied the campus police's order to break up. The crowd felt its power and was ready to go. All it needed was a spark to transform itself from an audience into what Bowling Green people called a riot. As we pointed out, *riot* means "roar," and roar it did.

The spark was the fraternity pledge's sneaking up behind Dean Taylor and hitting him on the head with a bag of water. This was such an outrageous, aggressive act that the audience was immediately changed into a political crowd. The boldness of this pledge had emboldened them. Once the crowd was formed

159

and moved into a protest mode, the rest was inevitable. The 1957 demonstration, dramatic as it was, had been a hollow ritual. It had no effect on the power relation between students and administration. But four years later the civil rights movement had taken center stage, Kennedy was raising a lot of hopes, and the civil liberties–civil disobedience culture of the sixties was in the air. This time the crowd had an unconscious that was full of these new currents, and it was just a matter of time before these new forces sprang into consciousness. When, on the second night, the two reverends introduced such ideas as grievances, civil rights, and tactical options, the culture of the sixties descended upon the students and the movement toward a campus victory was unstoppable. In McDonald's speech he spoke with distaste of the word *grievance,* and of the "oh-so-well-intentioned" speakers who had introduced the idea.

What had happened was that a campus that was secretly imbued with the blue-laws morality of its idiosyncratic president (the secret protected by drastic rules against snitching in public) had reached the end of the road. The secret was so powerful, the resentment of the students was so energized, and the historical moment was so ripe that all this had to explode. The way this explosion played out is described in our book. One thing led to another, and the culmination was in the resignation of the overconfident president. Some months later at a retreat for the BGSU administration, these grown men and women had an interlude in which they sang "Ding Dong the Witch Is Dead." Or so went the rumor. This rumor may have no more truth than the one about McDonald setting the prices at the candy counter. But sometimes myths have more meaning than the truth. In any case, this was a classic example of an overdetermined defeat.

A complex of waves hit the administration, each itself enough to cause defeat. It is not easy to disentangle this network of waves, but we will distinguish the following forces: feminism, disgruntled alumni, humanism, breezes from the sixties, and the collapse of a political Ponzi scheme.

Feminism. When a substantial community of women is unhappy about something, when there is a wave of feminist anger, it is not a good idea to get in the way of that wave. One of the forces that mowed down the McDonald administration was the early awakening of women's liberation. Historically, women had spearheaded the French (1789) and the Russian (1917) revolutions, in both cases proving the gutsier gender. They were at least as active as men in the Bowling Green uprising.

It should be remembered that the in loco parentis rules, on the basis of which colleges and universities attempted to control the personal morality of students, were used mainly to control women students. *In loco parentis* meant keeping girls on a leash. The various rules about dress, hours, dorm visits, alcohol, and cars, and the more slippery ones about expression of affection, were primarily restrictions on women students. To a great extent male students were regulated indirectly through control of women.

Before World War II these rules about women were acceptable to almost everyone. But as the late forties and then the fifties progressed, these rules became outdated and began to be recognized as restrictions on women's civil liberties. This means student protest in the sixties was largely a matter of liberating women, even though women's liberation as a formal social movement did not begin until the late sixties. Race relations, the Vietnam War, and poverty, to name a few, were also sixties issues. But a staple issue, and one that released vast amounts of student energy, was the simple matter of freeing up women to be adults.

How the feminist issue was handled varied from campus to campus. But since the BG administration was so extreme in their control of women, the issue popped open early on this campus. The McDonald administration's rules about alcohol and the expression of affection interfered with the private lives of students, and with the dating system in particular. These rules cast a pall of guilt and shame over the entire student body, particularly the women. Being human meant being bad, and being female meant attracting trouble. In particular, dating became more difficult, requiring sneaking around (e.g., making the twenty-mile drive to Toledo, where it was safer to drink, and then driving back to campus on a narrow, dangerous two-lane road; or kissing a date goodnight in a surreptitious way so as not to be turned in for an ethical lapse). Remember, dating is largely a women's game. It is the way guys court girls. College is, among other things, a place for the sexes to mingle and form pairs. At the present time, college is also a place for gays and lesbians to meet, but our case goes back several decades. For the women at that time and place, it was a way of falling in love, becoming engaged, and getting married.

This process involved increasing emotional and sexual intimacy. Before the sixties, young men were having their sexual experiences largely with prostitutes and a small minority of "bad girls." But once the sixties started, women began to catch up with men sexually; that is, the percentage of women having premarital sex began to approach that of men and eventually reached it. Sex, which was increasingly happening with the "girl next door," was now changing morally, from bad to (more or less) good. The psychology or meaning of sex was also changing, from a detached physiological experience to an encounter with the personhood of another human being. In other words, sex, as the sixties began, was finally being normalized. Any attempt to interfere with the relations between boys and girls was another futile effort to push back the tides of time.

To stigmatize the goodnight kiss and the holding of hands, suggesting they were tasteless or morally tainted, was an insult to the growing surge of feminism. The grievances concerning alcohol and the expression of affection were considered weak issues by the students, and maybe they were weak in the public arena. But the psychological meaning of these issues, especially for the female students, was anything but weak. During the protest itself women were right out there with the men. And they were not hesitant to talk to the press. As has been stated, five of the nine students who protested to the Senate and House committees on education were women

More generally, the mistake that McDonald and Bowling Green made was to overlook the fact that the 1960s would be the decade in which the liberation of women took off. It wasn't until 1970 that women's liberation reached the front page of *Time* and became an everyday talking point, but by 1960 the pot was already percolating.

The changing demography of women, as mentioned earlier, was part of this. By 1960 the divorce rate was going up, placing more women in need of jobs. Birth control (both the diaphragm and the pill) was becoming increasingly widespread. And the idea that women should control their own bodies was being voiced.

These trends were all at an early stage in spring 1961, but they were moving in the opposite direction from the McDonald administration. It was the beginning of a wave, but a massive wave of social change nevertheless. And the McDonald administration had placed itself squarely in the path of that wave.

Unhappy Alumni. A second cause of McDonald's defeat was the presence of disgruntled Bowling Green alumni in influential organizations. We printed part of William Day's letter explaining the 1949 demonstration. Writing for the *Toledo Blade,* the most important newspaper in BGSU's hinterland, he fully understood what was happening during the protest of 1961. The Block family, who owned the paper, took Day from this coverage when it became clear he could have a conflict of interest, but he still had indirect influence. The day McDonald resigned, Day told us, McDonald phoned Day and accused him of having caused his resignation. But Day was only the most obvious case. The rural Ohio press slowly turned against McDonald from week to week. And it seems quite likely that among these writers and their friends were included many unhappy Bowling Green graduates.

When Donnell the trustee assembled the Bowling Green alumni who worked for him at Marathon Oil, he was told negative stories about McDonald and the university. These unhappy BG alumni turned Donnell from a supporter of McDonald to a critic.

And the state legislature, which voted all but unanimously against McDonald, included BG alumni. So all in all, as the institutions of Ohio sat in judgment of the McDonald administration, this administration was given a thoroughly negative evaluation. We are not suggesting that these alumni allowed their unhappy experiences at Bowling Green to get in the way of truth. On the contrary, they knew more about Bowling Green than the average Ohio citizen, so they were actually closer to the truth.

Humanism. We are using the term *humanism* to refer to a complex of forces that elevate the human person to *a,* if not *the,* major value. When you have separation of church and state, humanism is the ethic of democracy. There was a student association of humanists on the Bowling Green campus at the time of the 1961 demonstration. These students attempted to gain a place on the campus Committee on Religion, which consisted of representatives of Protestantism, Catholicism, and Judaism. The humanists argued that they too were a religion. They also suggested that the separation between church and state required that they be included on this committee. President McDonald, who made all decisions of this nature, refused their request. So of course the student humanists were loudly vocal about the church-state issue on campus.

Both McDonald and his ally Father Ollivier flirted with defying the church-state distinction, and some of the legislators in Columbus were uncomfortable about this.

Quite a few of the faculty were also agnostics and atheists, despite McDonald's attempt to keep them off the faculty. These professors resented the religious tone McDonald had given to the campus, and they felt McDonald should not hold the office he held. Many of the one-third-liberal faculty were from this belief group, and they did what they could to weaken the McDonald administration.

Several of these professors, during the time of the demonstrations, went to the ACLU to initiate complaints against the McDonald administration, particularly concerning the mixing of church and state and the blackballing of nonreligious professors. McDonald resigned before these complaints were given much attention, but the newspaper story about the investigation called attention to the civil-liberties problems at Bowling Green.

In the state of Ohio generally there were also humanistic influences. Not every Ohio citizen was a religious believer. And the Jewish community, while obviously not nonreligious, could see that the church-state transgressions were not in their interest. For the "church" in question would be a Christian one.

Breezes from the Sixties. Once the protesting students got into a sixties state of mind, they completely outdistanced the administration in the race for control. The administration was still fighting with fifties bows and arrows, so to speak, while the students had sixties guns, and some pretty big ones at that.

The students, as we explained, had found civil rights, civil disobedience, civil liberties, feminism, and the Kennedy-King mystique. The administration was still using heavy-handed punitive measures and old-fashioned rules, including the unwritten ones. Then the administration got into a pattern of indecision, offering the carrot and then going back to the stick. McDonald wanted to use reform to win his battle, but his heart was not in it and he did not use this tactic consistently.

In Chapter 3 we contrasted the organizational power that Durkheim called organic solidarity with the communal or moral solidarity he called mechanical. Organization was a fifties weapon, and moral solidarity was the new sixties weapon. In a complete (e.g., a Nazi or Stalinist) dictatorship, organization will win every time, for it will simply machine-gun the opposition. Let Mario Savio jump onto the gears. We'll just grind him into hamburger and throw him to the dogs! But in a democracy you can't shoot people easily. You have to meet them on their terms. Organic solidarity, as in the McDonald university machine, cannot cope with moral solidarity. That's why McDonald milled around like King Lear in the night, while the students walked away with the trophy.

Collapse of a Ponzi Scheme. The McDonald regime fell quickly and decisively because it had weak foundations. It looked impressive, but it was built on sand. It was a political version of Charles Ponzi's famous investment scam of the early 1920s. When McDonald's wobbly structure, like Ponzi's, was pushed, it simply collapsed. In the original economic sense, "a Ponzi scheme is an investment fraud that involves the payment of purported returns to existing investors from funds contributed by new investors" (U.S. Securities and Exchange Commission website). A Ponzi scheme in general (i.e., the common denominator between the economic and political versions) is an organizational structure that is heavily in debt, in the broad sense of the word, but that hides this debt by constantly recruiting new resources, doing this by promising more than it can deliver. It is obvious how this works in a business-investment venture, but the political version is more complex and not widely understood.

Senator Joe McCarthy, notorious for "McCarthyism," was the best example of a political Ponzi scheme. In 1950 it looked as though he might not be reelected in 1952 to his U.S. Senate seat from Wisconsin. To gain more voter favor, he claimed, in a public speech, to have a list containing the names of numerous Communists who worked for the State Department. This was supposed to be a list of fifty-seven people, although on occasion he used larger numbers. At this jittery time in American history, his claim caused a sensation and increased his popularity. But when there were enough calls for him to disclose the list, and he sensed his power slipping away, he claimed that those questioning him were also subversives. Later, when further pressed, he claimed to have an even longer list. His successive lists were like Charles Ponzi's (or Bernie Madoff's) waves of investment. Each wave was fraudulent and could be paid for only by a constant influx of new resources. Every new list and new threat allowed him to "borrow" more power, although these debts had time limits and his scheme kept getting more complicated and shakier. Finally, in the Army-McCarthy hearings of 1954, the Army's attorney James Welch deflated McCarthy's Ponzi scheme. At this point McCarthy was claiming the list contained 130 names of Communists or subversives not in the State Department but in defense plants. Attorney Welch publicly challenged McCarthy to disclose the list "before the sun goes down," using the same dramatic tactics that McCarthy had used. McCarthy could not meet this challenge, and in this way he was shown publicly, on TV, to actually have no lists. His tactics were also shown to be bullying and in violation of civil liberties. As a result of the Army hearings McCarthy's political house of cards quickly fell. This fall included a censure by the Senate later that year.

Ralph McDonald had a similar power scheme. His resources were successive waves of incoming students, their tuition, the appropriations of the legislature, and what seemed to be satisfied graduating classes and loyal alumni. What had to be kept quiet, to keep this loop intact, was the intense dissatisfaction of the students and the secret system of threats and punishments that kept the public from knowing about this dissatisfaction. There was also some pluralistic ignorance in which the students did not actually know how widespread and intense this dissatisfaction was. McDonald's secrecy functioned like McCarthy's threats to his critics and like Charles Ponzi's secret profit-and-loss books. These practices kept the lid on.

When the BG students at the water fight became a protesting crowd the secret was revealed. The suppressed information began to pour out of the campus, and the lid, which had kept the loop functioning, flew off. The press and the legislature would now see how morally bankrupt the campus actually was, and McDonald's Ponzi scheme would fall of its own weight.

The five factors we have mentioned were intertwined. They operated together. This was why McDonald fell so fast and so decisively. When McDonald insulted the legislature for considering the bill to expand his board of trustees, suggesting that he had delusions of grandeur, he verified all the rumors about the campus. He also caused the acceleration of all five of the forces listed above, embracing his own dissolution.

We have now shown that the forces against the McDonald administration were far too much for it to do battle with. The administration did not know what was hitting them or where the blows were coming from. Their defeat was overdetermined.

Appendix A

Statement on Student Grievances

WE WANT TO BE

A. Individual Expression

The University has traditionally been the center of such creativity and expression.

B. We desire the possibility for such expression.

High academic standards would eliminate (or at least delimit) the necessity for such a myriad of regulatory rules. Is the rule to be more important than the individual?

C. We object against the idea that every phase of our life is being compartmentalized so as to make us feel little more than machines. We feel that the rules should be studied and that their purposes be evaluated.

D. We are being handed a "package-deal" education, which might fit into our society but into which we, as individuals, cannot fit. We are not interested in abandoning rules in favor of anarchy. We are concerned that rules have been deified such that individuality has been eclipsed.

E. The rules have been used to establish an "air of purity" which is quasi-existent.

F. Students will only act as mature as they are treated.

Effective Communication must be established within the academic community.

A. All present communication is one way—from the top down.

B. We want dialogue—two way communication.

We feel that the *BG News,* which is a source of communication in appearance only, is an example of the one-sidedness of communication. It should be made an organ of this free dialogue and expression.

THIS IS THE TIME TO BE—IT IS NOW THAT WE MUST BECOME

The faculty, being the heart of any university, ought to have the controlling voice on policies impinging on the educational process and on their own rights as individuals! Policies ought never to be something handed down by the administration.

Appendix B

President McDonald's Address to the Faculty

There are three sets of notes concerning this speech in the university archives. The authors are unknown. We consolidated the three in a way that seems as close as anyone could get to the original address. Still, this version probably reads less smoothly than the original rendition. Explanatory comments are inserted, as needed.

Last night we had to resort to drastic action (declaring a state of emergency) we had hoped to avoid. We had been advised that students from other colleges and universities, whose records indicated they would be welcomed absentees, would be on our campus last night. Since there were indications there were several campuses involved, it appears there must have been some organization and communication.

Later in the evening there was some justification for this belief. On the campus were six from one institution and one each from two or three others. Under the circumstances you can see the kind of situation we might have faced. Many students had completed mid-terms by Friday, and they had nothing to do. A partial vacuum existed on campus for them.

Sunday was the most wonderful, balmy day of the year. And fraternity pledging was completed. Some of the fraternities were trying to bring their new members into a feeling of fellowship. Sigma Chi pledges and actives engaged in a water fight. This is a sight to behold, and an audience was soon there. The fraternity leaders eventually stopped the water fight but the observers wanted it to go on. Dean Taylor asked the fraternity to stop, and they did. But a substantial number of students had gathered. The time had to be filled with something.

One part of the crowd went to Founders. Someone said let's go in. When a larger than normal group gathers on campus we inform the Ohio State Patrol as a matter of routine. From experience in dealing with students, they recognize that the sooner the group can be dispersed, the better.

Founders doors were locked. Probably the first one said let's go uptown. More and more chimed in. I was in the Carnation Room in the Student Union until 7:15 p.m. I laughed in front of the Union with a good natured group. We chatted. It looked as though some activity would take place. They were talking and laughing. I asked, what's going on? Someone said, we had a water fight at the Row. I asked what's happening up here?

Some boys in a small group started chanting, "We want beer." I said, you're talking to the wrong person. They laughed. One boy said, Why do girls have to go in so early? I used to be that age myself, and I wondered too. I said, I don't know. I don't even know what time they have to be in. It's up to the Association of Women Students. A girl said, AWS doesn't do that. I said, I don't know then, because the authority is delegated to them.

In front of the library another group asked about the ATO housemother (fired for not reporting some students who broke a rule). I replied, Why don't you ask her. Other questions concerned early dormitory hours. The group was still well behaved. They left and I returned to the concert.

The president then talked about the effects of news reports. He had listened to the 8:00 a.m. news, WSPD by Jim Uberhart. Uberhart talked in terms of a riot on campus. McDonald had also heard a Walter Johns interview. He said this particular broadcast was an example of the worst kind of news abuse—"The fact that they claimed objects were thrown was sheer fabrication and contrary to the mood of the crowd. [The "object thrown" probably refers to the water balloon, with which the Sigma Chi pledge hit the dean. One of the authors actually saw this happen, so McDonald is evidently prevaricating at this point.] Then 'grievances' came into the picture. Words like riot, mob and grievances were hammered home by the press, radio and TV. There are students on campus for whom this kind of talk is music." He then praised Deans Taylor, Whitaker and Smith for their wisdom and understanding.

At 5:00 p.m. Monday there were 500 to 600 students who went downtown, including those who wanted to start something, some who were purely spectators and some by now concerned about the word "grievances." Sunday it was spring fever, but on Monday I didn't know what to expect. Still there was no violence. The group returned to campus Monday evening and got an audience. They went to the President's house. No property damage, only blocked traffic, in which case the blockers were arrested.

Several hundred finally wound up at the Union. Then oh-so-well-intentioned but inexperienced individuals (Rev. Trautwein and Professor Stanage, both acting as preachers) took over. When the loud speaker was set up in front of the Union, it gave a reason for students to stay there. Grievances grew, and that night the blueprint for Tuesday was made. Dean Smith predicted that on Tuesday 200 to 300 students would boycott classes.

Some professors advised students that professors would not mark them as absent if they skipped classes. These misinformed students just decided then that they would have a vacation. But classes were going on. In the afternoon attendance was normal, even above normal. Students were growing weary of the demonstration. Student and faculty councils passed resolutions. Meanwhile the authorities had decided on a course of action because of the outsiders. The hard core was no longer attracting the students, and they would have to resort to other methods.

Tuesday evening after the state of emergency was declared, about 50 students and others who resisted directions given by peace officers were detained. The President then discussed things that were asked of him Sunday and Monday— things that could not be changed, such as drinking rules.

He said he told students, "We assume you are mature enough to decide for yourself whether you will be inconvenienced by not drinking and by being required to attend classes. I assume you exercised mature judgment in accepting BGSU. You are just as free to attend other institutions as you were free to enroll at Bowling Green. We put in the catalogue a clear statement of policy and you're asked to consider thoroughly whether this university climate is what you want." And then he quoted the catalogue about the drinking regulation, thinking it over with parents, etc.

One boy said to him, "I don't drink but I'm opposed to the rule on principle."

I said, You've never had a drunken roommate? Well I have. Some students come here and drink anyway. What would you do if your roommate was drunk. This would disrupt your schooling.

What about class attendance? The state of Ohio has a certain number of dollars invested in their classrooms, from $2.60 to 2.70 for that one hour for one person to occupy that seat. You asked to be enrolled so you could sit there. If you don't want to be, someone who has been turned down could have gone. In the beginning grievances consisted of beer and early hours for women. And later, high sounding issues. Regulations are essential if we want to be fair.

The fundamental, underlying problem, the basic factor, is one which makes me increasingly pessimistic. We are a university with 6,000 students who must daily use a library only big enough for about 1,500. Thus we need a system of rules for the library. Students must be packed and squeezed into some buildings. Some professors have classes of 50 and 60 in rooms suitable only for 30.

There is a shortage of educational space due to the number of students and the amount of floor space. We have been lacking adequate facilities since 1939. We are growing too fast. The shortage of space is increasing precipitously. Enrollment demands ever more. We have only one source for capital improvements—state appropriations. From 1954 to 1959 one fifth of all the increased enrollment in the state took place at Bowling Green. Yet Bowling Green was allocated only 10 percent of the money. From 1954 to 1959 we had an increase of 2,300 students. We have increased three times the average of the other state universities. We should have 50 percent more faculty members, and we could use double. The students cannot see enough of their professors outside of classes, now.

Year after year we have pleaded with the general assembly for money. We have been advised, however, that no money is available. Ohioans have more money for anything they want to do, but they don't want to pay taxes to support higher education. It is a terrible thing to say. Members of the General Assembly will do anything for Bowling Green and higher education except vote for more taxes. They believe they were elected for just that reason, not to increase taxes.

With so many students, it is inevitable that we should have tension. Space constraints cause regulation which can cause riots. For while they are wonderful students, they are put under constant pressure. That is why I am depressed. The tiny regulations are the ones that beset the students. But there is no way we can operate without systematizing.

Concerning crowdedness, McDonald said, "We should take a lesson from the old lady who lived in a shoe and had so many children she didn't know what to do. So she spanked them all soundly and sent them to bed.

"It is a terrible thing to have to exercise responsibility." McDonald "prays every night that he will be relieved of it, if it is the will of God, when difficult decisions are at stake."

He said that when the students returned, the faculty should exert an influence that protected the institutional atmosphere.

Some students have said some of the professors are in league with them, that they will not check class attendance. But they will become what you encourage them to be. The demonstration so far has been orderly and non-violent. This is because the students are from good homes and because they are in daily contact with a faculty that influences them well.

Appendix C

Interview with Robert Brinza on the Student Trip to the Legislature

INTERVIEWED BY NORBERT WILEY

I met with Robert Brinza on March 7, 1998, for about two hours over lunch to discuss the BGSU student demonstrations of spring 1961. We met at the Fog City Diner, a legendary restaurant on the San Francisco waterfront. Bob had been one of the nine or so Bowling Green students who visited the state legislature on April 3, 1961, just a few days after the demonstrations themselves. The students met with the House and Senate education committees to present their grievances with the university.

Bob had not thought much about the Bowling Green story for a long time, but he had read our manuscript and had done a lot of preparation for this interview. By the time we met he had remembered a great deal of what had happened, and as we talked he remembered more. For a long time he has been a computer programmer in San Francisco, a general rather than an applied one, and his analytic skills showed in the interview.

Bob was easy to talk to. Although the story was intense, he was neither highly emotional nor emotionally flat. He was just right for the situation, and he had a lot of facts at his disposal. He had also known some of the important professors in this story. In the years after the demonstration he had taken several reading courses in English literature from Dick Carpenter, one of the leaders of the liberal faculty, so he knew him well. He had also taken philosophy courses from Tom Tuttle, a somewhat idiosyncratic bachelor professor. Tuttle liked to go to concerts in Toledo, but he rarely got to, because he could not drive. He worked out a plan with Brinza where Bob would drive him to the concert and Tom would pay for Bob's ticket and dinner—at a Chinese place they both liked. After Bob switched his major from English to philosophy he also took courses from Sherman Stanage. He spoke of being at an ACLU meeting at Sherman's house several years after the demonstration. Someone had been selling a left-wing newspaper on the streets of Bowling Green. The police had arrested this person on a technicality, but with an obviously politically motivated intent. While the ACLU was meeting in Stanage's home concerning this incident, someone was seen taking down the license-plate numbers of the people attending the meeting. But this may have just been some unauthorized crank.

Bob had a canny sense of what we wanted in this research and he was skilled at placing details in the larger context. I guess I am saying I found him to be likable as well as a knowledgeable informant. And any sociologist would notice his resemblance to the well-known theorist Randy Collins. He looked a bit like Randy, was about the same age, and had Randy's feel for the overview.

Thomas Brundrett was the organizer of the student delegation. Although he was only a freshman, Tom had been a thorn in President McDonald's side for some months, frequently initiating formal complaints about the university. Brinza's recollection was that most of the group were freshmen. He thought this was significant, and he explained this by saying that each new freshman class at BG seemed to be more liberal than the previous one. To him this meant the direction at BG was inevitably one of liberalization, and it was only a matter of time before the strict and somewhat outdated McDonald administration would have to fall. If it hadn't begun on the unexpectedly warm day in March 1961, it would have been the following spring or the one after that. Of course, Bob and the other members of the delegation were the ones who ended up hastening, if not downright enacting, this fall.

Glenn Schmidt, also one of the nine, had been on a Lima, Ohio, radio station the day before the visit, urging BG students and alumni to join the delegation. Bob Brinza drove down from Bowling Green to the statehouse with Brundrett and Brundrett's girlfriend, Marjorie Levin. Marjorie was one of the students who spoke to the press in the capitol, along with another group member, Susan Ericksen. Women were kept under close control, much more so than male students, at Bowling Green, so for these two young women to take public roles and act as leaders was a noticeable instance of feminist courage.

These four people and Bob Brinza are the only names that have ever surfaced from this three-month-long demonstration. Other students were mentioned in the press because they held formal office in student government, but these officeholders were not active participants or leaders of the uprising. Other than the five just mentioned, the hundreds of demonstrators, from a student body of some six thousand, were all anonymous. There was no Mario Savio (Berkeley), Mark Rudd (Columbia), or other big-name leaders. Just these five gutsy kids.

Bob thinks the Brundrett family knew one of the legislators, possibly Ross Pepple, the chair of the Senate Education and Health Committee. Pepple later sponsored the board-expansion bill. This bill was so vigorously, and perhaps foolishly, opposed by President McDonald that it was blown up into what was in effect a no-confidence vote. Since the Senate eventually passed the measure 31 to 1 and the House passed it unanimously, it forced McDonald's resignation. It is pretty obvious that there was a causal line between this student trip to the legislature and the eventual resignation of McDonald. Perhaps the legislature was miffed with McDonald in the first place for some reason, and the student trip to the statehouse gave them the occasion to discipline him. This is speculation. But Ross Pepple's trustee measure was introduced on April 5, just two days after the student visit to the capital, and it was this piece of legislation, along with McDonald's clumsy response to it, that sealed McDonald's fate.

Glenn Schmidt was from St. Mary's, a small town near Lima, and this district was represented by Ross Pepple. For Schmidt to find the clout to go on the radio, and to do so in Ross Pepple's district, makes me wonder if perhaps the Schmidt family too didn't have some kind of relationship with Pepple. Pepple, long deceased, left no papers, so we are left with guesswork. At this point one cannot but harbor the hunch that President McDonald had done something to anger Senator Pepple. At least we can say these students were using everything they had, and they were a lot more effective than the university administration they were denouncing.

Brinza recalls beginning the visit in the House or Senate gallery, along with the other visitors to the legislature. Then they were asked to go into a smaller room, where the Senate Education Committee was meeting. Bob remembers others in the room, for the business of the Senate involved various people. Sitting next to Bob was the president of Ohio State University, Novice Fawcett, waiting to present his budget to the committee. He was in the room during the presentation of the students, thereby getting fresh information about the Bowling Green disturbances. It seems likely that he would have talked to his friends and peers, including other university administrators in the state of Ohio, about the unfolding Bowling Green story. Bob recalls Brundrett doing most of the talking during this meeting. The legislature had asked the group to elect a spokesperson, and they immediately all leaned toward Tom. He had organized the visit. If there was a single major leader at Bowling Green who made the demonstration succeed, it was the freshman Tom Brundrett.

Brundrett ran through the gamut of student complaints. Then the legislators specifically asked him about a matter he had been trying to avoid, the alcohol issue. This avoidance was because this issue made the students look self serving, and McDonald, calling the demonstration a beer riot, had tried to use it against them. Brundrett said it was not a major issue for them, but that the students wondered about a seeming contradiction: How it could be legal for eighteen-year-olds to drink weak beer in 3.2 bars in the state of Ohio but not legal if they happened to be attending Bowling Green State University?

At this point Bob remembers one legislator interrupting and saying, "Let me stop you for a moment and see if I have this straight. Are you saying that even though the laws of the state of Ohio allow 3.2 drinking for eighteen-year-olds, and unrestricted drinking for twenty-one-year-olds, at your university there is a rule that forbids this drinking?" Brundrett said yes. The legislator then said, in a disgusted manner, "Your administration is making its own laws on that campus." The implication was that only the legislature makes the laws, and other bodies cannot make rules that contradict those of the legislature. Bob sensed that a strong point had been made. The students had thought alcohol was their weakest issue, for it played into President McDonald's put-down of the demonstrations. But instead this issue suggested to the legislature that an institution they funded with tax money was using the money to, in effect, question the law-making authority of the legislature. Perhaps it had also gotten out that McDonald, in his speech to the faculty, had blamed the legislature for the demonstrations.

The legislators were not all friendly in their questions, but they tended this way. In particular Ross Pepple seemed quite welcoming to the students, and he suggested the possibility of a legislative investigation of the Bowling Green situation.

The next day the students, perhaps five of them, met with President McDonald at his request. What appears to have happened is that the students told Senator Pepple they might be expelled for petitioning the legislature. So they asked Pepple to phone McDonald and request his permission for the students to visit him. Evidently McDonald, who must have deeply opposed this idea, was trapped into saying yes. If he had said no, he would have been showing Pepple the very censorship that the students were accusing him of. Part of the package deal was for McDonald to receive the students the next day.

At that meeting, McDonald asked the students their grievances, and they freely told him. McDonald said he thought there was a lot to say for their ideas, but then he talked in such a way that he seemed not really to agree with them after all, or to have even heard them. He would make no changes, although he spoke in a flattering way to the students. To Brinza it was obvious that McDonald was just going through the motions of having a dialogue, and that he would do whatever he wanted.

Still, when these two or three days were over a lot had been done:

1. Students had communicated with the legislature and presented their grievances in that forum. This was completely unprecedented at BGSU and a far cry from the fearful silence that had always existed in the past. Moreover, President McDonald had given his approval, even if against his will. This meant the "no negative public statements" rule was rescinded. This was a green light for going to the press, and it opened the floodgates.

2. The legislators got direct information from the students, and they were impressed with how bad conditions seemed to be at Bowling Green. Ross Pepple was soon to introduce his bill to expand the BG board of trustees, first from five to nine and then, more moderately, from five to seven. But it was still an attempt to take power away from President McDonald and restore it to the board, and McDonald perceived it that way from day one.

3. One of the BG alumni represented the university with the legislature as an informal, part-time lobbyist. McDonald's complaints about the legislature's stinginess suggest he may have needed a real lobbyist. Also, such a person may have been able to neutralize the student visit to the legislature. But as it was, the students got what they wanted, and the interests, if not the needs, of the administration were sharply undercut.

4. The newspapers throughout the state, along with the wire service that circulated in the state, carried the story of the student visit. Throughout Ohio people knew that students were in the capital lobbying for their goals. This was a far cry from spring fever, a beer riot, or something ephemeral. It was clearly a long-term and politically astute project for the students. Having the president of Ohio State present meant he also probably passed the Bowling Green story along in important channels. No doubt dissident students on other Ohio campuses noticed the story too.

5. The raising of the level of dignity of the student cause cast light on their grievances, for now they could be looked at carefully and articulated more persuasively by the students. They were, in a sense, lawyers now, and they would plead their case with all the energy and drama of the courtroom.

OTHER POINTS FROM THE INTERVIEW

1. Bob was struck by the contradiction between raising the academic status of BGSU (trying to make it the "Harvard of Ohio") and maintaining

strict rules. To Bob, a higher academic status meant more-liberal rules. The administration didn't realize their campus was a contradiction. They never had any idea what was, in Bob's words, "going on."

2. The ten-story administration building that McDonald broke ground for before his resignation and that dwarfed the rest of the campus was known irreverently by the students as "McDonald's last erection."

3. Bob agreed that there were several important unwritten rules on campus and that they were, if anything, even more powerful for being unwritten.

4. He thought the administration interpreted "in loco parentis" in a far more strict way than most parents did.

5. Catholics thought Fr. Ollivier would excommunicate them if they took philosophy classes at BGSU. When Bob Goodwin came, from a Catholic university, to replace Stanage, he was expected to be a puppet of Father Ollivier, but Brinza said he was actually an excellent and quite fair teacher.

6. Ollivier continued to say Latin masses long after English was permitted. He opposed the liberalization of the Church.

7. Bob thought there was town-gown tension, in particular owing to the fact that the town was quite conservative on the issues of sex and alcohol for the students. This is complicated because the town newspaper (the *BG Sentinal-Tribune*) was anti-McDonald. And he hated that newspaper. So the town must be distinguished from the newspaper.

8. There were day students from Toledo and Findley. Bob assumed these students would follow whatever drinking rules they could get away with in their own communities. He also suggested that being day students might make them more dissident, though there is no data on this as yet.

9. Why so little national press for the BGSU demonstrations? Bob thought the lack of a charismatic and highly visible student leader, which the press could glom on to, was partly the reason. No celebrity, no story.

This is a good question, and I'd like to pause and mention some other possible reasons the BG story went so unnoticed.

It occurred at a university that was minor, to say the least. Since, nationally, no one had heard of Bowling Green, the story lacked pizazz.

There actually were spring-vacation beer riots in Fort Lauderdale, Florida, on the same day the Bowling Green demonstration began. This story displaced the Bowling Green story in the national press. It also suggested that maybe the Bowling Green demonstrations were mere beer-fueled riots.

The Bowling Green administration vigorously denied that the demonstrations were legitimate and newsworthy. The Ohio press mostly went along with the administration's story, at least for some days.

The story was spread out over several weeks. It lacked immediacy and punch for the press. In particular Sherman Stanage's rebuttal of President McDonald and his defense of the students was kept from the press. This news blackout was not only maintained by the administration but also by Stanage and his allies. Both sides thought publicity was against their interests, at least at that time.

This was not a traditional riot story in any sense. It was not a mindless, destructive riot, which was the kind of eruption the press certainly understood. Nor was it the sort of ideological demonstration associated with the major universities, such as the anti-HUAC demonstration at San Francisco in May 1960. It was a new kind of student statement. It was a demonstration against strict lifestyle rules but it gradually morphed or got re-framed into a freedom of speech–focused, ideological demonstration. The press was not ready for anything this complex and subtle.

The Bowling Green story was transitional in another sense. The issues were transformed over time and the leadership also changed over time. The demonstration began with the fraternity boys. It was their water fight and one of them hit the dean with a balloon full of water, thereby beginning the demonstration. But when someone in the crowd yelled "Founders" and switched the direction in which the crowd was going, the leadership passed from Greeks to independents. Since there were no actual leaders, and the riot tradition at BG had always been associated with the student elites, the press called on the existing student leaders, on the assumption that they were somehow also the leaders of this demonstration. But actually there were no leaders, in either the celebrity or the student-elite sense. This resembled the "revenge of the nerds," in that the student elites were bypassed and ordinary, average students conducted this action all by themselves. Again, this was much too subtle for the press to know how to headline and package it.

References

Abcarian, Gilbert, H. Theodore Groat, Arthur G. Neal, and Sherman M. Stanage. 1964. "Crisis, Charisma, and the Imputation of Motives: Student Responses to the Assassination of President Kennedy." *Revista Mexicano de Orientacion* 1: 47–67.

Adorno, Theodor W., Else Frenkel-Brunswik, Daniel J. Levinson, and R. Nevitt Sanford. 1950. *The Authoritarian Personality*. New York: Harper.

Austin, J. L. 1962. *How To Do Things with Words*. Oxford: Clarendon Press.

Bakhtin, Mikhail. 1984. *Problems of Dostoyevsky's Poetics*. Minneapolis: University of Minnesota Press.

Barkan, Elazar. 2000. *The Guilt of Nations: Restitution and Negotiating Historical Injustice*. New York: W. W. Norton.

Bellah, Robert. 1967. "Civil Religion in America." *Daedalus* 96: 1–21.

Bierstedt, Robert. 1966. *Emile Durkheim*. New York: Dell.

Bird, Kai, and Martin J. Sherwin. 2005. *American Prometheus: The Triumph and Tragedy of J. Robert Oppenheimer*. New York: Alfred Knopf.

Blauner, Bob. 2009. *Resisting McCarthyism: To Sign or Not to Sign California's Loyalty Oath*. Palo Alto: Stanford University Press.

Bowling Green Sentinel-Tribune. 2001. "100 Days that Changed BGSU." March 26, 27, 28, and 29.

Brokaw, Tom. 1998. *The Greatest Generation*. New York: Random House.

Cohen, Mitchell, and Dennis Hale, eds. 1967. *The New Student Left*. Boston: Beacon Press.

Cohen, Robert. 2009. *Freedom's Orator*. Oxford: Oxford University Press.

Collins, Randall. 1982. *Sociological Insight*. Oxford: Oxford University Press.

———. 2004. *Interaction Ritual Chains*. Princeton: Princeton University Press.

Dahrendorf, Ralf. 1959. *Class and Class Conflict in Industrial Society*. Palo Alto: Stanford University Press.

Day, William. 2001. Letter to Norbert Wiley. July 9.

Dean, Dwight G. 1961. "Alienation: Its Meaning and Measurement." *American Sociological Review* 26: 753–758.

DeMartini, Joseph R. 1976. "Student Culture as a Change Agent in American Higher Education: An Illustration from the Nineteenth Century." *Journal of Social History* 9: 526–541.

Durkheim, Emile. 1964/1933. *The Division of Labor in Society*. New York: The Free Press.

———. 1973/1898. "Individualism and the Intellectuals," in Robert Bellah, ed. *Emile Durkheim on Morality and Society*. Chicago: University of Chicago Press.

———. 1995/1912. *The Elementary Forms of Religious Life*. New York: The Free Press.

Ehrlich, Paul R., Carl Sagan, Donald Kennedy, and Walter Orr Roberts. 1984. *The Cold and the Dark: The World After Nuclear War.* New York: W. W. Norton.

Feuer, Lewis. 1969. *The Conflict of Generations.* New York: Basic Books.

Foner, Eric. 1998. *The Story of American Freedom.* New York: W. W. Norton.

Fromm, Erich. 1951. *Escape from Freedom.* New York: Rinehart.

Gitlin, Todd. 1987. *The Sixties: Years of Hope, Days of Rage.* New York: Bantam Books.

Givens, Stuart. 1986. *The Falcon Soars.* Bowling Green, OH: Bowling Green State University Popular Press.

Glynn, Patricia, and Daniel Glynn. 2006. Letter to Norbert Wiley. April 10.

Gordon, James R. 1965. "The One-Hundred Days of Bowling Green: March 26–June 26, 1961." Unpublished manuscript.

Greene, John T. n.d. "A Study of Salary Increases at Bowling Green State University: 1960–61 to 1961–62." Report to BGSU chapter of the American Association of University Professors.

Grinspoon, Lester, ed. 1986. *The Long Darkness: Psychological and Moral Perspectives on the Nuclear Winter.* New Haven, CT: Yale University Press.

Groat, H. Theodore, Evelyn C. Kniseley, and Arthur G. Neal. 1975. "Contraceptive Nonconformity Among Catholics." *Journal for the Scientific Study of Religion* 14: 367–377.

Habermas, Jurgen. 1984. *The Theory of Communicative Action, Vol. 1: Reason and the Rationalization of Society.* Boston: Beacon.

Hamilton, V. Lee. 1978. "Who Is Responsible? Toward a Social Psychology of Attribution." *Social Psychology* 41: 316–327.

Harrington, Michael. 1962. *The Other America: Poverty in the United States.* New York: Macmillan.

Harvard Crimson. 1949. "Olivet Spawns Rebel School: Six Fired, Twelve Instructors Quit." May 25.

Heider, Anne, and R. Stephen Warner. 2010. "Bodies in Sync: Interaction Ritual Theory Applied to Sacred Harp Singing." *Sociology of Religion* 71: 76–97.

Hess, Gary R. 2010. *Bowling Green State University: 1910–2010.* Virginia Beach, VA: The Donning Company.

Hofstadter, Richard. 1955. *The Age of Reform.* New York: Vintage Books.

Jeffries, Vincent, Ralph H. Turner, and Richard T. Morris. 1971. "The Public Perception of the Watts Riot as Social Protest." *American Sociological Review* 38: 443–451.

Keniston, Kenneth. 1960. *The Uncommitted: Alienated Youth in American Society.* New York: Dell.

———. 1969. "The Sources of Student Dissent," in James McEvoy and Abraham Miller, eds. *Black Power and Student Rebellion.* Belmont, CA: Wadsworth.

Kerr, Clark. 1963. *The Uses of the University.* New York: Harper Torchback.

Kinsey, Alfred, Wardell Pomeroy, and Clyde Martin. 1948. *Sexual Behavior of the Human Male.* Bloomington: Indiana University Press.

Kinsey, Alfred, Wardell Pomeroy, Clyde Martin, and Paul Gibbard. 1953. *Sexual Behavior of the Human Female.* Philadelphia: W. B. Saunders.

Korda, Michael. 2009. *With Wings Like Eagles.* New York: HarperCollins.

Lance, Larry M. 1966. "Conceptualization and Measurement of Collective Morality." Master's thesis, Bowling Green State University.

Lipset, Seymour Martin, Martin Trow, and James S. Colemen. 1956. *Union Democracy.* Glencoe, IL: The Free Press.

Lipset, Seymour Martin, and Sheldon S. Wolin. 1965. *The Berkeley Student Revolt.* Garden City, NY: Anchor Books.

Mack, John E., and Roberta Snow. 1986. "Psychological Effects on Children and Adolescents," in Ralph K. White, ed. *Psychology and the Prevention of Nuclear War.* New York: New York University Press.

Maloney, David K. 1981. "The Eye of the Storm: Bowling Green State University and the Student Unrest of the 1960s." Master's thesis, Bowling Green State University.

Marx, Gary T. 1972. "Issueless Riots," in James F. Short and Marvin E. Wolfgang, eds. *Collective Violence.* Chicago, IL: Aldine.

McCrae, Frances B., and Gerald E. Markle. 1989. *Minutes to Midnight: Nuclear Weapons Protest in America.* Newbury Park, CA: Sage.

McLuhan, Marshall. 1965. *Understanding Media.* New York: Mentor.

Mead, George Herbert. 1964/1913. "The Social Self," in *Selected Writings: George Herbert Mead.* Indianapolis: The Bobbs-Merrill Co.

Mead, Margaret. 1974. *Ruth Benedict.* New York: Columbia University Press.

Michael, Robert T., John H. Gagnon, Edward O. Lauman, and Gina Kolata. 1994. *Sex in America: A Definitive Survey.* New York: Warner Books.

Mills, C. Wright. 1956. *The Power Elite.* New York: Oxford University Press.

———. 1956b. *White Collar: The American Middle Class.* New York: Oxford University Press.

———. 1962. *The Marxists.* New York: Dell.

———. 1963. *Power, Politics and People: The Collected Essays of C. Wright Mills.* New York: Ballantine Books.

Myrdal, Gunnar. 1944. *An American Dilemma: The Negro Problem and Modern Democracy.* New York: Harper and Brothers.

Neal, Arthur G. 1970. "Conflict and the Functional Equivalence of Social Movements." *Sociological Focus* 3: 3–12.

———. 1998. *National Trauma and Collective Memory: Major Events in the American Century.* Armonk, NY: M. E. Sharpe.

———. 2006. *National Trauma and Collective Memory: Extraordinary Events in the American Experience.* Armonk, NY: M. E. Sharpe.

———. 2007. *Sociological Perspectives on Modernity: Multiple Models and Competing Realities.* New York: Peter Lang.

Neal, Sister Marie Augusta. 1965. *Values and Interests in Social Change.* Englewood Cliffs, NJ: Prentice-Hall.

Nettler, Gwynn. 1957. "A Measure of Alienation." *American Sociological Review* 22: 670–677.

Overman, James Robert. 1967. *The History of Bowling Green State University.* Bowling Green: Bowling Green State University Press.

Popkess, Barry. 1980. *The Nuclear Survival Handbook: Living Through and After a Nuclear Attack.* New York: Collier Books.

Powledge, Fred. 1991. *Free at Last? The Civil Rights Movement and the People Who Made It.* New York: Harper Perennial.

Riesman, David, Nathan Glazer, and Reuel Denney. 2001/1950. *The Lonely Crowd.* New Haven, CT: Yale University Press.

Rosenblatt, Charles A. 1962. "Relationships Between Alienation Variables and Qualities Associated with Political Leaders." Master's thesis, Bowling Green State University.

Rosenthal, Edward C. 2005. *The Era of Choice: The Ability to Choose and Its Transformation of American Life.* Cambridge, MA: MIT Press.

Rudd, Mark. 2005. "Why Were There So Many Jews in SDS? Or, The Ordeal of Civility." *Fast Capitalism* 1, no. 2. http://fastcapitalism.com.

———. 2009. *Underground: My Life with SDS and the Weathermen.* New York: William Morrow.

Schaar, John H. 1961. *Escape from Authority.* New York: Basic Books.

Schudson, Michael. 1992. *Watergate in American Memory: How We Remember, Forget, and Reconstruct the Past.* New York: Basic Books.

Shay, Jonathan. 1994. *Achilles in Vietnam: Combat Trauma and the Undoing of Character.* New York: Antheneum.

Snow, David A. 2004. "Framing Processes, Ideology and Discursive Fields," in David A. Snow, Sarah A. Soule, and Hanspeter Kriesi, eds. *The Blackwell Companion to Social Movements.* Oxford: Blackwell. Pp. 380–413.

Snow, David A., Burke Rochford, Steven W. Worden, and Robert D. Benford. 1986. "Frame Alignment Processes, Micromobilization and Movement Participation." *American Sociological Review* 51: 454–481.

Snow, David A., and Robert D. Buford. 1992. "Master Frames and Cycles of Protest," in A. D. Morris and C. M. Mueller, eds. *Frontiers of Social Movement Theory.* New Haven, CT: Yale University Press.

Snow, David A., and Sarah A. Soule. 2010. *A Primer on Social Movements.* New York: W. W. Norton.

Snow, David A., Sarah A. Soule, and Hanspeter Kriesi, eds. 2004. *The Blackwell Companion to Social Movements.* Oxford: Blackwell.

Spock, Benjamin. 1960. *Baby and Child Care.* Boston: E. P. Dutton.

Stanage, Sherman M. 1974. *Reason and Violence: Philosophical Investigations.* Totowa, NJ: Littlefield, Adams.

Stouffer, Samuel A. 1955. *Communism, Conformity, and Civil Liberties.* Garden City, NY: Doubleday.

Taylor, Telford. 1992. *Anatomy of the Nuremberg Trials.* New York: Alfred E. Knopf.

Teller, Edward. 1987. *Better a Shield Than a Sword: Perspectives on Defense and Technology.* New York: The Free Press.

Terkel, Studs. 1984. *The Good War: An Oral History of World War II.* New York: Ballantine Books.

Thompson, Graham. 2007. *American Culture in the 1980s.* Edinburgh: Edinburgh University Press.

Time Magazine. 1949. "Education Purge." January 24.

Turner, Ralph H. 1969. "The Public Perception of Protest." *American Sociological Review* 34: 815–830.

University of Michigan. 1962. "Report of the Special Study Committee for the Office of Student Affairs."

Van Dyke, Nella. 2003. "Crossing Movement Boundaries: Factors that Facilitate Coalition Protest by American College Students, 1930–1990." *Social Problems* 50: 226–250.

Weber, Max. 1968. *Economy and Society.* Vol. 1. New York: Bedminster Press.

Westby, David. 2002. "Ideology, Strategic Discourse." *Mobilization* 7: 287–304.

Whyte, William H. 1956. *The Organization Man.* New York: Doubleday.

Wiley, Norbert. 1967. "America's Unique Class Politics." *American Sociological Review* 32: 529–541.

Wilkinson, Doris Yvonne. 1970. "Tactics of Protest as Media: The Case of the Black Revolution." *Sociological Focus* 3: 13–22.

Wilson, Sloan. 1955. *The Man in the Gray Flannel Suit.* New York: Simon and Schuster.

Znaniecki, Florian. 1968/1934. *The Method of Sociology.* New York: Octagon Books.

Index

About the Authors

Norbert Wiley, Professor Emeritus of Sociology at the University of Illinois–Urbana, is a prize-winning sociologist and the author of several books.

Joseph B. Perry Jr. was Emeritus Professor of Sociology at Bowling Green State University, President of the North Central Sociological Association, and author of several books.

Arthur G. Neal is Emeritus Distinguished University Professor of Sociology at Bowling Green State University. His recent books include *Sociological Perspectives on Modernity: Multiple Models and Competing Realities* (2007).